Ingrid Seward has been editor of *Majesty* magazine since 1983 and has written for many publications throughout the world. In 1986 she assisted on a film about the Princess of Wales for Fuji Television in Japan and was chosen to commentate on the wedding of the Duke and Duchess of York for Cable Television News. She has covered many royal tours and interviewed members of both British and foreign royal families. Ingrid Seward is married and lives in central London.

INGRID SEWARD

Diana

GRAFTON BOOKS

A Division of the Collins Publishing Group

LONDON GLASGOW
TORONTO SYDNEY AUCKLAND

Grafton Books
A Division of the Collins Publishing Group
8 Grafton Street, London W1X 3LA

Published by Grafton Books 1989

First published in Great Britain by
George Weidenfeld and Nicolson Ltd 1988

A CIP catalogue record for this book is available from the
British Library

ISBN 0-586-20647-7

Printed and bound in Great Britain by
Collins, Glasgow

Set in Melior

For my husband

Contents

Acknowledgements

In compiling this book about the Princess of Wales I have drawn on my sources and experience gained from my involvement as editor of *Majesty* magazine for the past five years. In that time hardly a day has passed without my witnessing some incident regarding the Royal Family or having it related to me. The problem, as always, has been to sort out the fact from the fiction and I am grateful to the many people who have helped by giving their own account of circumstances as they actually happened.

I would also like to thank Jean Payne and Rachel Weller at Hanover Magazines for their tireless help in transcribing the work on to the word processor and to Harry Darton for all his encouragement when things went wrong.

I owe special thanks to: Derek Shephard, the publisher of *Majesty* magazine, who decided to employ me as editor, thus enabling me to be in a position to write this book; my mother for her painstaking efforts to file and record clippings about the Royal Family over the years; Alan Frame who conceived the idea in the first place and my agent, Judy Chilcote, for getting it off the ground.

The photographs in this book are reproduced by kind permission of:

Alpha Photographic Press Agency Ltd: 1 above, 1 below (Tim Anderson), 2 (John Rigby), 3 below (Jim

Bennett), 7 (Jim Bennett), 9 below (Jim Bennett), 10 above (Jim Bennett), 10 below, 12 above (Tim Anderson), 12 below (Dave Chancellor), 13 above (Dave Chancellor). Robin Nunn: 3 above, 4, 5, 6, 7, 8, 9 above, 11, 13 below, 14, 15. Photographers International: 16.

Prologue

If compromise is marriage's essential ingredient, it is especially vital to the Royal Family. For them there is no escape and it is a small world its members inhabit. They live together and vacation together and in their personal affairs have only each other to turn to for comfort and support. And living on top of each other emotionally as they do, each must make allowances for the other if life is not to become so claustrophobic as to be unbearable.

The Queen and Prince Philip made their accommodations early in their union and their marriage has been a success because of it. They are often apart, sometimes for months, but it does not matter. They remain close and even after four decades the Queen's face will light up when he enters a room.

It is an example Diana and Charles are learning to follow. And it has brought a spring back into their relationship. Seven years ago the dew of naivety was still upon Diana. Things are different now. The child-woman has grown up and the growing has not been easy. There have been tears and tantrums and arguments, and everywhere Diana looked the mirror of rumour was there to distort and exaggerate her difficulties. All she ever wanted to be was a wife and mother, but in marrying the man she chose to make her both, she put herself under a spotlight of unremitting scrutiny. It has made hers the most famous and photographed face in the world. But it has also picked up every nuance, every trace of disharmony in her life.

The world may love a fairy-tale, but it also has a
voracious appetite for soap-operas – and the Waleses,
by their wealth, position and titles and Diana's spectacular glamour, are the leading characters in the greatest soap-opera of them all. It required character and
nerve to keep in touch with reality when every action,
however slight and insignificant, was quickly con-
verted into the script for the next episode of fantasy.
To develop and mature and to come to terms with her
relationships was a daunting task.

It is the task Diana faced all those years ago when
she drove through the gates of Buckingham Palace to
start her career, as The Princess of Wales. It is the task
she is only now on her way to completing.

Prince Charles will never be the dominating figure in
Diana's life he once was. And gone forever is the
suppliant *ingénue* who responded to his every call and
instruction. But that is no bad thing; fairy-tales end
when the Prince marries his Princess. In real life people
must carry on and face the mundane concerns of each
day. It is the ability to cope with them that marks out a
successful marriage and belatedly perhaps, but at last
Charles and Diana are coming to terms with each other
in an adult and mature way.

It was noticeable on their Australian tour in the
January of 1988. The subtle sniping which had become
a feature of their public times together was gone, to be
replaced by mutual understanding and friendship. By
the nature of their work the Royal Family are adept at
putting on a show, but this was genuine.

Diana is never going to share all her husband's
interests. She is never going to follow his example and
spend a couple of days in a crofter's cottage in the sea-
swept wilds of the Outer Hebrides, planting potatoes
and tending the sheep. Charles is unlikely to draw a

close friend out of the set Diana now moves in, nor to develop a liking for the designer restaurants she now favours. They have their own interests and they will become more noticeable and that means they will see less of each other than they did in the early days of their life together.

Work too will keep them apart. No matter what pressures or strains she is under, Diana never lets her duties slip: they are important to her and will remain so. As is her family; she is a dedicated mother and were it not for the discomfort she suffers during pregnancy, would probably already have had a third child. But whatever turns and twists her future might hold, Charles will remain the central figure in her life. That is her destiny. One day he will be her King. And when that day comes she will be his Queen . . .

1

The Marriage Today

The wind sweeps on to Lochnagar from the west bringing with it the faint scent of stag. On a day when the air was crystal and the cloud wracks had blown through, the Prince of Wales could see across the Grampians almost to the Western Isles.

For much of September and, but for one day, for all of October he was there: a hillman with nature for his companion and 3,786 feet of what Byron called the 'frowning glories' of Lochnagar for his inspiration.

From first light until the sun surrendered itself to the snow-tipped peaks in the west he was out on the 'hill' as the ghillies call it. Searching the crags and outcrops with his binoculars, crawling up ravines, wading through rushing burns and stumbling over rocks worn smooth by time's eternity, and all the time climbing higher and higher. It is a place for caution and concentration, for the monarch of this land is a wily and nervous creature that will take flight at the first sight or smell of man, however princely he might be.

For a man like Charles who draws spiritual comfort from a Highland majesty greater than his own it is a place for reflection. And in the autumn of 1987 Charles, Prince of Wales, had much to reflect on.

Diana was not there to share his thoughts. She was in London, in Kensington Palace. She was having lunch with girlfriends, she was playing tennis, she was going to dinner parties, she was working, she was playing bridge, she was happy.

Charles was not. It was more than 500 miles that separated the Princess of Wales from her husband.

By now the marriage storm clouds had been gathering for some time and towards the end of October concern over the marriage between Diana and Charles had reached up as far as the echelons of the British Cabinet.

This was not how a romance which had begun as a fairytale was meant to end. But to even the most casual observer it appeared clear that the threads of affection that bound the world's most famous couple together were becoming dangerously loose.

The experts were more specific.

Research psychologist Dr David Lewis, casting his eye over a video of Charles and Diana together, remarked: 'The emotional temperature is very, very cold. There's nothing there, not even at the most basic level.

'It seems as if she's trying to cut him out of the picture entirely, to pretend he isn't there. It's not the sort of behaviour one would expect from a close, happily married couple living normally as man and wife.'

As in all marriages, Diana's relationship with the man she had married had gone through its fluctuations. She had loved him, rowed with him, kissed him, borne him two sons and squabbled with him again. And every change on the emotional barometer had been duly recorded.

And along the way there had been stories – some true, others the product of imaginations fertile with invention – of her breakdowns and threats of separation.

But this time it was different. This time the rumours came supported by a foundation of hard evidence. As the doyen of the Rat Pack of newspaper reporters who make their living recording the Royal Family's every cough and sneeze remarked: 'For once we don't have to make the story up.'

One of the Royal Family's ladies-in-waiting agreed. 'There is trouble,' she said simply.

Publicly, ministers of the Crown were steering well clear of the future. Then in October a maverick Tory MP tried to force a debate in the House of Commons on whether the Prince of Wales should – by the right of primogeniture of being the eldest son – automatically succeed to the throne. It was a sneaky way of trying to raise the Waleses' marital problem in Parliament but the British government's Front Bench sat as impassively as ever. As it had to: parliamentary procedure precludes such discussions of the Royal Family.

Privately, however, senior ministers – including Kenneth Baker, the Secretary of State for Education – were asking just what exactly was going on. It was a question of some constitutional importance. Charles will one day become King and Head of the Church of England. Diana will be his Queen. And with the popularity of the Royal Family slipping in the opinion polls, there were those who wondered whether the British electorate would tolerate a separation – even a private one – or worse, a divorce.

A secret two-page 'background paper' was passed down the corridors of Westminster Palace from MP to MP. Then, in the first week of November, the Executive Committee of the powerful 1922 Committee of Tory Party Backbenchers concluded that the Royal Family was in urgent need of better advisors – and that certain 'younger members' should make strenuous efforts to avoid criticism in future.

Certainly the Buckingham Palace press office's

record in damage control is not an impressive one. In 1957 Sir Michael Adeane, the Queen's Private Secretary, had tersely announced: 'It is quite untrue that there is a rift.' He was referring to the four-month separation of the Queen and the Duke of Edinburgh who was aboard the royal yacht *Britannia* on a world tour. His statement, however, had only fuelled the gossip and since then the Palace has followed the example of the ostrich and worked to the principle that if it said nothing, the problem would simply go away. It is a policy that has on occasion led to a breakdown of trust between the people who are the Monarchy's official spokesmen and the reporters they are supposed to be speaking to.

On this occasion, however, the Palace was not at fault. For thirty-eight days Diana had remained in London while Charles prowled the hills around Balmoral, gun or fishing rod in hand, and speculation about the rift had reached the elevated level of the Independent Television News. It had made the network news in the United States. It had even made the front pages of the usually staid *Sunday Times* and *Sunday Telegraph*.

On the advice of the Queen Mother, who had been so instrumental in bringing Diana together with Charles, it was arranged that the Prince of Wales would fly down from Scotland to join his wife in Wales to comfort the victims of a recent flood. They met at the RAF base at Northolt, just outside London, and flew together to Swansea and then drove on to the disaster area at Carmarthen on the river Twyl.

It was a chance, and one carefully stage managed by the royal advisors, for the couple to show the world how happy they were. It was a chance Charles refused to take. They were together only six hours. And that

night, and against the best advice of his Household
who had expected him to spend the night with his wife
at Kensington Palace, he insisted on flying back to
Balmoral.

The reaction was predictable. 'Charles Leaves Di
Again,' the front page of the *Daily Express* announced.
The *News of the World*, never at a loss for a pithy
phrase, simply announced: 'Marriage IS on the rocks.'

The Royal Family have many duties. But above all
else they are expected to be the embodiment of stability
of those finer virtues of family and home and parenthood, even if only for appearances' sake. It is a task the
Queen performs brilliantly. It is her example that her
subjects demand her son and his wife should follow.
'The royals,' *The Sunday Times* wrote, 'are not
"allowed" to have personal problems.'

If that is the rule, then the Prince and Princess of
Wales were breaking it. So what, as those concerned
government ministers were asking, was going on that
autumn?

There is their oft-mentioned difference in age. It was
something that caused Diana some concern in their
courting days but one she had chosen to ignore.

'The gap just does not matter,' she said on the day
their engagement was announced. Charles joked:
'Diana will certainly keep me young.'

She hasn't. Nor, conversely, has he aged her. Now in
her middle twenties, she has – despite all Charles's
discouragement – a well-developed interest in rock
music and discotheques and chatty lunches with girlfriends in the kind of designer-label restaurants her
husband hates.

He, on the other hand, gives a convincing impression
of sinking into a premature, cerebral middle age. He
likes delving into books on philosophy and history

(Diana prefers the less demanding entertainment of romantic fiction). He is a countryman at heart; Diana, like most people of her age, enjoys the bustle and adrenalin rush of the city.

And so the list adds up to build a picture that would suggest that they have absolutely no common ground at all. Indeed, when they were married, a team of marriage guidance counsellors in Dallas, Texas, presented with 'blind' personality profiles of the pair, concluded that they were in need of urgent professional help.

'If this was an ordinary couple coming to see me I frankly don't think they'd have a very good chance of making it,' said Maria Molett of the Marriage and Counselling Centre. 'I would recommend counselling immediately.' The trouble, they said, lay in their disparate backgrounds. He, they pointed out, was a university graduate. She was a high school drop-out.

She was expected to break away from her family – but he still sought his mother's advice and required her permission on just about every major decision he might have to make. He had set a pre-nuptial standard for her that he never declared for himself. And for the rest of her life, she would be expected to walk through doorways *behind* him.

Then there was the fact that he had never held a proper job – and neither, the counsellors pointed out – had his father.

'Here is a man who has spent his whole life playing second fiddle to his mother,' said one of the Dallas counsellors, Dr Mervyn Berke. 'He needs to examine that and how it is going to affect his relationship with other women – especially his wife.'

It was never quite as bad as that of course. Like the rest of the world, Charles was captivated by his bride's beauty, her refreshing innocence and openness and her easy, attractive charm. She also had a model figure with excellent legs, and Charles, in his old-fashioned way, has never been ashamed – even in this feminist age – of being attracted by such things.

Diana for her part was in love with her husband. She admired his athleticism and his comparative intelligence and the sensible way he looked at life and its problems. And the fact that he also happened to be a prince with the means to provide her with the most gilded nest was not a handicap.

Her affection showed. She kissed him at polo. She embraced him tightly on dance floors. She held his hand. And when she looked at him it was with eyes that shone.

But in a way those American counsellors were right. There were differences, and quite profound ones, and as the years passed they started to show. Diana can be wilful. She is a woman who will demand her own way and can become obstreperous if she doesn't get it. That grated with Charles. He had lived all his adult life as his own epicentre. Remarked his former valet, 'For the first time he had to consider someone other than himself,' and he found the adjustment a difficult one.

He was easily irritated by his wife's demands. He was unhappy at the way she had taken over the running of what had been *his* household and the way retainers who had been with him for years were leaving the royal employ, adding to the disruption in his routine. He also developed the less-than-admirable habit of criticizing his wife in front of people. It is a habit he still has.

Says a friend, 'He sometimes seemed to take pleasure in putting her down with little asides.'

And sometimes she took pleasure in turning the

tables on him. At a dinner party one night Charles was talking about Rudyard Kipling, the great imperialist author and poet.

'Do you remember the *Just So* stories?' he enquired of his wife.

'Just so what, Charles?' she replied.

'You know, the *Just So* books by Rudyard Kipling,' Charles said.

'Just so what, Charles?' she replied again.

All newly-weds encounter such problems, especially if they have not had the opportunity or the inclination to develop an intimate relationship before marriage. It is part of the process of compromise, of fine-tuning one's reactions and personality to fit in with the other person. What made it difficult for Diana was that she was expected to do this in the full glare of the most intense scrutiny any couple have ever been forced to endure. Charles had been trained from birth to expect this and although it could make him angry, he knew how to handle it. Diana did not, and by 1982 the word was circulating that the marriage was steering through troubled waters.

Said Stephen Barry, valet to Prince Charles: 'All the rumours in the summer of 1982 that Princess Diana was unhappy, and that the marriage was having problems, were quite true. Everyone at the Palace was worried that the fairytale romance was going to collapse.

'There was no question that Charles would do his duty. But the Princess – at that time volatile, happy and unhappy by turns, imperious and then pathetic – was the unknown quantity.

'It was not the Princess who had doubts: it was the Prince. He was concerned that he might have married someone who could not do "the job" as he calls it, but he was also experiencing a disruption to his entire life.'

The Queen, too, was concerned by the disturbing turn of events. Senior editors of Britain's newspapers were called to Buckingham Palace and kindly asked if, out of consideration for Diana's mental health, they would order their reporters to rein back on the intrusive attention they were paying her daughter-in-law. Most gladly agreed.

It was only a year since they had rattled back from St Paul's Cathedral in the 1902 State Landau to Buckingham Palace; only a year since they had stood on the balcony and kissed ('Go on, why not?' Diana had said), before a worldwide television audience of 700 million people.

It was only twelve months since they had sailed off into the Mediterranean on a three-week honeymoon cruise aboard the world's largest private yacht, *Britannia*. A company of 21 officers and 256 ratings were on call to give the royal couple the most romantic, most memorable beginning to their life together. From the moment Prince Charles leant across his wife and pushed the Dressing Bell beside the double bed, the ship was on full alert.

They slept in Prince Philip's bedroom, in a special large bed Charles had ordered aboard, and Diana had the Queen's special permission to use her bedroom as a dressing room. For the first time in his life Charles actually stayed in bed until past 8 o'clock before they headed out to take their breakfast on the Verandah Deck.

Diana, full of energy, would rush around, sometimes putting tapes on the stereo, at other times consulting with the chef on the meals for the day.

Charles would laze on an old-fashioned sunbed,

soaking up the rays. He used to use Bergasol sun cream until someone told him untruthfully that it caused cancer. Now he would just lie there. And when his valet enquired, 'Sir, would you like some oil?' he would answer: 'No, my skin can take the sun.' And it could.

There were picnics of salad and lobster, cold meats and fresh local fruits and cheese carried in large old-fashioned wicker hampers and eaten on sandy beaches in secluded coves.

In the evening they dined by candlelight, alone, or with some of the ship's officers, off beautiful old Irish linen brought from the old royal yacht, *Victoria and Albert*. And a small orchestra played medleys of musicals for them and Charles wore his tropical mess kit, Diana a simple long frock and some of her new jewellery.

'There were no rows on honeymoon,' said Barry. 'They kept those for later . . . after the honeymoon it went downhill.'

Not beyond the point of redemption however. Nowhere near it. As the Queen's action with the editors acknowledged, those first few months of married life had been marked by traumas of one sort or another and there were indeed times when first Charles, then Diana, wondered what they had let themselves in for. But there was no question, not then, of them going their separate royal ways. She was young, he was understanding. She was also pregnant and suffering terribly from morning sickness. That, of course, exacerbated the situation. But when William was born a vital bond was forged and the marriage settled down into a steady and steadied routine.

Diana adored her young son. So too did Charles. And when two years later Harry arrived, even the Rat Pack of royal watchers started talking with resignation about hanging up their binoculars and going back to the more mundane business of train crashes and court reports.

They were good days. Diana was establishing herself as the world's most stylish woman, to be copied and imitated and admired, who at the same time had the fulfilment of a young family to care for. Charles was getting on with the business of being the Prince of Wales. It was, he sometimes complained, a role without definition.

Nor, by the restrictions placed on a constitutional monarchy, was Charles always allowed to say exactly what he really felt for fear of breaking the rule of political neutrality all members of the Royal Family must obey. This could worry Charles. He is a man with firmly held convictions whose politics are well to the left of Thatcherism. He would bring his concerns home to his wife. She, it must be said, was not particularly interested. If Diana has any politics at all they are of the High Tory kind traditional to the old landowning class she was born into.

But if that was a cause of occasional stress, it hardly registered against the woes of unemployment and mortgages and urban despair many newly married couples were having to face. There were always nannies and cooks, valets and maids, gardeners and housekeepers to help ease the domestic strain. And not many young wives start their married life with a mansion in the country, a home in a palace in London, not counting the country retreats in Scotland and Norfolk and Windsor (even if the last lot did come with the in-laws).

Even by the standards of the landed aristocracy Diana had married well. In fact she couldn't have married better. On paper that is.

There is a price to be paid, however, for membership

of the most exclusive family in the world. There is the constant attention – at first fun and flattering, then annoying – which can induce claustrophobic depression.

There are subtler club fees to be met. The Royal Family is all-embracing. Upon joining, newcomers must surrender themselves to the protocols and habits already established. Holidays are pre-planned by tradition and for Diana to persuade her husband to take those summer breaks in Spain with King Juan Carlos constitutes a major breakthrough. Newcomers to the fold are expected to discard old friends and old ways.

And spontaneity is frowned upon except in the most carefully pre-arranged circumstances like a visit to a children's hospital where Diana is expected to embrace a child 'spontaneously'.

In older times, before the advent of the telescopic lens and the long-range microphone, the Royal Family could more or less do what it wanted, provided its members remembered to turn up at the requisite State occasions. They could hunt and shoot and drink and smoke and wear extravagant furs secure in the knowledge that their private life would remain private. They could maintain their mistresses, and the Queen's great-grandfather, Edward VII, maintained several.

Since the reign of George V, however, propriety in all things has been expected – indeed enforced – by weight of public opinion. Britain, like every other Western society, suffers its share of divorce and drunkenness and marital indifference. At the same time it has learned to accommodate the social trends of feminism and equal opportunity and gay rights and 'liberation' in the sexual and intellectual sense of the word. They are movements that are supposed to have passed the Royal Family by. It is supposed to remain in a

permanent time warp, a nice suburban middle-class
family peeking out at life from behind the net curtains
of the 1950s.

To be cast in this role by the accident of birth has
proved difficult enough. For Diana it has proved a
strain that at times has verged on the intolerable.
Glamorous and beautiful, wilful and just a little bit
spoilt (and with at least twenty servants on call it
would be hard not to be), Diana must have felt that her
young life was passing her by in a labour of official
banquets and boring dinner parties with an older
husband who, as a friend says, 'didn't or wouldn't'
understand her urges and interests.

By some accounts Diana was an emotional disaster
waiting to happen and stories started appearing, in
both Britain and America, telling of disharmony and
tantrums and 'malice in the Palace'. They were an over-
dramatization. Diana, a wife and a mother almost
before she became a woman, was simply growing up.
The *ingénue* peeking out from under a schoolgirl fringe
of hair had been replaced by someone more sophisticated, much more assured who was no longer prepared
to follow, doe-like, where her husband chose to lead.

It was here that the 'Fergie Factor' came into play.
Sarah Ferguson has approached marriage to Prince
Andrew with a singular determination to maintain her
independence and it is an example that Diana has
followed. She began going out more – without Charles.
She started inviting *her* friends back to Kensington
Palace for late night supper parties. She discovered, as
if she didn't intuitively know it already, that she had
much more in common with the crowd of 'Sloanes'
that Fergie introduced her to than she had with the
Laurens van der Posts so favoured by Charles.

Charles did not approve. But Diana had set her

course. From now on, she told a newspaper reporter who has known her for ten years, she and her husband would be going their own ways 'more and more'.

The first indication of precisely what she meant by that remark came in Switzerland during the winter of 1987. Charles and Diana were staying in a rented chalet at Wolfgang near Klosters. At night Diana would go out to discotheques while Charles, who was not impressed by the 'Hooray Henry' antics of some of his younger fellow guests, stayed behind and retired early to bed.

There was, of course, an acceptable explanation for this. The Princess of Wales likes nightclubs and dancing. Charles does not. 'I always end up paying the bill,' he grumbles, 'and I hardly ever drink anything.'

When she returned to London, however, while Charles stayed on for a few extra days, he suddenly started turning up in the clubs he had refused to visit with his wife.

One night he was to be found buying £30 bottles of champagne for his party of fifteen and £4 bottles of beer for his security men at the Funny Room in the Aaba Hotel. And when he took to the dance floor to dance the rhumba with a pretty girl, recalls the hotel's manager, 'everyone in the room started to clap'.

And on to this unsettled marital horizon strode the handsome figure of one Philip Dunne.

He is tall and dark haired with a well-developed appreciation of his own good looks. Educated at Eton and a godson of Princess Alexandra, he is the son of the Lord Lieutenant of Hereford and Worcester and his family home is stately Gatley Park near Leominster. He was a good friend of Fergie. And although ensconced in a live-in relationship with Katya Grenfell, the former wife of conductor Oliver Gilmour, he bore with him a reputation as a lady's man.

The Princess of Wales was smitten. And when the 28-year-old Dunne joined the royal party in Klosters it was obvious that the two got on very well together.

Diana is naturally flirtatious and had become increasingly aware of her ability to interest very good-looking men. One evening after skiing everyone joined in an after-dinner party which culminated with Diana lying in the bottom of a large chest of drawers pretending to be asleep. She called out that the first person to kiss her would become a prince. Dunne stepped forward and obliged.

It was all good hearty fun. So too was the visit Diana paid to Gatley Park. She was not there alone, for amongst the other guests was David Waterhouse, the Major in the Household Cavalry who has known Diana 'since she was a schoolgirl'.

The drumbeat of rumour had started, however. First in the better salons of London and then in the gossip columns, stories circulated of Diana's attachment to the young merchant banker.

It did not help appearances when Dunne turned up by Diana's side at Royal Ascot.

Then came the wedding of the Duke of Beaufort's son, the Marquis of Worcester (a gangling figure known as Bunter), to the actress Rachel Ward's sister Tracy. It was a splendid affair, held in a marquee in the grounds of the Ward family home in Oxfordshire. There was a discotheque and dinner and as much champagne as the guests cared to consume.

Charles and Diana, accompanied by the Duke and Duchess of York, arrived early for the dance while their hosts were still having dinner. In certain higher reaches

of the British aristocracy the Royal Family are regarded
with an indifference that can border on contempt (they
are regularly referred to as 'the Germans' or 'the
Krauts', references to the Windsors' Hanoverian ante-
cedents). And a number of the revellers failed to rise to
their feet as protocol demands.

But if the royal arrival went almost unobserved, the
other events that evening did not.

One of the guests was Charles's former girlfriend Anna
Wallace. Their relationship had been ill-starred; on a
visit to Windsor Castle some years before, for instance,
Charles had scuttled away in search of the champagne
Anna had asked for, only to return a long few minutes
later with a bottle of brown ale he had commandeered
from one of the Guardsmen and the sad explanation,
'Mummy's got the key to the drinks cupboard.'

The two still keep in touch, however, and see each
other occasionally when they are both out hunting with
the Belvoir. They saw each other that night and interior
designer Nicki Haslem, who knows both Charles and
Diana well, was dispatched across the canvassed room
to instruct Anna to prepare herself to dance with the
Prince of Wales. Mick Jagger, who witnessed the scene,
was heard to comment: 'Don't think much of her
"weekend house-party" disco dancing.'

Once back at his own table, Charles then locked
himself in conversation with Camilla Parker-Bowles,
the wife of the Colonel of the Household Cavalry. There
had been a time when Diana would have been enraged
by her husband's behaviour. Prone to jealousy, she had
always shown signs of unease when Charles spoke to
any woman with whom he had once been linked. And
for the first few years of their marriage, Diana had
pointedly excluded Mrs Parker-Bowles – who, married
though she was, had been a close friend of the heir to

the throne during his bachelorship – from Kensington Palace and Highgrove.

Now Diana was unconcerned. Her husband could speak to whom he liked. And whilst he did, she went off to enjoy herself. She danced furiously with gallery owner David Ker. She dragged someone she had never met on to the dance floor and engaged him in fifteen minutes of frenetic arm wavings and leg kickings – much to the embarrassment of the young man who did not find her 'windmill' style of dancing aesthetically pleasing.

'She seemed to be having a wonderful time,' one of the guests remarked afterwards, but, 'It was not the way you'd expect to see the future Queen behaving.'

Charles left early and, by one salacious account, he stopped on the way to tell Anna Wallace that he was not happy with his life. Diana carried on dancing until 6 o'clock in the morning, pausing only long enough to wipe her forehead on the hem of her gown.

And one of her dancing partners was Philip Dunne.

His name cropped up again when it was mistakenly reported that he had accompanied her to a David Bowie concert at Wembley. In fact her escort was Major Waterhouse, who took the muddle up with gentlemanly good grace. 'I find the whole thing amusing,' he said afterwards.

Then, on a more serious note, he added: 'There has been a lot of talk about the Princess and Philip. It is absurd to say they are having an affair. The allegation is totally untrue.'

Diana's friend, newsagent heiress Kate Menzies, agreed. 'It's nonsense,' she said.

They were telling the truth. That Diana found Dunne an engaging and attractive companion, as many other women have, is not in question – not that he wasn't flattered by her flirtatious attention. And it was no secret amongst her friends that Diana was intent on enjoying herself and in her own way more than she had done previously.

But she is a devoted mother. And after seven years of marriage she knew full well her royal parameters. To stray beyond them would have been all but inconceivable for a young woman who has the example of her own parents' marital disaster to remind her what the consequences could be. But if Diana's friends were convinced of her propriety, Prince Charles was more circumspect.

He is a thoughtful man, aware of his destiny and resolved to fulfil it. Old-fashioned – and some would say old before his time – he has an inbuilt understanding of the need for 'appearances', especially when it comes to the family business of royalty. He was appalled by the publicity the speculation on the state of his marriage had engendered. Some of that was the consequence of his own behaviour: serious minded, he was not always able to appreciate his wife's enthusiasm for what he dismisses as the 'flighty', and at times could be unbending and severe when flexibility would have been a more productive tactic. Others were naturally inclined to place the blame for his deteriorating situation at Diana's doorstep (or 'Diana's dancestep' as one wag referred to it).

But if all this was bad enough, worse was to follow. Prince Charles since his earliest youth has gone out of his way to avoid confrontations. Brought up to contain his emotions, it is only on the rarest of occasions that his temper – which can be vile – is allowed to get the better of him. He is unwilling to follow ire down its uncharted pathways, preferring orderly retreat to the dangerous waters of verbal combat.

On 22 September he flew north to Balmoral. Diana remained behind in Kensington Palace. They were not to spend a night together under the same roof for well over a month. Such separations are fairly common to the Royal Family, and both Charles and Diana have very full agendas of official engagements which can take them hundreds and often thousands of miles away from each other. But as the *Sunday Times* observed: 'What characterizes many of Charles and Diana's recent times apart – he is on his painting expeditions to Florence, she visiting restaurants, cinemas and clubs without him – is that they are avoidable.'

The ensuing furore this separation generated was not. Like Walter Cronkite counting up the days the American hostages had been held in Iran (and in so doing, counting out the presidency of Jimmy Carter), the newspapers published a daily account of the time the royal couple had been apart.

'*Just what is going on?*' Sir John Junor, the authoritative and respected columnist in the *Sunday Express* wanted to know. He went on to write: 'Prince Charles is far too sensible not to be aware that a four-week absence from his wife and children would be bound to arouse comment.

'*Why then did he permit such a long absence to happen?*

'His Press Secretary assures us that the couple are as much in love as ever they were.

'*Really?*

'In that case unless they wish to do lasting damage to the Royal Family, shouldn't they begin to show it?'

On the last Saturday in October Prince Charles came down from Lochnagar and flew south to attend the wedding of Earl Mountbatten's grand-daughter, Lady Amanda Knatchbull, a woman who it had once been suggested would make him an ideal wife. The Queen was there. So was Prince Philip and the Duke and Duchess of York, and Viscount Linley and Lady Sarah Armstrong-Jones.

The Princess of Wales was *not* there. And that night Charles did not return home to her, preferring instead to sleep over at the home of his brother Prince Andrew's father-in-law, Major Ronald Ferguson.

Was this the end? Was Britain about to witness what the politicians feared it would not accept – the end of the royal marriage? Not yet. That weekend, the couple flew off together, all smiles, on an official visit to West Germany. Had the royal goldfish bowl once again distorted reality to create an image of crisis when there was none? Not quite. The problems had been real enough and the Queen herself – as reluctant as she is to interfere in the lives of her family – would be forced to point out the dangers of the course her son and heir and his wife were following.

It was obvious that adjustments were going to have to be made in the relationship between Charles and the woman who will one day, God willing, be his Queen.

2
Charles

To understand Diana and the role she plays, it is important to understand something of her husband.

It was Charles who made her a princess and will one day make her Queen. It is Charles, the tetchy, old-fashioned conservative with hair that was never long, in trousers that never flared or quite fitted, who has taken the back seat as Diana sets about – unconsciously perhaps but still definitely – reshaping the image of the Royal Family with her style and glamour and personality.

It is Charles who was born to be King. But it is Diana that the crowds turn out to see. As he readily admits. And it is a situation to which he acquiesces, by his nature and training.

To the public at large, he was the action prince, forever parachuting out of aeroplanes and diving under polar ice-caps and riding his polo ponies into break-neck confrontations, pausing only long enough to slake his supposedly prodigious romantic thirst with yet another leggy blonde.

The reality, however, never quite matched the image the media so determinedly bestowed on the prince they nicknamed Action Man (a sobriquet, incidentally, he detests). For behind all the bravado, traces of the shy youngster who never really knew what to say to a girl, are still discernible. The veneer is so smooth and sophisticated. But the man behind it has an attitude and approach to women very different from the ones his list of so-called conquests would suggest.

Raised in a matriarchy where the men, even someone as overtly chauvinistic as Prince Philip, must defer to the women and most particularly to one woman, Charles was brought up to regard the female sex with deep respect. It did not make him a mother's boy, far from it. But it provided him with little preparation for the rugged, all-male world he encountered at Gordonstoun. And Gordonstoun, in its turn, was no training ground for the princely Lothario the popular imagination would brand him.

His years spent there, on the wind-swept coast of the Moray Firth, were not the happiest time of his life.

He had been put into Windmill Lodge where his housemaster, Bob Whitby, did little to make life easy for him. Brusque, opinionated and seemingly always angry, Whitby made it a point of principle to shout loudest at the boys he liked best, especially new boys. He had been ordered by Prince Philip to treat the heir to the throne as he would any other pupil and it was an instruction he carried out with relish. It was not surprising that the first couple of years Charles spent so far away from the family he so depended on were lonely and tearful.

He was not academically exceptional and it took him three attempts to pass Maths 'O' level. Even history, the subject which he is so fond of and the one of which he says, 'I honestly believe that the only real way one can hope to understand and cope with the present is by knowing and being able to interpret what happened in the past,' could prove perplexing. On one occasion his tutor, the exuberant Robin Birley, felt moved to shout at him, in front of the whole class, 'Come on, Charles, you can do better than this – after all, it is the history of your family we're dealing with!' But it was an episode one must presume Charles would not want to see repeated: his 'A' level form was studying the reign of the executed King Charles I.

Nor did he shine on the sporting field. As a polo player he has worked and trained himself up to a creditable four handicap player. At rugger and athletics and cricket he was disappointing.

The London newspapers, already making their first stab at creating their action prince, would write how well he was doing at this sport or that, and how it would only be a matter of time before he made the Rugby First XV.

Gordonstoun fielded four rugby teams which travelled the north of Scotland to engage schools like Strathallan and Aberdeen Academy in sporting combat. Charles never made any of them. Instead, he spent miserable, morose, wet afternoons with the infirm and unathletic playing for a motley Windmill house side. He cut a forlorn figure, often to be seen standing apart from his team mates with his hands clasped behind his back, taking little part in the unskilled action eddying around him.

He had few friends and anyone who did try to strike up a conversation with him was instantly accused of 'sucking up'.

His lot was not improved by the resentment his arrival had generated amongst many of his fellow pupils. Gordonstoun is peculiar to the British public school system in that it is, to a large extent, run by the boys themselves. The senior prefects, called colour bearers, meet periodically to revise the rules. And, in theory at least, the headboy, called the Guardian, enjoys equal powers with the headmaster. He can grow a beard and is allowed to marry (practice, of course, was rather different; one of the Guardians who succeeded Charles was promptly expelled when he was found with a woman in his rooms).

This independence was underscored by the kind of boys who went there. It has been called a reform school for expelled Etonians and the boys who went there certainly tended to be wilder and more independent and more adventurous than the kind usually encountered in other public schools.

Charles's arrival, however, brought with it the introduction of a whole new and stricter set of regulations. For instance, the boys were now forbidden to go into the local town of Elgin without specific permission.

This was hardly Charles's fault but not all of his 400 fellows were convinced and he found himself the butt of the inevitable jokes. One – and one often repeated – concerned his marmalade.

To supplement their spartan diet of black pudding and porridge and a bi-weekly helping of haggis, the boys were allowed to order a few luxuries from the school suppliers, Gordon and McPhail. (Gordon and McPhail are also the bottlers of many of the finest Glenlivet malts but these were never allowed on the tuck list.) Charles would order Robertson's marmalade and many was the morning when someone would pick up his jar and point to the 'By Appointment to H.M. The Queen' on the label and proclaim, 'Oh goody, mummy approves.'

Charles resented the jibes. If he wanted anything other than to be away from the place, it was to be accepted, to be treated like everyone else. But no matter what Prince Philip may have ordered, and no matter how aggressively Whitby tried, Charles could never be just another boy. Gordonstoun was a school well-stocked with sprigs of the aristocracy, but no one was allowed to use their title and everyone was addressed by their surname – except Charles who was always called 'Charles', a title in itself.

And the three classmates who, down in London together at the end of one term, had prankishly telephoned Buckingham Palace and asked to be put through to their contemporary, found themselves 'gated' and confined to school grounds in punishment for their impertinence when they returned to Gordonstoun. To add to his sense of isolation, his father had the disconcerting habit of flying in to see him and landing his helicopter on the lawn of Gordonstoun House – and this at a school where even the richest parents would never dream of arriving in a Rolls Royce for fear of embarrassing their son.

It was around this time that the notorious cherry brandy incident took place.

Every year, the boys went off on 'expeditions', either walking through some isolated part of the Highlands, or cruising through the Western Isles on the school yacht, *Pinta*. It was a break from the normal routine and was greatly anticipated for it represented the opportunity to – hopefully – meet girls or perhaps to sneak into a local pub for a clandestine pint of beer. And the hills were alive with the sight of masters and boys playing an often farcical game of hide-and-seek as a result.

Charles got caught. The *Pinta* called in at Stornoway on the Isle of Lewis in the Outer Hebrides. Charles walked into an hotel bar and for want of anything better to say, asked for a glass of that sickly, sticky liqueur because, 'having never been in a bar before, the first thing I thought of doing was having a drink. Being terrified and not knowing what to do, I named the first drink that came into my head – which happened to be cherry brandy because I had drunk it before when it was cold and I was out shooting.'

By misfortune, a freelance journalist was sitting in

the bar and an innocent schoolboy transgression became front-page news.

'I wanted to pack my bags and go to Siberia,' he recalls. He was exaggerating: where he really wanted to go was to Birkhall, the Highland home of his grandmother the Queen Mother.

It was really only on stage that Charles came to life and into his own. He auditioned for the role of Shakespeare's Henry V in the school play and only just lost out to David Gwillim who went on to make acting his career and played the role again in the much praised BBC television production of the play. Eric Anderson, the master in charge who went on to become headmaster at Eton, explained that Charles was passed over because he did not want to be accused of favouritism and because it was just possible that the young prince might have failed to live up to the promise he had shown in rehearsals.

Anderson had no such misgivings when he cast the future King as Macbeth. It was faith well justified: Charles was superb. And Anderson – a caring, intelligent man who encouraged the boys to express their thoughts and opinions, and can be considered the first of the older 'gurus' to have so influenced Charles – considered him to be the finest Macbeth he had ever seen. Only by playing someone else, it seems, was Charles truly able to play himself.

But then role playing has been the corner-stone of his life.

He has had to live up to the role model provided by his father, a hardy, athletic man always on the go and intent on instilling in his eldest son a sense of the machismo he deems so important. Prince Philip was a hard act to follow and one Charles was always uncomfortably in awe of.

Then there was the role forced on him by the British press. By the chance of birth, he was the 'most eligible bachelor in the world' and the reporters employed to report on his activities were determined that he should live the part to the full.

Certainly he has an appreciative eye for a pretty face, and the well-rounded figure of an attractive woman can still excite his interest, even now.

But in neither his home life nor his education were the makings of the rampant bed-hopper the papers chose to present. Childhood had taught him to respect women in a way that is uncommon amongst the British upper classes. Gordonstoun, with its enforced separation of the sexes, had made him a little self-conscious in the presence of girls of his own age. He had never followed the example of some of his contemporaries known as 'shades', who used to sneak into Elgin to pursue clandestine romances with the local girls. And those who did, during the production of Gilbert and Sullivan's *Pirates of Penzance*, remember him as shy and self-conscious.

His spell Down Under at Geelong Grammar had rounded out his character, but it had also reinforced his inhibitions. Australia, in the days before improved air communications and immigration had eased the national psyche, was still a place where men gathered on one side at a party and the women on the other and any male who made the crossing was instantly labelled a 'poofter', a homosexual.

It was therefore a distinctly old-fashioned attitude towards women that Charles took with him to Cambridge and one of his contemporaries at the university where he read history was quoted as saying, 'When he first came up he was astonishingly naive about girls.

He really thought that girls who slept with their boyfriends weren't "nice".'

Like most undergraduates, though, he soon discovered that university has more to offer than academic
study. He became friendly with Lucia Santa Cruz. The
daughter of the former Chilean ambassador to London,
she was at Cambridge helping Lord Butler, the Master
of Trinity College and Charles's university guide, to
write his memoirs.

She was an unlikely choice for a royal companion.
Exotic, foreign, Catholic, four years his senior and with
political opinions far to the right of Charles's own (it
was only on Lord Butler's stern advice that the future
King was dissuaded from joining the university's
Labour Party). But the attachment was serious enough.
And according to biographer Anthony Holden, Lord
Butler said, 'The Prince asked if she might stay in our
lodge for privacy which was a request we were very
glad to accede to.' The implication in that is obvious.
Clearly the school of life was modifying Charles's view
of relationships. And Earl Mountbatten of Burma was
encouraging the change.

'I believe in a case like yours, a man should sow his
wild oats and have as many affairs as he can before
settling down,' Uncle Dickie wrote to his favoured
great-nephew.

Charles's oats were never sown as wildly as they
might have been, however. He is not a natural woman-
izer and many of the girls he went out with were
simply friends.

Georgina Russell was one whose name was linked to
his in those early days. The daughter of Britain's former
ambassador to Madrid, she is bright, intelligent and
socially acceptable. She wore mini-skirts and on occasion the see-through blouses fashionable at the time.

Her hair was long and blonde. She was invited to spend the weekend up at Balmoral, but that is as far as it ever went. Some years later when she married Baronet Sir Brooke Boothby, the prince saw her wedding photograph in a society magazine and declared in astonishment: 'Good God, her hair is black. She's not a blonde at all!' A remark hardly revelatory of intimacies past.

It was the same with Fiona Watson, the attractive daughter of Lord Manton. She too was declared to be 'the girlfriend' and, according to legend, it was only the unfortunate discovery that she had once displayed her ample figure in all its naked splendour in the girlie magazine *Mayfair*, that ended their affair.

That was not what happened. Always 'very cautious and very careful' about committing himself emotionally, he would often leave it until the last moment before asking a girl out and Fiona was not the kind to sit at home on the off-chance that he might telephone.

She had other boyfriends. And when Charles did ring one evening, Fiona, after first dismissing his call as a prank being played by one of her friends, told him, no, she had already made other arrangements. It was the end of the affair which had never started.

There were, of course, others who were prepared to cancel everything for an evening out with the Prince of Wales. But as they soon discovered, it was not the most exciting of occasions. An evening at the opera perhaps. Or a dinner in his chambers on the second floor of Buckingham Palace.

That was not quite as romantic as it sounds. The girl would be asked to make her own way there, for Charles – excused the normal conventions – never picked up his dates himself and rarely arranged for his detective or valet to do the collecting for him.

And once there she would find that there were always servants on hand, serving the food – usually a cold supper – clearing away afterwards, hovering in the corridors, their ears always pricked for the faintest hint of gossip. There is also the point that as far as the Royal Family is concerned the Palace is the Queen's home. That puts a brake on everyone's behaviour, and having been smuggled in through the basement, the girls usually found themselves on their way out again to make their own way home well before midnight.

For the twelve years leading up to his marriage to Diana, his valet was Stephen Barry who recalled, 'If he was meant to be in his bed in the morning when I went to wake him up – he was in bed. Alone.'

Barry added, 'Buckingham Palace was totally unsuitable for anything indiscreet to take place. It would have been impossible for a girl to have spent any time there without a footman or his policeman or me not being aware that she was there.' They never were. Which prompted Barry to remark, 'I sometimes thought the limitations on his privacy were part of the reason for his participation in so many energetic activities.'

That is not to say that Charles did not enjoy a private life. He did. He had his girlfriends, drawn from the utterly discreet stream of Britain's aristocracy and upper middle class, combined with an occasional exotic diversion like Laura Jo Watkins, the daughter of an American rear admiral.

They had met in California in 1974 at a cocktail party on one of the ships Charles served aboard during his spell in the Royal Navy. She called him 'sir', but in an off-hand, light-hearted way, and Charles was enchanted by her outgoing American personality and her uncomplicated sense of humour. She visited him in London and went through the entrance-via-the-basement routine before exiting again and returning to the American Embassy where she was quartered. She witnessed his maiden speech at the House of Lords where Charles addressed his fellow peers on the dangers of too much government interference in sport.

In the end, however, the romance died its inevitable death. Laura Jo returned to the United States, but continued to correspond with the Prince. He managed to see her again during one of his stop-overs in America, and when he went to a big charity ball in Miami, she joined him. It was all very discreet and Charles went to the ball accompanied by his secretary Rosie Taylor, who acted as a decoy. Laura Jo was smuggled in to the party in a flower van and remained out of sight until all the Miami matrons had had the chance to have their photograph taken with Prince Charles. That's all they seemed to want and by 10 o'clock, had all gone home. Charles and the rest of his group, including Laura Jo, then stayed on and had their own private party – it was quite a party and they ended up dancing on the tables before returning to the house of a rich American couple where they were staying.

Charles, said Laura Jo, 'is a great guy'. The strictures of his life, however, were 'unliveable for kids like us'.

The same applied to his brief dalliance with actress Susan George, who had appeared in the violent and, for the time, sexually explicit *Straw Dogs*. She described him as 'romantic and loving'.

He was also very taken with beautiful blonde singer Lynsey de Paul, whom he met a couple of times at charity dinners. Once again the situation was impossible and in spite of press stories of a romance, they never progressed further than some witty banter in the full view of several hundred other people.

It would have been saliently out of character for a prince who, unlike his brother Andrew, has never felt comfortable making flamboyant advances, to move away from his bevy of blue-blooded British blondes. For if there has been a watch word in Charles's relationships, it is discretion. And discretion certainly characterized his relations with Lady Tryon and Camilla Parker-Bowles.

Both are married to men he has known for years and who consider him their friend. Lady Tryon, the former Qantas air hostess Charles nicknamed Kanga, is the wife of merchant banker Anthony Tryon; Camilla's husband Andrew is Colonel of the Household Cavalry, the Queen's Silver Stick-in-Waiting and a former escort of Princess Anne. Neither has ever spoken publicly of their relationship with the Prince, but both in their way provided him with the companionship and feminine comfort he sought.

The object of courtship, of course, is to find a suitable mate. For the future King it was a necessity and however close he may have been to Mrs Parker-Bowles or Lady Tryon, they could never be more than a footnote in his romantic development.

So, to the entertainment of his future subjects, a succession of more or less suitable young women rolled into, and out of, his horizon, to be scrutinized and dissected and subjected to the pressure of being, if only for the moment, 'the girlfriend'.

Finding someone fitted for the role of future Queen had its unique problems. As Mountbatten had advised, 'For a wife (you) should choose a suitable, attractive and sweet-charactered girl before she has met anyone else she might fall for.

'I think it is disturbing for women to have experiences if they have to remain on pedestals after marriage.'

In other words, virginity was, if not exactly a pre-requisite, a distinct advantage – no easy criterion to meet in this modern age, especially as Charles grew older and so inexorably did the age of any potential match.

It was her past that put paid to Davina Sheffield's chances. Although she always insisted 'I never had a relationship with him, it was a friendship', there is no doubt that at one time she was close to Charles. Blonde, elegant, with a worldly sophistication, she was exactly his type. The relationship ended, however, when her previous lover, Old Harrovian powerboat enthusiast James Beard, felt moved to reveal all about their live-in affair.

The pressures of the goldfish bowl of royal life put paid to Lady Jane Wellesley, the highly intelligent and very beautiful daughter of the Duke of Wellington. She would have made an excellent consort for the Prince, but very quickly decided that the future offered by Charles was not for her. 'I have a title already – I don't need another one,' she stoutly declared before setting off to make a career for herself in television production.

Temperament took Anna Wallace out of the frame. The vivacious, sexy daughter of a substantial Scottish landowner, she fitted well into Charles's essentially rural lifestyle. She hunts (they met whilst out riding with the Belvoir), and she is a fine horsewoman. She could pass the 'Craigowan test' as it was known to the Royal staff – those weekends spent fishing in the cold and rain of the Balmoral estate. It was a test Georgiana Russell had failed: she had nearly died of boredom.

But Anna was never as close to the Prince as is now widely assumed. She had had a flat in Chelsea but Charles only visited there once. It was to attend a formal dinner party and he left before midnight.

She had other boyfriends – a fact that did not go unnoticed by the policemen assigned to look after their royal charge. They saw it as part of their duties to check into the backgrounds of the young women Charles took an interest in.

Also Anna has a mind of her own. She has very clear ideas about how she should be treated. And when Charles took her to a birthday party for the Queen Mother at Windsor Castle and then went off to talk to the other 400 guests – as his duty required – she became deeply irritated. Declaring that she would not be treated like that, she left.

Others were unsuitable in other ways and did not match up to the Royal Family's idea of what was suitable. No one ever passed a direct opinion on Charles's fancies. They didn't need to: they had other ways of making their thoughts known, which they did most pointedly when Charles arrived at Balmoral with Sabrina Guinness, the free-wheeling brewery heiress whose past had included a spell in Hollywood where she had worked for Ryan O'Neal as a nanny looking after Tatum.

The whole Balmoral experience, she says, was 'terrifying'. On arrival she remarked that the car that had collected her from the station looked like a 'black maria'. To which Philip had unkindly replied that she should know all about black marias. She hardly ever saw Charles. And when she was about to lower herself into a chair, the Queen had told her sternly, 'Don't sit there. That's Queen Mary's chair!'

Sabrina was out.

There were also the ones who simply did not 'fancy' Charles. One was the red-haired Lady Sarah Spencer, daughter of Earl Spencer – and Diana's oldest sister. They got on well together and Charles gave his support when she was struggling with the slimmer's disease, anorexia nervosa. But that, as far as Sarah was concerned, was as far as it went.

'He's a fabulous person but I'm not in love with him,' she firmly declared. 'I think of him as the big brother I never had.'

By now Charles was moving into his thirties and there was a mounting undercurrent of concern, not least amongst his own family, about his continuing bachelorhood. Some supposedly 'informed' members of society, pointing to the proliferation of gays amongst the staff at Buckingham Palace and the alleged bisexuality of Earl Mountbatten, even postulated that he would never marry.

That was nonsense, of course. Charles had had his girlfriends. He had plenty of what one called 'Hanoverian enthusiasm'. And girls did make it past the inquisitive eyes of the servants to his rooms – including, on one spectacular occasion, more than one.

But the Prince who had once written a booklet advising on how to chat up women, could still be unsure of himself in their company. His relationships need time to develop. And time, private time, was in the shortest supply. 'People don't make it easy for him to marry, do they?' Lord Mountbatten observed. 'I mean, what chance has Charles to woo a girl? He can't even stop to joke with one without being married off the next morning.

'You've got to get to know her – and that's not easy if you are a royal.'

Charles didn't make it easy for himself. Determined to live a life as normal and outfront as possible, he insisted on conducting his romances in the full public spotlight with the predictable consequence that most of them collapsed before they had properly begun.

Princess Margaret, however, had little sympathy for his predicament. The Prince did not, as has sometimes been suggested, have a secret 'love nest' in Notting Hill Gate – or anywhere else. But as his aunt would remind him, the Royal Family does have at its disposal a large collection of houses and hideways where he could take a girl, leaving the world none the wiser. That he chose not to is a measure of his honesty – or his reserve.

Lord Mountbatten, his eye always on the look-out for a chance to promote his own dynasty, inevitably had his own solution to the problem – his grand-daughter Lady Amanda Knatchbull.

It would have been the realization of all his ambitions. And, but for his tragic death when he was blown up by an IRA bomb in 1980, the man who succeeded in marrying his nephew to the future Queen might yet have pulled off the coup of marrying another member of his family to the future King. People who knew him and Charles well were convinced he would.

But with Mountbatten's powerful influence removed, the proposed union never got past the starting gate. Intelligent and pretty as Amanda was, she wasn't Charles's type. There was also the point that they had known each other since earliest childhood and were too much like brother and sister to make the quantum step to being husband and wife.

Amanda went on to work in estate agency. Charles went back on his circuit of tall, attractive blondes. And, in rejection of his aunt's counsel, he continued to conduct his courtships in public, turning up with the latest 'Charlie's Angel' at polo or Ascot, setting off the next round of speculation.

As intrusive as that was, it did serve some purpose. As Charles once candidly admitted to a reporter, 'You can afford to make a mistake but I've got to get it right first time. If only I could live with a girl before marrying her . . .'

But he couldn't. Instead it was left to the press to drag up her past, to test her character with remorseless pursuit. Charles claimed that all the attention infuriated him and he accused the press of 'cheap sensational writing'. He ingenuously insisted, 'It's got nothing to do with anyone else who I might want to marry or anything like that.'

If Charles believed that, he was the only person who did. The people he will one day reign over had an understandable and justifiable interest in the identity of their future Queen.

So too did his friends and family. If Charles was happy in his bachelor ways, they were not.

One story that did the London rounds is that a group of his chums, including his cousin the Earl of Lichfield and his equerry Nicholas Soames, grandson of Sir Winston Churchill, met one evening and drew up a short list of blue-blooded virgins to submit to him for his perusal.

Another is that the Queen Mother and her friend Lady Fermoy discussed the situation over afternoon tea.

And the name that emerged out of those romantic premeditations was one Lady Diana Spencer.

3
Childhood

The Duchess of Marlborough was determined that her favourite grand-daughter, the beautiful Lady Diana Spencer, should marry the Prince of Wales, and offered him a dowry of £100,000 which he was glad to accept.

The Prime Minister, however, objected. He had other plans for the Prince. He forbade the marriage. The Spencers of Althorp would have to wait another two-and-a-half centuries for one of their daughters to wed a Prince of Wales. And by a twist of historical coincidence, her name was also Lady Diana Spencer.

But if that first union was kept unconsummated by the dictates of politics, it was the beginning of a long, occasionally scandalous, and unusually worthy association between the families Spencer and Royal.

Descended from a fifteenth-century farmer, who had by-passed the local butchers and wool merchants to sell his sheep direct to London and in so doing had set the foundations of a fortune that enabled them to buy their first peerage from King Charles I, the Spencers lived in the grandest of splendour in their Jacobean mansion in Northamptonshire. The men spent their years in courtly, if low key, attendance to the sovereign of the day. And their women – gay, beautiful, enchanting – regularly caught a succession of royal eyes.

This close and often romantic link to the Royal Family had begun with Sarah, Duchess of Marlborough, wife of the first Duke, who defeated Louis XIV's forces at Blenheim, and forebear of Sir Winston Churchill. She rose to become the richest and most powerful

woman in England and Queen Anne's Lady of the
Bedchamber in much more than name alone (the two
women exchanged passionate love letters which they
signed Mrs Freeman and Mrs Morley).

It was a love affair that profoundly shaped the course
of British history. Anne had wanted her exiled half-
brother, James Stuart, to succeed her. Sarah, a fervent
Whig intent on securing a Protestant succession, was
committed to the Hanoverians and in the end she got
her way. She may have failed in her ambition to marry
her grand-daughter, the first Lady Diana, to the Prince
of Wales, but it was her action that ensured that Charles
was Prince of Wales when he married his Lady Diana.
And when she died she left the bulk of her vast estate
to her grandson, the first Diana's brother Jack, father of
the first Earl Spencer.

In the next generation Lady Georgina Spencer,
daughter of the first Earl, became the closest friend
with Prinny, the Prince of Wales who succeeded to the
throne as George IV; so close that when she fell pregnant his constant and suspiciously paternal visits
caused her husband, the Duke of Devonshire, 'some
emotion'.

It continued into this century; Diana's grandmother,
Cynthia, had been seriously courted by the Prince of
Wales (who abdicated as Edward VIII to become the
Duke of Windsor), before she married the seventh Earl
Spencer in 1919.

When they weren't being romanced by the Royal
Family the Spencers were usually to be found serving
it, and being honoured in return.

Edward VII was godfather to Diana's grandfather. His
wife, Cynthia, daughter of the Duke of Abercorn, was
the Queen Mother's Lady of the Bedchamber.

Diana's father, 'Johnny', was equerry to King

George VI and to the Queen, whose sister Princess Margaret he once dated.

Her family on the maternal side was also closely linked with the throne. Her mother's father, Lord Fermoy, was a shooting and tennis-playing friend of George VI. His wife, the redoubtable Ruth who would play such an encouraging role during Diana's courtship by the latest Prince of Wales, is the Queen Mother's lady-in-waiting and best friend.

It is an association which prompted one cynic to describe the Spencers as 'ten generations of Royal groupies'.

More kindly, it bestowed in Diana a natural ease in the presence of the Royal Family. When asked, back in her courting days, if she ever felt uncomfortable in the presence of the Queen she had replied, 'No, why should I be?' There was no reason. She had known its members from earliest childhood. There had never been a time when she didn't know them; the first meeting with the man she would marry took place, she recalled, 'when I was still wearing nappies. I've known him all my life.'

Those nappy days and the years that followed were spent in Norfolk at Park House, a ten-bedroomed Victorian mansion on the edge of the Queen's Sandringham estate. Built by Edward VII to accommodate the overflow of guests from Sandringham, it had come into the family through Diana's mother, Frances, whose father had rented the property from George V. Shortly after Frances married the seventh Earl Spencer's heir Viscount Althorp, Lord Fermoy died and the newly-weds took over the lease. And it was here, late in the evening of 1 July 1961, that Diana Frances Spencer was born. She weighed 7lb 12oz, 'a superb physical specimen,' as her father recalls.

Park House was ideal for a young family: large and rambling, overlooking the royal parkland, and hidden from the road by woods and shrubs. Like their mother before them Diana and her elder sisters Sarah and Jane and, later, her brother Charles, enjoyed a traditional country childhood with walks in the woods, building tree dens and playing games of hide-and-seek.

There were always a lot of animals in attendance. Horses and ponies and rabbits, and the hamsters and gerbils Diana was so fond of and, of course, their father's gun-dog, Bray, and a springer spaniel named Jill and a cat called Marmalade. There was also a swimming pool which Viscount Althorp had installed for his children's amusement during the summer holidays.

It was a rustic and, in the Spencers' minds, a simple existence. 'We are not at all grand,' Diana's mother would say.

That depends on your definition of grand. Park House was certainly not as grand as Althorp (pronounced 'Althrup' according to some, pronounced as it is spelt by Diana) where her crotchety grandfather lived in opulent splendour until his death in 1975. But there were six servants including a full-time cook, and from an early age the children were fed pheasant for lunch. There was also a private governess, Miss Gertrude Allen, who had taught Lady Althorp, and who gave her lessons in what had once been the butler's pantry. And Janet Thompson, Diana's nanny for two-and-a-half years, recalls that 'the Althorp children never tidied their rooms or made their beds'.

Another nanny, Mary Clarke, felt that she was 'seeing a bit of old England that was dying fast', and she was right – life at Park House was very much in the

'Upstairs, Downstairs' tradition, almost Edwardian in its order and routine.

'The children were brought up in the old-fashioned way,' Nanny Clarke remembers, 'with ideals clearly stated. Manners were very important.'

They were something the Althorp children did not always find easy to acquire. Sarah, six years older than Diana, was particularly wild, forever getting herself into scrapes. It often proved too much for the over-worked women who were charged with the duty of turning her into a young lady, and nannies came and went with indecent frequency – a cause of concern to her parents who belong to a social class where nannies are regarded as an essential part of the family and often raise several generations, staying on past retirement and on to death.

The turnover at Park House, however, was fast. 'I can't remember exactly how many but it was a lot,' says Sarah, with amusement.

Jane was much quieter, but Diana did her bit to make up for that. She locked one nanny in the bathroom. In a fit of mischievousness she threw another's clothes out on to the roof. And no amount of persuasion could ever make her do something she didn't want to.

'She wasn't easy,' Nanny Thompson remembers. 'Some children will do as they are told immediately. Diana wouldn't. It was always a little battle of wills.' Obstinacy remains a characteristic of Diana to this day – to the occasional embarrassment of her royal relations – and there were numerous occasions when the 'spirited' little girl was dispatched to her room as a punishment.

She didn't like going for walks, much preferring to ride along on her bicycle. She didn't like having her long blonde hair washed.

'I had to talk her round each time,' says Nanny Thompson who had charge of Diana's upbringing until she was nearly six. 'My method was to lay her down in the bath, leaning her on my arm with her hair trailing in the water. But it was always a bit of a struggle. She would say, "Oh, not hair wash time again."'

She didn't much like horses. Riding is an essential part of country life. But when she was eight Diana fell off and broke her arm. It took three months to mend.

She again fell off her bay Romany a couple of years later when the pony caught its foot in a rabbit hole and tripped. Diana, Nanny Clarke believes, was not concentrating 'or she wouldn't have fallen'.

'We walked the rest of the way home and the doctor checked her and said she was fine.' Psychological damage had been done, however, and it was only very recently, and under pressure from her husband and mother-in-law, that Diana could be persuaded back into the saddle.

But if life had its occasional bumpy downs, it also had a lot of ups. There were romps with their father in the nursery, 'a wonderful room for playing bears in. We used to play bears there on our hands and knees,' Lord Spencer recalls.

There were bedtime stories from Nanny with animal and school tales being Diana's favourites. In the summer there would be trips to the seaside at Brancaster to build sand castles on the beach. There were shopping expeditions into King's Lynn which Diana adored. Even at that young age she had a passion for clothes. There was also the round of children's parties.

'The children were socializing all the time and Diana loved parties,' says Nanny Thompson.

One was at Sandringham. With her hair washed and neatly brushed, and wearing a new frock, five-year-old

Diana and her brother Charles set off for the 'big house'
for tea with Prince Andrew and Prince Edward, who
succeeded in covering himself with honey. And when
the tea was finished Nanny Thompson found her young
charge and six-year-old Andrew engaged in a frantic
and completely informal game of hide-and-seek in the
corridor – with the Queen.

There were times, though, when mood won out over
even Diana's love of parties: when she was ten, for
instance, and had been invited to a post-Christmas tea
party at Sandringham with the royal children. She
emphatically refused to go, claiming that she had a
headache.

By then, however, Diana's childhood idyll had come
to a savage and heartbreaking end. Her parents had
separated and Lady Althorp had left home.

In the summer of 1966 Frances had met wallpaper
heir Peter Shand-Kydd. He was everything her husband
was not.

Lord Althorp was quiet and kind and unassuming,
and preferred animals to people. He was, as far as his
wife was concerned, something of a bore who spent too
much of his spare time attending to the various local
charities he was involved in and not enough time with
his wife who liked parties, the theatre and people.

Shand-Kydd, a graduate of Edinburgh university and
a former naval officer, was extrovert and attractive with
an uncanny ability to make people laugh.

He also happened to be married with three children
but that proved no impediment to the desire of the
heart. According to the first Mrs Shand-Kydd the two
became lovers at an address in South Kensington.

Lady Althorp moved out of Park House and into an
apartment in Cadogan Place in Belgravia taking her

two youngest children with her. Diana went to day school, Charles to a nearby kindergarten.

Lord Althorp was devastated. His wife's decision to leave him, he says, came as a 'thunderbolt'.

The couple had married in considerable pomp in Westminster Abbey. The Queen and the Duke of Edinburgh and the Queen Mother were among the 1500 guests who attended at the Abbey and at the reception at St James's Palace afterwards. They had appeared the ideal couple. But how many of the fourteen years they had spent together had been happy ones? Lord Althorp wondered. 'I thought all of them – until the moment we parted. I was wrong.'

Lady Althorp returned to Park House with her two youngest children for a 'family' Christmas. It was the last one they would share together. Lord Althorp also put his foot down on the matter of Diana and Charles.

'He refused to let them return to London,' said her mother.

In all the free-wheeling morality of the sixties marital break-ups had become increasingly commonplace and by 1978 even the Queen's sister, Princess Margaret, made it into the divorce court. The old strictures, which even fifteen years before had denied a divorced person entrance into the Royal Enclosure at Ascot, were gone.

The Althorp divorce was different, however. Frances was branded an adulteress. Worse, she was perceived as having deserted her young family, and when the matter made its sad way into court she was refused custody of her children, which was awarded to their father. Even Frances's mother, Lady Fermoy, had turned against her, lending her moral support to her son-in-law and the comfort of her physical presence to Sarah and Jane and Charles and Diana. When Charles said, as he often used to, 'I was told that before you marry the daughter you should first look at the mother,' he clearly did not have Lady Althorp in mind.

Diana, in particular, was 'seriously affected' by the split, Nanny Clarke says. The young girl, once so lively, became introverted and developed her nervous blush and the habit of always looking down. This was when she started locking the women employed to look after her in bathrooms and throwing their clothes out of the window. And she would say to Mary Clarke: 'I'll never ever marry unless I really love, really love, someone. If you're not really sure you love someone, then you might get divorced. I never want to be divorced!' She was confused.

So was her father, who suddenly found himself as the head of a single-parent family and without the skills to cope. He would join his children for tea in the nursery but it was, says Mary Clarke, 'very hard going. In those early days he wasn't very relaxed with them'.

He tried to break through the barrier by asking them questions about what games they had been playing and how their school work was going, and about their pets, 'but they only answered his questions. They never started a conversation.'

After a few weeks Miss Clarke suggested that it might ease matters if the children, rather than being confined at the top of the house, were allowed to join their father for lunch in the dining room in future. Lord Althorp readily agreed, 'and the children became more relaxed.'

The confusion would remain in their young minds for some time to come, however. The Althorp divorce became absolute in April 1969 and within a month Lady Althorp had married Shand-Kydd. They moved into an old farmhouse near Itchenor in Sussex where Diana would go to visit her mother on the odd weekend and during the vacations. When she returned to Norfolk she was always 'awkward'. And she would test her nanny's loyalty by making unfavourable remarks about her father.

'I knew she meant none of it and would always change the subject.'

It was after one such visit to Sussex that Diana had stamped her stubborn little foot and refused to attend the royal children's tea party at Sandringham. She had become more solitary and was spending long hours in the nursery, dressing her teddy bear in her little brother's old baby clothes.

The change was not a dramatic one but it was there; the little girl the staff had affectionately nicknamed 'Duchess' for her imperious manner had been deeply upset by the sad, irreparable turn her short life had taken. Both her parents had done their best to shield their offspring from the malice that inevitably marks a marriage break-up but this divorce had been a particularly nasty one. It had set Lady Fermoy against her daughter, it had separated Lady Althorp from her children, it had virtually ostracized Lady Althorp from society, it had left Diana confused and unhappy. The feuding and the legal haggling had also dragged on for two bitter years, and no matter how hard Johnny Althorp and his former wife tried to confine the bitterness to their solicitors' offices, the children had inevitably caught its strong scent and it sickened them emotionally.

Diana did not talk about it except to say, over and over again, that she would only marry for true love because she never, never, wanted to get divorced.

4
School

When Diana was nine years old her parents decided that it would be in her best interests if she went to boarding school.

It was, her father recalls, 'a dreadful day'. That day the little girl was driven forty miles from Sandringham across the flat, monotonous Norfolk countryside and left at Riddlesworth Hall near Diss with her pet guinea pig 'Peanuts', and her trunk marked 'D. F. Spencer' packed with her uniform of pleated dresses, white shirts and her 'Sunday best' cherry-red dress the girls called 'prickles', all of which her mother had bought at Harrods, the school's outfitters.

It wasn't such a good day for Diana either.

She had been to school before. After being tutored at home by her mother's old governess Ally Allen, she had spent two years at Silfield in nearby King's House. But that had been a day school and every evening she had had the warmth and familiarity of Park Lodge to come back to. Now she was away from home with lots of other little girls who were away from home, many for the first time, and for the first few nights the dormitory was filled with the sound of them quietly weeping into their pillows.

And school, even at the best of times, was not an institution in which Diana would shine, at least not academically. Ally had called her a 'real trier' and a 'conscientious worker' who was interested in history (she liked stories about kings and queens). At Silfield the headmistress, Jean Lowe, who had given evidence on Lord Althorp's behalf in the custody battle, had been impressed with how well she could read and how clear her writing was, at the same time noting that she dedicated all her pictures and drawings to 'Mummy and Daddy'.

But she had been young then. At Riddlesworth her education moved from the nursery games of infancy and on to the harder curriculum of grammar and arithmetic and history lessons which were about dates and facts, not fairy-tale kings and queens. She was, Miss Lowe remembers, 'extremely average'.

The British boarding school is, however, a strange institution. It can be a horror. Yet by its very routine and insistence on rules and order it can give a sense of security, and Diana, like many other children from broken homes, found a stability there she might otherwise have missed.

She soon settled in and her mother and father would come to visit her on alternate weekends, bringing with them the ginger biscuits and Twiglets and cream eggs she was so fond of. She never did rise to any noticeable academic heights but she came to excel in other ways.

'The things that particularly stand out in my memories,' Miss Lowe recorded in the school's magazine in 1981 when Diana became, by marriage, the most famous of her old girls, 'are kindness to the smaller members of the community, her general helpfulness, her love of animals and her excellence at swimming and indeed her considerable prowess in general physical activities.'

Riddlesworth had taught her the necessary level to pass the Common Entrance examination which gave her passage to her next school. With the inevitability of family tradition, she went to West Heath, the all-girls public school near Sevenoaks. Founded in 1865, its aim was to 'train the students to develop their own minds and tastes and realize their duties as citizens'.

Prince Charles's great-grandmother, Queen Mary, had been a pupil there. It was where Diana's mother had been educated. She had risen to become 'captain of everything' and it was where Mrs Shand-Kydd had decided to send her own daughters. With mixed success.

The middle girl, Jane, was a senior girl when Diana first arrived, and enjoyed it. Not so her eldest sister Sarah.

Like her mother, an excellent tennis player who had qualified for junior Wimbledon only to be struck down by appendicitis, Sarah was an excellent sportswoman. She had played lacrosse and netball and cricket and tennis. She had captained the swimming team and was famous for her prize-winning dive, the Spencer Special which left barely a ripple in the pool.

But she was also headstrong and rebellious. Though now teetotal, she also developed a youthful taste for strong liquor.

'I used to drink because I was bored,' Sarah recalls. 'I would drink anything. Whisky, Cointreau, sherry, or most often, vodka because they couldn't smell it on my breath.'

One day they did and Sarah was firmly told to pack her trunk and depart the school – and not to return.

Diana was never in that league – but she did have her moments.

The headmistress, Ruth Rudge, who retired recently, was Australian and her intention was to 'develop character and confidence'. The girls had to wear a uniform of navy jumper, pleated skirt and black stockings ('Oh look,' said Diana, enviously, when she went back to open a new sports hall in 1987, 'I see you are allowed to wear coloured tights now'). They slept in dormitories they nicknamed 'cowsheds'. Diana's was decorated with a portrait of Prince Charles, though it was Prince Andrew whom her contemporaries would jokingly say she was going to marry.

As part of their 'duties as a citizen' everyone was expected to take part in community work and Diana would visit an old lady in Sevenoaks every week to sit and chat, do some shopping and help tidy up. She also paid a weekly visit to a nearby home for handicapped children.

Music and sport were also emphasized and Diana was good at both. She played tennis well enough, though not as well as her mother. She won the diving prize. She excelled at netball because, as she says, 'it was much easier for me to get the ball in the net because I was so tall'.

She danced tap and ballet and went for long walks through the attractive grounds that surround the Georgian mansion which is the main school building.

And like all children at boarding school she had her holidays to look forward to. Diana's were particularly pleasant. Whatever her father may have thought of his former wife (and not surprising in the circumstances, it wasn't a lot), they were still determined to spare their children from as much of the lingering bitterness as possible and vacations were divided between Norfolk, Sussex and, later, the Isle of Seil on Scotland's West Coast where the Shand-Kydds had bought a thousand-acre sheep farm.

Scotland was an idyllic retreat for a young teenager who was still rather young for her age. There was swimming in the warm waters of the Gulf Stream which sweep into the Firth of Lorn and lobster pots to be baited and occasional trips to the cinema in Oban where Frances Shand-Kydd ran a small gift shop.

From the age of fourteen onwards Diana also had the rather grander alternative of Althorp, the Northamptonshire seat of the Spencer family.

In 1975 her grandfather, the seventh earl, died and her father succeeded to the house – a magnificent mansion two hours' drive out of London set in 2000 acres of rolling countryside. Portraits of Diana's ancestors, including works by Sir Joshua Reynolds, hang in the 115-foot gallery. There is a library stocked with some of the rarest books in Europe, and on the ground floor is the porcelain collection.

Lord Althorp was now Earl Spencer. And upon his elevation to the peerage his daughter moved up from being plain Miss to become Lady Diana Spencer. This social elevation did not curtail her stubbornness and occasional naughtiness. Back at school if she didn't like a particular sporting activity she had been known to smear blue eye-shadow on her knees and pretend it was bruising. And there were, she remembers, dormitory romps and pillow fights and midnight feasts and custard-pie throwing.

When she was caught she was punished by being made to 'run six times round the hall which has to be preferable to the lacrosse pitch or weeding the garden which I became a great expert at'.

This expertise did not extend to her schoolwork. At Silfield she was awarded a prize for trying hard. At Riddlesworth she won the Pets' Corner Cup.

West Heath rewarded her social work with a 'special award for service', which, as Miss Rudge emphasized, was only given to outstanding pupils.

The examiners who marked her 'O' level papers were

not so charitable. She failed them all. And when she went back to take them again, she failed them all again.

On her return to the school in 1987 to open the new £250,000 sports hall, she said, 'In spite of what Miss Rudge and my other teachers may have thought, I *did* actually learn something.' It was not enough, however, for Diana to continue her education. At the age of sixteen and without any tangible qualifications, she left West Heath.

There then followed a brief, though not highly productive, stay at the Institut Alpin Videmanette, an expensive Swiss finishing school.

She was supposed to improve her French. Instead she spoke English with Sophie Kimball, another English girl, and became desperately homesick. The school imposed a reign of terror forbidding anyone to utter a word of anything but French. Pupils were supposed to take a bi-lingual secretarial course and acquire cooking skills, but if they failed to understand anything that was going on it made their lives very miserable indeed. At night they were locked up and the only boys they ever saw were the ones from the local village. Young for her age, Diana did not fit in well with the European and more worldly pupils and although she enjoyed the skiing she hated everything else. One day, and after many tears, she left and flew home to her mother's London apartment in Chelsea.

But Diana was not the only pupil to leave. Melanie Green, who attended the school a short time after Diana, recalls: 'I hated it. I can quite understand why she left. I have never been so miserable in my life and I left too.'

For many youngsters so under-qualified, the future would have offered nothing but a wasting life in the dole queue. Diana was spared that indignity. She was

born an aristocrat with a cushion of family money to
support her. She moved into her mother's home and
attended a cookery course and took dancing lessons.

And when Mrs Shand-Kydd decided to sell the
house, her family trust, supplemented by a tidy bequest
left her by her American great-grandmother, Frances
Work, enabled Diana to buy a flat, 60 Colherne Court,
on the borders of Kensington and the rather more
down-market area of Earl's Court.

Sophie Kimball moved in as a flatmate. And when
she moved out she was replaced by Carolyn Pride, a
school friend from West Heath, who was studying at
the Royal College of Music. Joining them were Ann
Bolton who is now married to Australian Noel Hill,
and the extrovert Virginia Pitman who has hitch-hiked
through Africa.

They got on well together, buying their groceries at
the little Indian-run shop on the corner, eating at the
local bistros, occasionally entertaining friends to
supper (Virginia usually did the cooking, and Diana,
ever the tidiness fanatic, did the washing up).

There was also money that had to be earned. Ann
Bolton, for instance, was an estate agent's secretary.
Diana had to make do with more lowly employment –
for a year she worked as a daily maid and a baby-sitter!

Her sister Sarah was also living in London, in an
apartment she shared with Hampshire landowner's
daughter Lucinda Craig-Harvey.

Lucinda is now a West End theatre producer. She
recalls: 'She worked for me as a "daily" three days a
week. She did everything. She dusted. She cleaned.
She did the washing up. She cleaned out the bathroom.
She scrubbed out the loo. She did the lot. And she was
very good. Well, good enough. She lasted a year and

Sarah, as her older sister, would have soon got rid of her and got someone else if she hadn't been.

'I'd mark her a good eight out of ten.'

In the evenings the world's most successful char-lady – not many cleaners rise to become Princess of Wales – would baby-sit. Her clients included an American couple, Patrick and Mary Robinson, who remember her as 'refined – and wonderful with children'.

It was working with children that gave Diana the most satisfaction. Her ambitions to become a dancer having ended when she grew too tall, she had nurtured the hope of becoming a ballet teacher instead. For a short time she had worked at the Vacani School of Dancing round the corner from her flat in Kensington, teaching infants their first rhythmic steps. She did not, however, have the dedication to make a career out of it. 'She had rather a full social life,' Miss Vacani recalls.

She had, however, been popular with the children. And when Kay Seth-Smith, a contemporary of her middle sister Jane at West Heath, offered her a job at the Young England Kindergarten she helped run in Pimlico, Diana jumped at the chance.

'She got along very well with the children and the parents liked her,' Kay recounts.

Her job was to help the children with their pictures and picture books and bricks, to give them simple dancing lessons, to comfort them when they cried, to change them when they wet themselves. It was work she did well. As her mother had once remarked, 'Diana was a positive Pied Piper with children'.

But that full social life which Miss Vacani had been talking about was getting much fuller. For a young man had come on to her horizon, and that man was the Prince of Wales, the 'most eligible bachelor in the world'.

Diana was flattered and charmed. Her flatmates were quickly caught up in the excitement of the romance and became involved in the subterfuge and the plots and the plans that went with it. And when it became clear that Diana's friendship with Charles was more than just a passing thing, the excitement grew and acquired a life and momentum of its own. Would Charles call tonight? Would Diana be invited to Balmoral? Was Charles too old for her? Diana would ask the girls who shared her home. Did he love her? Did the girl who had sworn that she would never marry someone she didn't truly love, love him?

In this frenzy of royal courtship there was little time for clear or introspective thought. That would only come later.

In 1987 Carolyn Pride was interviewed for Australian television. 'What', she was asked, 'did Diana and Charles have in common?' Her mouth dropped open as she stumbled for a reply.

It never came. Diplomatically Carolyn's reaction was cut off the tape and never broadcast.

5
Courtship

In the days before Diana became accustomed to daily hairdressers, high fashion and expertly applied make-up, she looked her best when she was wearing her least. No frilly blouses concealed her elegant neck, carefully cut skirts her long legs, or bulky sweaters her well-rounded figure. She was young and not fully aware of just how attractive she could be. But if she wanted to impress a young man, any young man, she always made it a point to go swimming or sailing or, at the very least, play a game of tennis.

When Prince Charles saw her aboard *Britannia* at Cowes in the late summer of 1980, he wasn't however particularly interested. She belonged to his younger brother Andrew's set, and had come aboard, not at Charles's invitation, but with Lady Sarah Armstrong Jones, his cousin and sixteen years his junior.

Diana was three years older than Sarah, but still almost a generation away. And besides, Charles had his mind on other things – most particularly the break-up of his romance with the beautiful but oh so self-willed Anna Wallace. There was also the fact that if he noticed Diana in anything more than passing, he thought about her as the sister of one of his former girlfriends – Lady Sarah Spencer – who had recently married (he hadn't attended), and whatever others might have been plotting he most certainly was not thinking of renewing his romantic links with the Spencer girls.

But if Charles was not instantly enchanted by the

fresh, gambolling nineteen-year-old who spent some days aboard the Royal Yacht, his staff were. 'She was so unassuming and so natural,' one recalls. And in the manner of all servants, particularly ones who are in the employ of the bachelor Prince, they inevitably started speculating amongst themselves if she was the one for what they called 'the job'.

So, it seems, did Diana. At the age of sixteen she had jokingly told a friend that she was 'out to get' Charles. But that may have been just romantic fantasizing on the part of a young girl whose main reading was the soapy romances penned by her step-grandmother, the redoubtable Barbara Cartland. The Prince's late valet, Stephen Barry, insisted however: 'She went after the Prince with single-minded determination. She wanted him – and she got him!'

She had, of course, met him many times before in the years of her childhood spent as a near-neighbour of the Windsors at Sandringham when Charles used to pop his head round the nursery door where she was having tea with Andrew and Edward, or during a shooting party on Sandringham Estate where at the age of sixteen she was reintroduced to him by her sister Sarah. More recently she had encountered him at polo. But then he had always been busy or with a girlfriend in tow. This time he was alone.

She made sure Charles was watching when she bravely followed his example and went windsurfing in the choppy and not-too-warm waters of the Solent. Naturally flirtatious, she made sure he noticed her long slim legs and trim figure. And he could not fail but start to take an interest – if only a comparative one – in the beautiful younger sister of a former girlfriend.

Accounts of this first meeting vary. Some claim that it is where the famous romance began. Others insist that his interest was but a mild one; that with Anna still in mind, the timing was wrong and he simply regarded her as a new and pretty addition to his surprisingly limited circle of friends.

But she had certainly impressed him enough for him to invite her up to Balmoral shortly afterwards. Diana accepted with alacrity.

At this stage of her development the young woman whose life was soon to go the way of a fairy-tale was inclined to lapse into a world of fantasy.

Under-educated, without a proper career to interest her and with an imagination fuelled by the Mills and Boon-style novelettes she was so addicted to, she was – like a Barbara Cartland heroine – simply marking time until she married and had children. And there were times when she could not but feel that her life was uninteresting and, above all, desperately lacking in the kind of romance she was seeking.

She did have admirers amongst her set of well-connected young Sloanes. They included Old Etonian Simon Berry, a member of the family of St James's wine merchants, and George Plumptree, six years her senior, who now writes books on gardening. They would dine out together in one of the Chelsea restaurants favoured by her set. Occasionally they would eat in and Diana, who had attended a Cordon Bleu cookery course, would make scrambled eggs. She went skiing in France with Berry and sixteen other friends. But for whatever reason, none of the men she met quite matched the identikit which Diana had mentally drawn for herself.

The Prince of Wales, on the other hand, fitted her romantic notions perfectly and the more he dismissed her as a 'little sister', the more intrigued she became.

There were no obvious signs, however, that her interest was being reciprocated during that first stay at

Balmoral. And her second trip north in October also passed without any romantic incident that anyone who was there at the time can remember.

Diana was not without her supporters, however. The staff were very taken with her. And on that second expedition to the Highlands she stayed with the Queen Mother at Birkhall on the Balmoral estate. Her grandmother Lady Fermoy was also there. Both ladies had always been fond of her and in the enclosed and female-dominated world that Charles lived in, the approval of those two grand dames was certainly no handicap to any young woman with a romantic interest in the Prince.

And Diana, it must be said, played the part demanded of her to ingenuous perfection. These days, she can hardly bring herself to visit Balmoral. Then she was cheerful and obliging. While Charles was out on the hill stalking stags, she would get on with her needlepoint until it was time to join the returning men for afternoon tea followed by evening drinks and dinner and perhaps a game of charades. She had sat the 'Craigowan Test' – and this was one examination Diana passed with honours.

It was now that Charles and Diana's relationship changed up a gear. Once back in London Charles invited her to join him for what he called 'cosy' dinners in his rooms at Buckingham Palace. He then paid her the enormous compliment of inviting her down to Gloucestershire to take a look at Highgrove, the eighteenth-century manor house he had bought for himself out of his income from the Duchy of Cornwall, for £800,000 in 1980.

If Diana was not overly impressed (and she wasn't) with the sparsely furnished and rather stolid house whose rooms, in a failure of imagination, Charles had painted all white, she did her best not to show it. The fact that she was there was enough. It could mean only one thing – that Charles was now beginning to take a serious interest in her.

It was in many respects an odd romance. Throughout his courting years Charles had kept within his own age group. Diana was almost young enough to be his daughter, a still unformed woman barely out of school. She shared none of his obvious interests.

There was also the contrast in their educational backgrounds. Diana, as the Americans say, is a high school drop-out. Charles, on the other hand, is a university graduate who likes nothing better than settling down with an intellectually taxing book on psychology or history.

Nor – and this was a rarity indeed amongst Charles's serious girlfriends – did she share his love of equestrian sports.

For all their differences, however, the couple were developing an obvious and genuine affection for each other. Perhaps it was because of them. Diana had a freshness that Charles found captivating. She was unspoilt and good humoured and even the vociferous press attention she quickly attracted failed on all but the rarest of occasions to disturb her unduly – unlike Lady Jane Wellesley who had been reduced to near hysteria by the hordes of paparrazzi who had attached themselves to her when she had first started walking out with the Prince of Wales.

There was another factor too which worked in Diana's favour. It was that time was running out for the 'world's most eligible bachelor'.

Left to his own devices, some of his friends believe that Charles might never have married. He enjoyed his bachelorhood and as the years passed he was becoming ever more set in his own self-centred routine. He had his sport and there was an army of servants always on hand to tend to his needs. He had his foreign travel. There was usually a pretty girl available to join him for dinner or accompany him to polo. He is a man who enjoys his own company, who indeed becomes irritable and depressed if deprived of the chance to spend time alone with only his thoughts for company, and the compromise a marriage demands did not entirely appeal to him.

But Charles was under pressure. When the press started worrying about his continued reluctance to take a bride, they were merely reflecting a public concern – and one that was growing. The Queen too was becoming unhappy with the situation. She is a woman whose whole life has been dedicated to upholding the Crown and one of the fundamental responsibilities of monarchy is to secure its own succession.

On a more personal level she was growing increasingly uneasy at the way her son and eventual successor was ending romantic escapades and eroding the dignity of the Royal Family.

This was hardly Charles's fault. If he had been born as little as thirty years earlier he could have dated whom he liked, secure in the knowledge that his romances would have been allowed to mature in private and not on the front pages of the tabloids. But the old barriers which hide the Royal Family from public view had fallen and Charles's love-life was looking disconcertingly like an episode out of a soap opera. The Queen was not amused.

Nor was Prince Philip who had made it his life-long habit to remind his son of his royal responsibilities. He reminded him of them now and kept pointing out that if Charles didn't make his choice soon there would be no one left to choose.

He was also concerned that Charles should not be seen to be leading a nineteen-year-old up a garden path to a still-born romance. It was a worry shared by Diana's mother, Frances Shand-Kydd. In a letter to *The Times* she complained:

'In recent weeks many articles have been labelled "exclusive quotes" when the plain truth is that my daughter has not spoken the words attributed to her. Fanciful speculation if it is in good taste is one thing, but this can be embarrassing. Lies are quite another matter and by their very nature, hurtful and inexcusable.

'May I ask the editors in Fleet Street whether, in the execution of their jobs, they consider it necessary or fair to harass my daughter daily, from dawn until well after dusk? Is it fair to ask any human being, regardless of circumstances, to be treated this way? The freedom of the press was granted by law, by public demand, for very good reasons. But when these privileges are abused, can the press command any respect or expect to be shown any respect?'

Mrs Shand-Kydd had underestimated her youngest daughter. Diana quite enjoyed the chase and with the connivance of her friends and Charles's private staff made a game for herself out of outwitting the pursuing Rat Pack of reporters assigned to cover her every move.

She would sometimes slip off to her grandmother's apartment in Belgravia's Eaton Square and then slip out again into a waiting car driven by Charles's valet, Barry, who would whisk her away to a rendezvous at Buckingham Palace or Highgrove. She would sometimes say she was going to one place and then double back and head off in another direction in her Mini

Metro. And if, as sometimes happened, the journalists succeeded in double guessing her, she always took the trouble to drop her head in that familiar way and award them the prize of a demure smile.

For despite what her mother might have thought she had been giving quotes – and quite genuine ones – to a number of royal reporters. She had established a friendly rapport with several and had sought the private, off-the-record advice of at least one journalist and had told him that she disagreed strongly with what her mother had written.

She also happened to enjoy the attention. Every morning she took delivery of the newspapers and would sit for hours with her flatmates giggling over the morning's quota of pictures and stories devoted to her.

The press in their turn adored her. She had won them over by a combination of charm and subtle co-operation and they had become her unquestioning allies in what in truth had become a courtship by newspaper.

It was weighed down with this backpack of public and private pressure that Charles entered the New Year and whatever his private thoughts might have been, the roller coaster was speeding towards what was now looking like an inevitable *dénouement*.

In keeping with royal tradition he went up to Sandringham in Norfolk. Diana went too. So, of course, did her fan club of royal reporters. Everyone was becoming very tetchy. Prince Edward fired a shotgun over the heads of photographers. Charles shouted to the waiting journalists that he hoped their editors had an unhappy New Year. Even the Queen was irritable and in an unprecedented break of temper shouted at the Rat Pack, 'Why don't you all go away!'

They didn't, needless to say. For by now just about

everyone who could had entered into the plot. It was reported that 'Kanga' Tryon and Camilla Parker-Bowles had 'vetted' Diana and found her acceptable. Questions were being asked in the House of Commons. Barbara Cartland declared: 'Prince Charles has got to have a pure young girl. I don't think Diana has had a boy-friend. That is marvellous . . .'

Giving more explicit expression to what people had come to believe was a prerequisite for any bride of the Prince of Wales, Diana's uncle, Lord Fermoy, went so far as to announce, 'She, I can assure you, has never had a lover.'

The Windsors, contrary to accepted opinion, have never held physical purity in quite the high esteem they are supposed to, as witnessed by the unproblem-atic way Sarah Ferguson was accepted into the Royal Family. And Lord Fermoy, who was never as close to his niece as he liked to think he was and who later committed suicide, was hardly in a position to know with true certainty what a young woman living unchaperoned in the centre of London might or might not have got up to.

But if purity is a public virtue, then Diana could provide. No ex-boyfriend emerged from the woodwork of the past to talk about love trysts in 'rose-covered cottages'. All that anyone managed to dig up was that she had once taken a shine to a handsome young lieutenant, Rory Scott, in the Scots Guards, and had used to take his shirts back to her flat to wash. But all in perfect romantic innocence as everyone was at pains to point out. There simply was no past to expose because, as Diana herself observed, she simply didn't have one. She had sat another test, this time before the jury of public opinion with the press presenting the evidence, and passed again with flying colours. Whatever reservations Charles may have harboured, whatever excuses he may have given himself, had run out. Diana had captured the greatest heart of all – the heart of the British public.

At the end of January, Charles flew off for his annual skiing holiday in Klosters. Diana had hoped to go with him and had been looking forward to the break. In the end, however, it was agreed that with all the constant attention, it would be better if she remained behind in Britain.

On 2 February Charles flew home. Two days later he made her an official proposal of marriage. Not on his knees, 'not on either of them,' he says, but over dinner in his private sitting room at Buckingham Palace just before she flew off for a vacation in Australia with her mother and step-father.

'I chose the moment so that she would have plenty of time to think about it, to decide if it was all going to be too awful,' he recalled.

Diana decided it wouldn't be and promptly said, 'Yes'. As he knew she would. For the couple had already discussed marriage, in a roundabout way, but in some detail over 'picnic' dinners of eggs and spinach eaten off a card table in the still-to-be-properly decorated discomfort of Highgrove. Charles can have been left in no doubt that the young girl, all of thirteen years his junior, was deeply in love with him.

Charles was more circumspect. 'Are you in love?' the television interviewer enquired. The Prince hesitated for a moment and then answered, 'Yes, whatever that may mean.'

It was not a dramatically romantic response. But then, for the man born to be King, marriage is as much an act of state as a declaration of the heart. For him there can be no going back, no divorce, no second chance. Love, whatever that may be, could all too often prove to be only infatuation, he had said. 'Creating a secure family unit in which to bring up children, to give them a happy secure upbringing – that is what marriage is all about,' he once explained. 'Marriage is more important than just falling in love.'

Diana made no such qualifications. Asked the same question she had answered instantly, 'Of course.'

To win a prince is one thing, to become a princess is something very different, as Diana was about to discover. In becoming engaged, she had made a reality out of every lovelorn schoolgirl's fantasy – including, it is fair to say, her own.

She was to discover what the price was. The engagement was announced at 11 A.M. on Tuesday 24 February. (*The Times* had had the story on its front page that morning, leaked to its editor, Charles discovered to his profound anger.) She became, for all practical purposes, a member of the Royal Family.

She was assigned a detective who from now on would accompany her everywhere, even into the Bond Street lingerie shop where she went to buy her silk knickers.

She moved out of her flat in Colherne Court, and not into Clarence House with the Queen Mother as was supposed at the time, but into Buckingham Palace, into a suite of rooms a tiptoe away from Charles's own chambers.

There was a very good reason for this. Charles and his wife-to-be had been walking out together for six months, but it had been a courtship conducted in a goldfish bowl.

'They hardly ever had a moment when they could be alone together,' one of Charles's aides told me. 'The

time between the engagement and the marriage was the
time when they could get to know each other – absolutely vital for two people who, after all, are going to
have to spend the rest of their life together.'

Again this might seem odd. Most people get engaged
after they have got to know each other, not before. But
that, even in this day and age, is not the royal way, not
if the royal in question is the future King.

On a more mundane level, Diana also had to learn
how to behave.

'We had a lot of problems with Diana at the beginning,' one of Charles's closest aides explains. 'She had
come straight out of the nursery school into the Palace
and she sometimes got carried away with it all.

'The most important thing we had to do was to calm
her down. She got very excited. She was always waving
and smiling – like a film star. But there is a difference
between being a film star and being a member of the
Royal Family. Everything has to be more discreet.'

The task of guiding her through the unseen pitfalls
fell to Charles's closest aides and to Lady Susan
Hussey, wife of the Chairman of the Board of Governors
of the BBC and Lady-in-Waiting to the Queen.

It was Lady Susan who would quietly and discreetly
advise her to wave now, but not to wave then, and how
to execute the royal handshake (always brief and never
too firm: the exercise gets very painful over the course
of a day after hundreds of hands have been shaken).

Oliver Everett, Charles's assistant private secretary,
taught her how to walk. For a while each day he would
parade the future Princess up and down the Palace
ballroom with yards of tissue paper attached to her
head and dragging along the floor behind her. This was
how she was prepared to walk down the aisle at St Paul's
with her wedding train. Everett, a polo player and

seventeen years Diana's senior, formed an immediate bond with the Princess. She was lonely and he was around far more than Prince Charles. He was later appointed her private secretary, but left in 1983 – some say it was because Diana was embarrassed by the close friendship she had formed with Everett, and that she threw him out after her marriage.

She was given a selection of royal biographies, books describing the lives of other women who in times past had married other princes of the realm, and she was expected to read them. 'It was a fast lesson in recent royal history,' an advisor explains.

There were inevitable hiccups and mistakes. Stephen Barry explained, 'There isn't a charm school for princesses. Diana had to learn by example.'

And if the example proved insufficient, subtle action had to be taken. As in her dealings with the household servants.

The Royal Family are as a rule most polite to the people who look after them and Charles always ends his orders with the words, 'If you don't mind?'

But there is always a distance between them, a chasm that is never crossed, and the relationship is never more than that of master and servant.

In those early days, however, Diana was too familiar. Lonely and left alone for long hours each day, she was forever popping down to the kitchens, looking for company, or engaging young footmen in conversation.

It was the senior staff who objected and took the matter in hand. They did not approve of these 'Scandinavian' practices. The British do not have a bicycling Royal Family and their employees, whose own lives are governed by a servants' caste system, do not want one.

Barry admonished a footman who was becoming too

friendly with her. The Yeoman of the Glass and China
gave her a sterner reminder of the social divisions of
her new role as the future Princess of Wales.

One day when the court was at Sandringham, Diana
again arrived in the kitchens.

The Yeoman saw her. He bluntly pointed to the door
and said, 'Through there is *your* side of the house –
and through here is *my* side of the house.'

Diana blushed a deep red and fled, never to return.

It was an ivory tower from which there was no
escape. One day she decided to go out. The moment
she got into her red Metro which was parked in the
quadrangle of Buckingham Palace, Paul Officer, one of
the policemen from the Royal Protection Squad,
climbed in beside her.

She said she could manage by herself, thank you. He
replied, 'I'm sorry but we're part of your life now.'

The staff called her the Princess in the Tower. The
Prince, returning from a day of royal duties would
anxiously enquire, 'Is Lady Diana all right?'

True to the old theatre adage, of course, it was all
right on the day and it was a radiant and beautiful
Diana who arrived on the arm of her father at St Paul's
Cathedral that glorious summer's day in 1981.

There were the little confusions. She got his names
round the wrong way ('Well, with four names it's quite
something to get organized' she explained afterwards).
He did manage to endow her with his worldly goods,
but only just. 'But it added a certain amount of amusement into the proceedings,' Charles said.

The night before, tens of thousands of people had
gathered in the Mall and sung *Rule Britannia*. Remembers Charles, 'It really was remarkable and I found
myself standing in the window with tears pouring
down my face.'

Weddings are a moment for hope and optimism; they represent a commitment to the future and when Diana and Charles married, a whole nation joined in the celebration.

'I found we were carried along on a wave of enormous friendliness and enthusiasm,' Charles recalls. 'It was remarkable. And I kept telling myself to remember this for as long as I could because it was such a unique experience.'

He added, 'Inevitably these things don't always last very long. But I think it made one realize that underneath everything else, all the rowing and the bickering and disagreements that go on the rest of the time, every now and then you get a reason for a celebration or a feeling of being a nation.'

Diana shares all those feelings. She also has one more private memory. She says, 'It was terrifying.'

A worldwide television audience of 700 million people had watched Lady Diana Spencer marry the Prince of Wales. They would be watching to see how the marriage would work. Diana was right. It was terrifying.

6
In-Laws

The Queen, senior members of the Royal Household assure me, 'thinks the world' of Diana.

So she does, though in her own regal way.

For all that stern public persona the Sovereign is in fact easy-going with a witty and, at times, wicked turn of phrase who enjoys a joke, a glass of wine and her children. She adores her grandchildren. And she is very taken with both her daughters-in-law.

She knew instinctively how to treat the young coltish aristocrat who married her eldest son and brought such glamour into the family business of monarchy.

One day when Diana came into her private sitting room in a state of high agitation, the Sovereign took one look and remarked, 'She's like a nervy racehorse. She needs careful handling.'

And the Queen has handled her carefully, encouraging her with her genuine affection and the occasional kindly word.

There is, though, another side to the woman who has spent almost all her adult life reigning over a fifth of the world's peoples. She is always regal, always a little reserved – even with her closest kin.

In the popular imagination, she is a woman who is always worrying over the behaviour of her offspring, forever calling them to account – an ermine-plumed mother hen fretting over her brood. In fact she is far too busy with her works of State, work she approaches seriously and with a single-minded dedication, to over-concern herself with the normal ups and downs of day-to-day life that might afflict other members of the Royal

Family. And for all the talk of the 'young royals', it is worth remembering that they are in fact adults, often with children of their own, and they are expected to deal with their own problems themselves. If there are any sharp words of advice to dispense, it is usually Charles – already on the threshold of middle age – who does the dispensing.

Indeed, there have been times when her own staff wondered if she was expecting too much independence from her family. For there were certainly times right at the beginning when Diana was in some need of the Queen's guidance but never got it.

Diana had moved into Buckingham Palace in preparation for her wedding. She was accommodated in a modest suite on the second floor, down the corridor from Charles's apartment. The Queen does not visit that part of the building – and it was by appointment only that Diana would visit her future mother-in-law in her private suite a mile of Palace corridors away. The appointments were few and far between.

It was confusing and not a little disconcerting to a young girl who was used to the companionship and informality of her own family. She was lonely. She felt isolated, and her confidence, as yet uncast by the mould of experience, began to erode. Diana, initially so relaxed and at ease in the Queen's company, went through a period when she was 'petrified' of her.

She felt herself under scrutiny, and she was. There were several occasions before the wedding, she admits, when she cried. There were similar occasions afterwards and at one point the Queen had cause to wonder if Diana was going to 'make it'.

It is easy to say the Queen should have done more. But the Queen, by natural shyness and a lifetime's training, has never been capable of giving tactile comfort and motherly love at the drop of a tear. And besides, the Royal Family have always held that you are either royal or you are not and if Diana was going to 'make it', as they put it so colloquially, she had to make it herself.

To everyone's delight and the Sovereign's particular pleasure, a marked warmth now characterizes the relationship between the Queen and the woman who will be a Queen herself one day.

Diana came to realize her power and her position and she began to feel more relaxed in the presence of her mother-in-law.

The Queen in turn is 'delighted' with the way Diana has developed. The Princess of Wales still joins the Queen for lunch or tea or a light evening meal, though only 'by appointment'. (No one, not even the Prince of Wales, 'drops in' on the Queen, a member of her Household points out.) Such exigencies of royal life notwithstanding, however, the relationship is 'first class'.

There are moments of exception as there are in all families. But it was more in sadness than in anger that the Princess and her husband were summoned to Buckingham Palace in the October of 1987. It was the time of the Balmoral estrangement and the estrangement was degenerating into royal crisis. Even the Royal Family, which lives most of its life cocooned in an ivory tower of indifference high above the speculations of the rabble, had come to realize that something had to be done to quench the bushfire of rumour and that only the Queen was in a position to do it.

Her Majesty does not like confrontation. In fact she detests it and goes out of her way to avoid it, as does her son. But eventually, after Diana had attended a fashion show and Charles had been to the opera, the Waleses left Kensington Palace and drove the few short miles across London to the Monarch's London HQ. Twenty minutes later they were on their way back home again.

It had been a terse exchange. But it had been at Charles and *not* Diana that the Queen's displeasure had been directed.

It is not easy to apportion blame when a relationship hits the skid pan. As far as the Queen saw it, however, Charles was the one who had to take the larger share of responsibility for that altogether unseemly situation.

'The Queen did not think Diana had done anything wrong,' says a member of the Household.

It is a measure that illustrates just how far Diana has come since her marriage and in what affection the Queen now holds her. She is not a newcomer any more. She is a fully integrated and immensely important member of the family and one whose side the Queen will take, even against her own son if the situation so warrants.

Perhaps more surprisingly, Diana is also on the best of terms with Princess Margaret. Bohemian but at the same time *very* Royal, the Queen's sister can be somewhat tricky. If she wants to stay up until 3 o'clock in the morning leading a sing-song from the piano, she does so – and everyone has to sing along with her until she grows tired. No one departs her royal presence until she retires herself. And that includes the servants. It even included the Queen's servants until, up at Sandringham one year, she enquired why her retainers were looking so tired. On being told that it was because they had been on duty almost till dawn, the Queen ruled that when she retired then her staff could retire too. (Those houseguests without the necessary stamina for Margaret's all-night sessions now follow the servants' example and make a discreet bolt for the door when the Queen gets up to go to bed.)

Amusing and a splendid mimic, Margaret can also exercise her tongue to withering effect. She does not suffer fools or bores lightly and many poor souls, talking on into tedium, have found themselves cut off in mid-sentence with the word 'Quite' which she uses as incisively as a surgeon uses a scalpel.

Princess Margaret likes to be entertained – and she is not an easy woman to please. Yet she is very fond of Diana. She was most impressed when the Princess of Wales took the trouble to send her butler, whom she hardly knew, a hand-written note and a potted plant when he was hospitalized with jaundice in 1987.

Diana also makes the point of bringing her aunt-in-law punnets of fresh raspberries she has picked herself on the Highgrove estate.

Margaret rarely entertains her royal relations, much preferring the company of actors and handsome property developers. The Waleses, however, are an exception. They are regularly invited to walk across the courtyard at Kensington Palace from their own apartment to hers for a fine gourmet dinner and she in her turn will be asked back for a rather simpler repast of fish and fruit.

It is an easy-going, informal interplay between two disparate women and Diana must take much of the credit.

The only time Princess Margaret really disapproved of anything Diana did was when she put her hair up in a classic chignon for the State Opening of Parliament in November 1984. She thought Diana upstaged the Queen and should have been sensible enough to realize what an uproar the new style would cause. Diana's former hairdresser, Kevin Shanley, who had refused to do the style and had left it to his assistant Richard Dalton, agrees:

'I knew it wouldn't suit her,' he said. 'Her hair wasn't long enough, but Diana got her own way – and at what a cost. That one hairstyle ruined everyone's fantasy of her.'

Her relationship with her sister-in-law the Princess Royal is much more complex. On the face of it they have absolutely nothing in common. Anne can be brusque to the point of rudeness: Diana, if not the Shy Di of the tabloid headlines, is always trying to put people at their ease. Diana is very aware of how she looks. Anne doesn't care. Jeans and jumpers and artificial-fibred shirts are her preference and more than one grand lady has been astonished by her chipped and unvarnished fingernails.

It is only on the most special of occasions and then only in the company of the most special of friends that she can be persuaded out of the country she loves and into a West End restaurant. Diana adores her girlie lunches in such fashionable London eateries as San Lorenzo and Launceston Place.

Anne has earned international respect for her work for the Save the Children Fund. Diana's work is simply to be the Princess of Wales – just being Diana is a job in itself.

There is also the eleven-year age gap. Anne was a fully formed woman secure in the role she had created for herself when she first met the gambolling filly who was destined to be her sister-in-law and, one day, her Queen.

'I am *not* Diana Spencer!' she shouted angrily at a photographer who tried to take her picture one day.

Inevitably, stories started to circulate in the salons of

Belgravia and Chelsea that the two did not get on, that
Anne regarded Diana with something approaching
barely disguised contempt.

The notable absence of Anne and her husband Mark
Phillips from the christening in 1984 of Prince Harry
did not help matters. Buckingham Palace described it
as unfortunate and explained that it was because of a
'longstanding engagement that had been fixed far in
advance'.

The longstanding engagement turned out to be a
rabbit shoot, organized by Mark Phillips's parents.

Diana did not feel it was necessary for Anne to be
made a godparent. But she was nonetheless upset
when Anne could not be bothered to attend the
ceremony.

The situation is not quite as bad as it may appear,
however, and recent months have seen a distinct
improvement in their relationship. They could never
be called best friends (BF as Diana calls it). But friends
they are.

In the television interview with Sir Alastair Burnet,
Diana, in reference to the estrangement, acknowledged,
'The story arose obviously as she wasn't chosen perhaps as a godmother for Harry, which had our child
been a girl, was a possibility. But Harry arrived, so we
went to a man.'

She emphasized, 'Princess Anne has been working
incredibly hard for the Save the Children Fund and I
am her biggest fan, because what she crams into a day
I could never achieve. And we've hit it off very well
and I just think she's marvellous.'

That is something of an over-statement. But Diana *is*
to be heard loudly praising Anne's indefatigable work
for the world's under-privileged children to her
friends. And when Anne is abroad, which she so

frequently is, Diana will drive the eight miles to Gatcombe Park to keep a surrogate mother's eye on little
Peter and Zara Phillips or invite them over to Highgrove for tea. What strains there were have been alle-
viated as the two came to accept each other's finer
points – a compromise all families make if Dallas-style
feuds are to be avoided.

There were never any problems between Diana and
Princess Margaret's daughter, Lady Sarah Armstrong-
Jones. It was Sarah who invited Diana aboard the Royal
Yacht *Britannia* – a visit that would eventually lead
Diana down the aisle of St Paul's Cathedral – and they
have been close friends ever since.

In those early days when Diana was still intimidated
by the stuffy formality of royal dinners, they would
slip away and take their supper together in the kitchens
at Balmoral.

Of course, once she had overcome her initial insecur-
ity, Diana's natural stubbornness quickly reasserted
itself. She can fight her corner – and loudly. She
remains reluctant to do what she doesn't feel like
doing. She cheerfully admits that she is no intellectual
athlete and if she believes in something, however
flimsy the foundations of her argument might be, it
takes a considerable effort to make her change her
mind.

These are traits that can be something of a handicap
in her relations with her husband. As far as Prince
Philip is concerned, they constitute a virtue.

The most outspoken member of the Royal Family,
the Duke of Edinburgh has spent his royal lifetime
putting his foot neatly into his mouth just about every
time he opens it – to the constant irritation of the
politicians who serve his wife and the subjects she
reigns over.

If he is angered, he will use expletives. If he is kept waiting he will complain. When annoyed, he can display an unfortunate disregard for the feelings of others.

At the Royal Windsor Horse Show one year, for example, he stood in line to receive his prize for four-in-hand driving, nodding and smiling to his fellow competitors. But the moment he returned to the sanctum of the Royal Box, he declared in a stage whisper that all the other prize winners were 'such snobs'. What had generated such royal opprobrium? Simply that the 'snobs', as he called them, had actually bothered to dress up to receive the medals they had worked so hard for.

The Queen Mother does not get on with him and they regularly pass each other on the staircase without exchanging so much as a nod. The Queen's dresser, friend and life-long confidante, Margaret MacDonald whom the Sovereign calls Bobo, has little time for him and has been known to walk out of a room when he walks in.

It is not surprising that at times relations between Philip and Charles have been fraught.

It was the currency of the Palace servants' realm that Anne and not Charles was the child whom Philip most identified with and who most lived up to his expectations. They were right. Philip's strengths – and for all his failings they are still considerable – lie in action and practicality. He has little sympathy and less time for intellectual navel contemplation, and Charles's Laurens van der Post-inspired contemplation of the 'mirror of the soul' leaves him cold.

He was always insisting that his son could 'do better', both at sport and at shouldering his share of royal responsibility (Philip is one of the hardest working members of the Firm). And when he didn't, Philip was quite capable of reducing his son to tears with his invective.

'My father is very wise about how one should look at life,' Charles has said. 'As I got older I began to realize that he was probably worth listening to. Then again, sometimes I disagree. It happens, you know.'

Those disagreements came to a head one day in an astonishing confrontation at Buckingham Palace. The two men were shouting at each other. Suddenly Charles rounded on his father and said, 'Just you remember who you are talking to. You are talking to the future King of England!'

He then turned on his heels and stormed out of the room – past a senior Palace advisor who had witnessed the whole incident through the open door.

This is where Diana comes into play. She is the peacemaker and, during particularly fractious moments, the go-between. Her own father can be difficult. Her grandfather, the seventh Earl Spencer was a real old grouch who would declare, 'I don't like people,' and would greet unwelcome guests at the door of Althorp holding a shotgun. Diana is used to difficult older men and she knows how to handle them.

Philip is extremely fond of her. He, notoriously, has an eye for a pretty woman, especially one with blonde hair, and he was charmed by her femininity and, of course, by her stubbornness.

'The Duke of Edinburgh gets on much better with the Princess of Wales than he does with his own son,' says a Palace advisor bluntly.

Philip also has a certain sympathy for the role marriage has forced on Diana. He sees in her situation a repeat of his own – an outsider marrying into the most difficult family in the world and then having to carve a niche for herself within the rigid confines of the royal protocol. And he approves of the way she has gone about that daunting task.

So, too, naturally enough, does the Queen Mother. It was she, after all, who with the help of her friend Lady Fermoy, connived to bring Diana and Charles together. An earl's daughter herself, the Queen Mother does love a good title and regards Diana as an eminently suitable consort for her favourite grandson. They speak frequently and the Queen Mother is always delighted when Diana brings round her children for the royal ritual of afternoon tea which, by Windsor family tradition, is always served at 5 o'clock.

It was the Queen Mother, rather than the Queen, who gave Diana some elementary advice when Diana was in training to be a princess. She had told her, over one of her many gin and french's, that a princess does not display plunging *décolletage*, referring to the black silk taffeta dress Diana wore to a poetry reading at the Goldsmiths' Hall in the City of London.

It had been a daring declaration of her independence. But there are royal rules, and Diana has to adhere to them. She is now a member of the Family. That does have its advantages, of course. There are castles and limousines and servants and jewels beyond the dreams of a young girl who came into married life with just a necklace with a gold D hanging on it. But there are restrictions.

There is also sacrifice. For those who marry into the House of Windsor may gain a family but they also lose one. Their own.

Inexorably their lives become consumed and taken over by the business of being royal. There are duties to perform and official engagements to attend and security to worry about. There is no longer time available to spend with the people one might want to spend time with and the process is as poignant as it is inevitable.

The attitude of the Royal Family does not help soften the separation. They are *the* Family, close-knit, self-contained, secure in their position and content in their own company. They are also isolated: as Charles warns, members of the Royal Family can only ever fully trust each other. There is little room in their self-sufficient round of holidays and high days for outsiders and new in-laws remain always the out-laws.

It was little noticed at the time, but Diana's father, Earl Spencer, was not invited to attend the marriage in Westminster Abbey of his daughter's brother-in-law Prince Andrew to his daughter's best friend, Sarah Ferguson. Nor were Mr and Mrs Peter Phillips, parents of Princess Anne's husband Mark and grandparents of the Queen's two eldest grandchildren.

After the Duke and Duchess of York had departed on their honeymoon, the Royal Family attended a supper party held by Lady Elizabeth Anson, the Queen's cousin, at Claridge's to look at a video of the ceremony and eat smoked salmon and scrambled eggs.

Fergie's stepmother Susan attended, so did Fergie's sister Jane and her half-sister Alex. The Major, however, left as soon as was polite to do so.

'I took the younger children home as soon as I could from the hotel, because I knew that the children had to get home – obviously – and, secondly, that night the village of Dummer were going to have a barbecue,' the Major explains.'Having been in the village since 1939, and they having supported Sarah enormously throughout the entire wedding and had great fun, my place was in the village that night – not at Claridge's hotel. That didn't go down terribly well with one or two people. But that's what I decided so that's what I did.

And I'm very glad I did because of the reaction from the Dummer village who had no idea that I was coming. When I turned up it made everything worthwhile. It was wonderful. They were amazed as they'd heard that there was a big party at Claridge's and they'd assumed that was where we were going to be.'

It was where everyone assumed Major Ferguson would be. But after an adult lifetime of royal service, Major Ferguson knows his place – and it was with the villagers at Dummer and not with the Royal Family.

This separation of families is not spoken about or defined. There are no written rules. It happens naturally. And it is not total.

Diana does see a lot of her sisters, particularly Jane. It would be hard not to – Jane's husband is Sir Robert Fellowes, the Queen's deputy private secretary – and with their three children they live almost next door to the Waleses in the royal housing estate better known as Kensington Palace.

Earl Spencer does not fare so well. An old man and infirm, one of his greatest pleasures is to see and play with his two grandsons. He does not see them as often as he would like. At Christmas, for instance, the Waleses follow the Queen's court, first to Windsor and then on to Sandringham for the New Year and January. Lord Spencer is not invited.

It makes the visits he does make to Highgrove all the more touching. One day William proudly showed him around Charles's farm – William excitedly running ahead, Spencer puffing along behind. They came to a five-bar gate.

'I can't open it, grandpa, you've got to climb it, otherwise the animals will get out,' William ordered.

And Earl Spencer did just that, remarking afterwards, 'William lectures me.'

He always tries to make sure that Harry, so much
quieter than his elder brother, is not left out and says,
'They're basically very affectionate children who get
on well together.'

Sometimes they come to visit him at Althorp where
they race down the long elegant corridors in their pedal
cars. But the visits are infrequent.

A courtier of the old school, Earl Spencer understands the all-embracing grip of royalty and says, 'I'm
just very happy that my daughter is happily married.'

So too is he. But that, unfortunately, does not make
communication between the Earl and his daughter and
her new family any easier.

Diana was fifteen years old when Johnny Spencer
fell in love and found someone to replace his first wife
Frances. It was almost a re-enactment of the bitter
marital troubles of the previous decade. For the woman
in question was Barbara Cartland's daughter, Raine –
and she was married to the Earl of Dartmouth, one of
Spencer's friends.

She left her husband, divorced him, and they were
married two months later in a five-minute ceremony at
London's Old Caxton Hall register office.

It was a case, says Spencer, 'of two very lonely
people who found each other and found happiness
together'.

His daughters did not share in that happiness. When
Raine moved in, the girls, led by Sarah, would sing,
'Raine, Raine, go away.' They resented her grand airs
and graces and the imperious way she had supplanted
their mother in their young minds.

The first time Lady Dartmouth, as she still was, came
to lunch at Park House, Nanny Mary Clarke 'feared
trouble due to misplaced loyalty towards the mother. I
remember feeling tense and trying to distract Diana

without success. Sarah was sent from the room and Diana followed her. We did not lunch together again with Lady Dartmouth.'

As the new Lady Spencer, Raine is credited with effecting a rapprochement between her husband and his cantankerous father. That, however, did not improve her relations with his children, and Lord Spencer, who still tries his best to paper over the cracks, has been forced to concede, 'No step-relationships are easy. It was hard on my children and hard on Raine, moving into a family as close as we are.

'You couldn't expect it to work wonders at the start.'

Lady Spencer has said, 'Sarah resented me, Jane didn't speak to me for two years, even if we bumped into each other in the passageway. It was bloody awful.'

One day she telephoned Diana in London and informed her about a memorial service she was due to attend. 'Be sure to wear something suitable – preferably black,' she said.

Diana took this as an immediate challenge and amidst much giggling defied her stepmother's wishes and went into Miss Selfridge and bought the brightest outfit she could find and wore it. When she appeared at the memorial service, Raine was livid, but chose to ignore her stepdaughter's obvious snub for fear of worsening the already rocky relationship.

Matters did improve slightly when, in September of 1978, Lord Spencer suffered a severe stroke. He went into eight comas and very nearly died.

'Raine saved my life,' he says simply. 'Without Raine I wouldn't have lived to see Diana married, never mind walking up the aisle of St Paul's. Raine sat with me for four solid months, holding my hand and even shouting at me that I wasn't going to die because she wouldn't let me.'

The girls were impressed with the love and care she lavished on their father and her iron-willed determination to pull him through.

But they were not so impressed with the way she had set about putting her imprint on stately Althorp, their family's home and their brother Charles's birthright.

Lady Spencer is a determined woman and a former member of the now defunct Greater London Council. She had never lived her life by the innocent precepts her mother espouses ('My mother's books are period books,' she says dismissively), and went through Althorp – where they moved after the death of the seventh earl – like a whirlwind.

Enormous hostilities were generated. The ex-chauffeur has recalled how she called the kitchen girls 'a pair of sluts', how she wanted nothing to do with a special Christmas party Lord Spencer organized for William and Harry, saying, 'It's your affair, not mine,' and how the staff are in terror of her 'because she finds fault in everything.'

It is her refurbishment of one of England's finest houses that has generated the most resentment, however.

On the Countess's instructions, eleven of the twelve Van Dycks have been sold, to be replaced by a gushy chocolate box portrait in pink of Raine herself. The Old Master drawings and 'quantities of rare eighteenth-century china, books, music and furniture' have been dispersed.

In all, it is estimated that some 300 irreplaceable works of art have gone from the house since Raine's reign began. And not always at a price commensurate with their real value.

For example Andrea Sacchi's picture *Apollo Crown-ing the Musician Pasqualini*, which had been pur-chased by the first earl in 1758, was sold in its original frame to Wildenstein's, the international art dealers, for £40,000. Wildenstein subsequently resold it to the Metropolitan Museum of Art in New York for £270,000.

The Earl Spencer defends his wife's actions. He insists, 'We had to sell. We had no money, just a huge overdraft.' The Countess says that they 'are very proud, that the turnover the 40,000 visitors generate a year has topped £400,000 which is a pretty big jump from the £2,000 a year it was in my father-in-law's day'.

That has not placated those experts who point out that as a Grade 1 listed house, Althorp had been well maintained by Raine's late father-in-law who in the fifties and sixties had carried out 'a thorough and exemplary' restoration with the assistance of Stephen Dykes-Bower, the surveyor of Westminster Abbey.

Every woman, it could be argued, likes to put her stamp on a house. But does that justify, ask her critics, turning such a fine mansion into a second-class 'coun-try house hotel' with fitted carpets and fake log fires in the grates?

In their damning catalogue of the Reign of Raine, Alexandra Artley and Thomas Dibdin wrote, 'If it were not so tragic, what has happened at Althorp would be . . . high comedy.' It explains why so many people have come to regard Johnny Spencer's second wife as the Wicked Stepmother who sold the family silver.

This is not how the great families like to operate. It is a tenet of the British aristocracy that beautiful things like houses and paintings and furniture are held in trust for succeeding generations. The dispersals for which Raine is so largely held responsible cannot have helped her standing with the younger members of the Spencer family.

Nor can the remarks so sneakily attributed to her. According to the chauffeur, Foy, Lady Spencer has been heard to remark, 'Jane's all right just as long as she keeps busy producing more children. That's about all she is good for.

'Sarah is okay while she sticks to hunting and shooting which is all she cares about.'

The future Queen has not escaped Raine's acerbic observations either. 'How can you have an intelligent conversation with someone who doesn't have a single O level?' she is said to have remarked to a friend. 'It's a crashing bore.'

Prince Charles, is, however, quite taken with his stepmother-in-law. Whatever her faults, she is intelligent and dynamic which he finds appealing.

Diana does not. As Stephen Barry recorded, 'There is not a great deal of love lost between the Princess and her stepmother.' And should Charles dwell too long in conversation with Raine, Diana will find an excuse to drag him away, and out of the house.

Diana has a new family now. She has her children and her husband. She may have been born a Spencer, but she is now a Windsor.

7

Homes

As they rounded the bend, the house that was to be Diana's future home came into view. The sand-coloured stone building, with its pillared porch and tall windows, was a disappointment for the girl whose head was full of fantasy and whose heart was hoping her dream man would have a dream house.

That was eight years ago and Highgrove, the nine-bedroomed Georgian house with 350 acres of land had only recently been purchased by the Duchy of Cornwall for Prince Charles for £800,000 from Maurice Macmillan, son of Harold Macmillan, late Earl of Stockton, the former Prime Minister.

Once inside, Diana's mood failed to improve. The house had only bits of furniture rescued from the basement of Buckingham Palace, where Charles had stored the collected booty from his many foreign trips.

Diana had been expecting, and hoping for, something a little more impressive from the first home of the heir to the throne, but she didn't say anything. Her face remained impassive as she went from half-furnished room to half-furnished room. For the girl who divided her time between her father's stately home – Althorp House, one of the grandest houses in England, boasting a 115-foot gallery and acres of beautiful parkland – and a cosy elegant flat near Earls Court, it was disappointing. Her flat in Colherne Court was an impressive apartment for an eighteen-year-old to own. Situated on the ground floor of the Brompton Road entrance to the block, it had two large bedrooms, a sitting room, bathroom and separate loo, and at the back was a beautiful pine kitchen with a round table, perfect for the small dinner parties that Diana used to co-host with her flatmates.

For a girl whose home and family are her most cherished possessions, the disarray of Highgrove was an immediate challenge. During the solitary hours she spent waiting for Prince Charles to return from hunting in the early days of their courtship, she formulated plans and ideas for improving the house. Even if she would never be mistress of it, she hated the thought of Charles living there in discomfort. He, on the other hand, quite enjoyed what he called 'camping' at Highgrove and was perfectly happy sitting on the sofa in the sitting room over a plate of scrambled eggs and thinking of ideas for the garden – which, he claims, was the reason he purchased the house in the first place.

'It was a challenge,' he says, 'to create something, and I did rather fall in love with it. The big cedar tree in the front and the walled garden finally made up my mind.'

It was also near to his sister. The Princess Royal's estate at Gatcombe Park is only eight miles away, set in the heart of the Gloucestershire countryside inhabited by his hunting cronies and close friends such as Andrew and Camilla Parker-Bowles. But, if Charles had had marriage on his mind when he first saw Highgrove, it is doubtful he would have bought it. Although it has four large reception rooms downstairs, a large kitchen area and extensive staff quarters, nine bedrooms on the upper floors and a nursery wing, it is small by royal standards. (For the Royal Family there is always Security Staff to be housed along with all the necessary domestics such as cooks and housekeepers.) But this was the house immediately available. And when they married they made the decision to move in, until something larger caught their eye.

The Queen, who once joked that Highgrove 'sounded like something in Wimbledon', would like her son and daughter-in-law to live closer to her at Windsor Castle, so that she can see more of her grandchildren. But, for the present, this seems unlikely to happen. Eight years after buying the house they are still there. And Charles, through his Duchy of Cornwall estates, has spent considerable sums improving everything at Highgrove, from the elaborate security system of closed-circuit cameras that scan the grounds to planting a wild flower border down the front drive. Recently he has even improved the outside of the building. And five months' work, completed at the end of 1987, gave a splendid new look to the eighteenth-century mansion. Decorative Ionic columns have replaced the plain ones in front of the house and a balustrade has been added to the roof. The front of the building now boasts a classical pediment – a low-pitched gable – with a round ornamental window in the centre.

Charles was anxious to move in as soon as possible and dispatched his various staff to get the necessary furnishings to make the house habitable. His valet was sent scurrying to Heals, the furniture store in Tottenham Court Road, to buy beds. He didn't get anything too expensive as the Prince didn't quite know how he wanted the house to be and, since he was engaged, wanted to wait for the wedding presents.

They were worth waiting for. At last Diana was able to have her dream kitchen – a German design – a swimming pool (from the estate workers at Althorp), wrought-iron gates from the village of Tetbury and more china and glass than they knew what to do with.

Meanwhile, Diana was doing her best to sort out the

interior of Highgrove and she engaged the assistance of
South African designer, Dudley Poplak. Diana's
mother, Mrs Shand-Kydd, had used Poplak on both her
London homes and both she and Diana liked his
attention to detail and traditional style.

The soft pastel colours and country chintz fabric that
dominate the colour scheme at Highgrove today are the
result of Poplak's influence.

Downstairs there are still the four reception rooms
mentioned in the original estate agent's particulars.
These consist of a comfortable sitting room for Diana
where she can escape from the activities of the household, a large formal drawing room for entertaining,
furnished with the most tasteful antiques, and a study
for Prince Charles. This is painted beige and has a
matching sofa with scatter cushions. On the side tables
are piles of magazines, books and family photographs.
There is also a dining room with a large table, but
when the Prince and Princess are alone they rarely use
it, preferring to eat in her sitting room in front of the
television.

In the early days of Highgrove life, Diana spent a
great deal of time watching television while Charles
was out hunting or working on his papers, which go
everywhere with him.

'Wales works very hard,' one of his cronies complained. 'Those bloody papers even accompany him
when he comes to stay for the weekend.'

The peach entrance hall of the house is wide with
polished wood floors. It runs from the front door right
to the back where french windows lead on to the
garden. There is a grand piano and a wide staircase
leading up to the bedroom suites on the floor above.
The staff quarters and the large kitchen area lead off
the hallway and an intricate pattern of back stairs joins

them up with the nursery suite on the top floor where
the windows are carefully barred to prevent any acci-
dents – like the one at Windsor Castle when Prince
William unwittingly dangled his little brother out of
the window, 'so he could have a better look'.

Weekends at Highgrove are relaxed affairs and the
royal couple try and organize their life so that they can
be there from Friday afternoon, after William has been
picked up from school, to Monday evening. Any staff
from London who are on weekend duty leave Kensington Palace early, and butler Harold Brown, cook
Mervyn Wycherly and one of the Princess's dressers
and a valet will travel together with the car piled with
provisions. Sometimes Charles and Diana have a late
engagement on Friday and will let some of the staff go
ahead with the children. They will drive down with
their detectives either late in the evening or early the
following morning.

Charles hates London and is always keen to get out
as quickly as possible and if he is playing polo in the
summer or hunting in the winter will snatch an extra
night in the country. Neither Charles nor Diana will
avail themselves of the red helicopters of the Queen's
Flight unless they can combine the trip with an official
engagement. Charles is reluctant to use any of the
Queen's transport that is funded out of the civil list
unless he has a thoroughly valid reason.

Princess Michael once pointed out to him that his
life would be made a lot easier if he used helicopters
instead of travelling by car. Charles thought for a
minute and said, 'but I can't do that, they are funded
by public monies'. 'But,' insisted the outspoken Princess, 'haven't you thought about buying one yourself,
you're easily rich enough.' It seems Charles hadn't and

he continues to battle with the traffic on the motorways when he has private engagements.

The day at Highgrove starts a little later than at Kensington Palace and if Diana wishes to take an early swim she asks the gardener Dennis Brown to remove the cover from the heated outdoor pool. She usually waits, however, until the family have had their breakfast together, with Charles buried in a copy of *The Times*, while she attempts to bring some semblance of order to William and Harry's table manners. Both children are very well brought up and well-mannered, but they do get excited and insist on talking instead of eating and trying to distract their father from his newspaper.

Charles is going through one of his periods of hostility towards the press, which is hardly surprising, as he says, 'considering the amount of rubbish that is printed about my wife'. In the last eighteen months he has had more than his fair share of criticism and it annoys him that the quality newspapers have stooped to the levels of the tabloids. And, during a visit to Brixton he was forced to admit: 'I don't believe much that I read in most of the newspapers. In fact I have great difficulty in reading them at all.'

After breakfast, which is always something simple and healthy such as grapefruit, bran flakes and toast, or croissants with honey for Charles and Diana, and cereals and milk for the children, Charles will often visit his farm Broadfield, which the Queen lent him the money to buy and where he practises organic farming methods and keeps a herd of dairy cows and sheep. Prince William loves to accompany his father on these visits and look at all the animals.

A few years ago it was the garden, not the farm, that absorbed most of Prince Charles's time, but now it is

almost completed. In June of last year Charles invited
members of the Worshipful Company of Gardeners,
who had just elected him a Liveryman, to a tree-
planting ceremony at Highgrove. It was a chance for
him to show off his most prized possession to fellow
enthusiasts, and his favourite part of the whole thing –
the walled garden.

Thigh-high grass filled with wild flowers inter-
spersed with narrow mown paths lead to the walled
garden, a few hundred yards from the main house. It
was once only accessible through a hole in the wall
where somebody had made a gap to get a tractor
through, but now it is a masterful creation of fruit,
flowers and vegetables – designed by Charles himself
with the help of a couple of gardeners.

The tranquillity of the beautiful garden is the perfect
place for Charles and Diana to escape from the pressures of the royal existence. Charles has even been
known to land a red helicopter of the Queen's Flight in
an adjoining field during a busy working day – just for
a couple of hours – to enable him to sit under the trees
and work or do some weeding.

'Very therapeutic – weeding,' he claims, 'and it's
marvellous if you can do enough to see the effect.'

'The thing I remember most about the garden,' a
visitor said, 'was the beautiful scent and the way the
paving in front of the french doors had little wild
flowers growing in between the stones. It was done so
beautifully it all looked perfectly natural.'

The garden is a paradise for the children. They have
a pet rabbit, who lives by the swimming pool, two little
ponies who are stabled in the yard next to the main
house, a climbing frame, a swing and a Wendy house
and acres and acres of land to play in. Both William
and Harry love meeting visitors and showing off their

little ponies. Prince William is very polite and will come up and say, 'Good morning,' while Harry sits shyly in the background. One visitor who had parked her car in the stable yard was talking to William when he noticed she had a little puppy in her car. 'Let me see the doggy,' he said, squealing with delight, and rode up on his pony to the car where he took hold of the little puppy and held it close to his chest. As soon as the dog started to struggle William got bored and trotted off into the long grass. He then played hide-and-seek with Harry who was not nearly as at home on horseback and still needed the assistance of groom Marilyn Cox and the leading-rein.

Beyond the walled garden and the stables are huge greenhouses filled with tropical flowers and scented plants for the house. These are out of bounds to William and Harry unless they have someone with them. Charles knows the children would rather be in the swimming pool or picking runner beans than in his greenhouse, but if anyone shows an interest he will rush them off for a tour. He knows all the complicated Latin names for the plants and is not shy about revealing his knowledge to fellow enthusiasts. Apart from the visual beauty of the garden, the Prince is keen to enhance the tranquillity with suitably restful sounds – running water for instance and tinkling bells.

During a trip to Italy he was entranced to see cows grazing with bells around their necks. He purchased some antique bells to try and simulate the effect and tied them round the necks of some of his cows. The experiment was not a success and the cows were terrified of the noise. Charles then considered smaller bells to be attached to the sheep that graze near their bedroom window. He loves the sound of bells and running water.

Diana is not so keen on the sound of the water, complaining it makes her want to go to the loo all the time!

'I have endless plans to do new things,' Charles says. 'Slight *folie de grandeur* – but I like to leave something better than I found it.'

Many of the things in the garden have been gifts from friends. The Sultan of Oman presented them with a dovecote which has been constructed at the far end of the main garden behind the back drive; musician Yehudi Menuhin presented them with a pond full of carp, and a women's institute with a herb garden. Diana finds her husband's fascination with organic farming and old-fashioned gardening a trifle eccentric – and she heartily wishes he hadn't made the remark about talking to his plants during the ITV series in 1986.

Charles, for his part, couldn't care less. If people wish to make him out to be a weirdo, let them. And, during the visit by the Liverymen of the Worshipful Company of Gardeners, he tested them out for reaction as he planted a young sapling.

'I must give it a rub to wish it luck,' he said, looking at the assembled company, adding wickedly, 'I sit here talking to the plants.'

An avenue of apple trees, a bank of shrubs and trees and the wild flowers he has planted have all benefited from a few words from the Prince of Wales. He has created a sanctuary for himself, his wife and children and for the variety of tiny wild creatures that choose to inhabit the peaceful setting of the Highgrove garden. When so much time and trouble has gone into a project it is hardly surprising that Charles and Diana like to spend as much time as they can outdoors.

In the summer, meals are taken in the garden,

weather permitting. Either a simple buffet lunch of
quiches, flans, salads and fruit-salad is prepared or a
delicate offering of poached eggs in tartlets, cold
salmon, some of Charles's home-made soups followed
by fresh apple pie, summer pudding or home-made ice
cream. Cheese and biscuits are offered at lunchtime,
never in the evening.

If Charles and Diana are spending the weekend alone
they will sometimes have supper in front of the TV on
a folding table laid with a beautiful linen cloth and the
best silver, but if they have guests they eat in the dining
room. Dinners in the country are informal by royal
standards – they still have staff to wait on table and the
finest delicate dishes are prepared by the cook but the
men don't wear black tie and, as a rule, the ladies wear
simple dresses and low-heeled shoes. The conversation
might be about the day's hunting or polo, or sometimes,
when Sir Laurens van der Post and his wife come to
stay, take on a more serious note. Another guest,
Armand Hammer, head of Occidental and the man
whose financial contributions have kept Atlantic Col-
leges – one of Prince Charles's main interests – was a
guest at Highgrove with his wife Frances. He describes
a typical summer lunch with great relish. 'Charles was
tremendously proud of everything we ate,' Hammer
explains. 'Fruit, vegetables, meat, dairy products – had
been grown or prepared in his gardens and on his farm.
We ate on a table on the lawn and Prince Charles was
at his most informal and unregal.

'When we were about to leave, Prince Charles suddenly disappeared and returned to present us with
several boxes of plump, sweet strawberries which he
had picked himself. He was more delighted to give us
berries he had grown, and picked with his own hands,
than if they had been jewels from the family vault.'

Sometimes Andrew and Fergie come for the weekend, which brightens things up considerably for Diana and while the men are swopping stories over the port the two ladies will retire to the sitting room and have a good giggle (Sloane habits die hard). Diana finds Fergie's company exhilarating and it gives her an excuse to have a good gossip without the ever-constant fear of anything being repeated. These country dinners do not linger long into the night and the assembled company are usually in bed by midnight at the latest. Charles sometimes works for a couple of hours in his study before retiring, but Diana has tried to dissuade him from this, explaining that he must have a break from his work or he will never be able to relax.

Now that both the children are at school – William is at Wetherby in Pembridge Villas and Harry at Mrs Mynors' in nearby Chepstow Villas – Monday mornings are a time both Charles and Diana can have to themselves. Sundays are not a day of rest in the Waleses' household because from May to September Charles usually has a polo match at Windsor or Cowdray. More often than not Diana will accompany him, following in her own car with the children and nanny Ruth Wallace. Although she confesses 'to enjoying polo', it does rather break up her weekends and there is always the posse of photographers anxious to get photographs of her and the children in those off-guard moments. Sometimes the match is held in aid of one of her charities, such as Birthright, and then it's another day's work for the Princess as she chats to the sponsors in the hospitality tent after the match, longing to get back to Highgrove and a dip in the pool. I have watched Diana at these polo matches on some hot Sundays and felt sorry for her, for, although Fergie is sometimes

there to brighten things up, polo is not really a spec-
tator's sport unless it is at top level and Diana would
clearly rather be relaxing in the garden at home. As
soon as she alights from her car, parked behind the
pony lines, a crowd of photographers follow her to the
royal box, running backwards in their efforts to get a
good informal picture. Depending on her mood she is
either co-operative with them and smiles and poses for
the picture or if she is feeling fed-up she will keep her
eyes downcast, and hurry to the royal box as quickly
as possible. Once there it's another round of cocktail
party conversation and she will delight in any
distraction.

During the 1987 Cartier International she was chatting to a paraplegic in the ambulance car when the
actor John Hurt sidled up to her and poked his head
into the vehicle. A little the worse for the excess of free
drinks dispensed by Cartier, he struck up a conversation with the Princess without seemingly realizing who
she was. Diana was delighted. Not only does she love
show-business personalities, but the hilarity of the
situation appealed to her. 'Anything for a change of
routine is fun,' she tells people. 'I love it when something unexpected happens,' and John Hurt's visit to the
ambulance was certainly unexpected.

William and Harry love going to the polo to watch
the man they call 'papa' play. But they are not always
on their best behaviour and when William was first
introduced to polo he was impossible – running here
and there and demanding all Diana's attention. Finally
he had to be taken home in disgrace.

He is better behaved now and when he and Harry get
bored there are many other things to do. Feeding the
ponies with sugar lumps, playing doctors and nurses
in the ambulance car, treading in the divots (the lumps

of turf pulled up by the ponies' hooves) at half time
and stroking any one of the many dogs belonging to
players and spectators. At Smiths Lawn, in Windsor
Great Park, where Charles plays most weeks, there is a
wonderful character called Ginger, whose duty it is to
look after the Prince. He enjoys looking after William
and Harry too and, when Nanny isn't looking, will
tempt them with sugar lumps and encourage them to
stroke the ponies standing in the lines waiting to play.
William likes to go into the hospitality tent and help
himself to a plate of strawberries or raspberries and
then both little boys will sit under the trees with their
nanny and tuck in.

During the polo season Prince Charles will play at
least a couple of times during the week as well as
weekends. In the week he leaves from Kensington Palace
in his convertible blue Aston Martin – he also has a new
£80,000 model, a gift from the Amir of Bahrain – with
his detective in the back and one of his favourite operas
blasting on the car stereo system. He has been criticized
because polo seems to consume so much of his time, but
his polo manager, Major Ronald Ferguson, father of the
Duchess of York, springs to his defence.

'It's unfair criticism. He's like any other young
person who is physically fit and who happens to enjoy
a game. It doesn't mean that he cuts down on his public
engagements. It means that he has more to do in one
particular day than before. It's my job to see he gets the
maximum number of matches in.' The Major goes on
to explain, 'If he didn't play polo he might want to play
golf or tennis. He'd get into something, he'd never
become a lump, he's not that sort of person.'

When Charles hasn't got any sporting activities
arranged, he will work out to a routine of exercises
devised by the Canadian Air Force. These only take a

few minutes a day and gradually build up your strength and stamina – the joy of them being he can do them anywhere, even in his cluttered study at Kensington Palace.

Kensington Palace, the London home of the Prince and Princess of Wales, is situated in an attractive part of central London between Kensington High Street and Bayswater Road and adjacent to Kensington Gardens. A field – convenient for helicopters – divides the rambling palace from a private road of embassies. You can walk up the private road, but only drive up if you are going to one of the embassies or Kensington Palace.

Built nearly 400 years ago of warm red brick, it was the home of William and Mary and the birthplace of Queen Victoria, and today it is a royal village, 'the aunt heap,' Charles once dubbed it – the home of no fewer than fourteen members of the Royal Family.

To gain access to any of these private apartments, the visitor has to pass a police sentry box where there are always two policemen on duty. They ask your name and, if you are expected, know yours. Then the security comes into full swing and a telephone call is made to the apartment you are visiting and you are allowed to drive through. Closed-circuit television cameras monitor your route up the gravel drive, passing the Duke and Duchess of Gloucester's apartments on the right – they have a 35-room apartment for themselves, their three children and the Duke's mother, 87-year-old Princess Alice. A clocktower guards the entrance to 1A Clock Court where Princess Margaret now lives alone in the courtyard of the old stables, and then finally at the top north end are apartments 8 and 9, which belong to Charles and Diana. Their immediate neighbours are the Prince and Princess Michael of Kent who live in apartment 10 and the Kents' cars share the partly walled courtyard with the Waleses and a police sentry box.

Because several intruders have been found within the enclave of Kensington Palace over the past year, security has been stepped up. Charles and Diana have armed policemen sleeping in their apartments who are highly trained, so, in the unlikely event of an intruder gaining access to the apartment, he would get no further.

Once you have parked your car out of the way by the police sentry box, carefully remembering to leave the keys inside in case the police want to move it, you have the impression you are in a beautiful old village, complete with the old-fashioned gas street lamps of which Charles is so fond. In the summer, roses climb the walls of the courtyard and in autumn the country smell of burning leaves hangs in the air. It is hard to believe you are only a few minutes' walk from the hustle and bustle of Kensington High Street.

Once you are inside the Waleses' three-storey L-shaped apartment – either entering up two stone steps to the front door or, if you are not known to the Prince and Princess, via the side door under the stone arches at the back of the house – you have the impression of being inside a country mansion where vast oil paintings dominate the walls and vases of flowers fill every available corner, including some very stylish dried flower arrangements. A sweeping staircase leads from the entrance hall to the rest of the house and the carpet is green with a grey Prince of Wales feather motif. When Bob Geldof visited Prince Charles at Kensington Palace to discuss his Band Aid project, he noticed the carpet and, typically, remarked on it:

'Don't think much of the carpet,' he said and Prince

Charles, amusingly enough, agreed with him. 'Yes, it is
rather garish, isn't it?' he replied.

As early as 1975 Prince Charles was given two
apartments at the north end of the building by the
Queen, to use as his London residence. The apartments
in Kensington Palace belong to the Queen and are
known as 'grace and favour', i.e. rent free, but the
occupants have to pay some of the upkeep, and the
rates, being those of central London, are high.

Princess Margaret pays about £10,000 per annum for
her apartment, her chauffeur's cottage and a flat for her
cook and butler. The others pay similar rates, depending on the size of the residence. Diana's sister, Lady
Jane Fellowes, has a cottage in the complex with her
husband, Sir Robert Fellowes, the Queen's assistant
private secretary. Sir William Heseltine, Diana's private secretary, also has an apartment, as have the
various staff necessitated by the running of the Palace.
Those not so lucky are housed in apartments in Kennington, South London, part of the Duchy of Cornwall
estate.

When they became engaged Diana was anxious to get
Charles out of his bachelor apartments in Buckingham
Palace as soon as possible and employed the services
of Dudley Poplak to supervise the interior. Like most
women, she kept changing her mind as the building
took shape and decided to have an extra bathroom in
the master suite so that she and Charles would not trip
over each other in the mornings. At one time it was
considered moving both Charles's and Diana's offices
into Kensington Palace, but there was not room so for
many years they commuted between Buckingham
Palace and Kensington Palace – larger meetings involving both Charles and Diana being held in Kensington
Palace.

Sadly, for the casual visitor and people involved in running the royal couple's various interests, those days are over. Diana found that the house was always full of strangers, so much so that she could hardly set foot out of her own suite of rooms without fear of bumping into someone. So at the beginning of 1988 the Waleses moved their office and office staff into St James's Palace, into the suite of rooms formerly occupied by the Lord Chamberlain. Now the twice-yearly engagement meetings, lunches and audiences with politicians and captains of industry are held there, where there is ample room for everyone and a dining room for official lunches.

So, 'KP', as Diana calls it, is a home again. Charles still has his study on the first floor, which is dominated by a large desk covered in a profusion of papers and pens and where he works late at night and early in the morning. Diana still has her sitting room, with the wallpaper specially commissioned by Poplak to include the Prince of Wales feather motif, where she watches her favourite television programmes and videos. Designers will still visit her here and it is her favourite room for the very small informal suppers she sometimes hosts. And, for larger gatherings, there is the dining room which has a circular mahogany table that can seat sixteen, and the beautiful drawing room that holds at least sixty people.

The drawing room, with its yellow wallpaper, marble fireplace and collection of antiques and tapestries, has been the setting for occasions as diverse as the meeting with Indian Prime Minister Rajiv Gandhi to the more recent party hosted by Charles and Diana for pop stars who had played at charity concerts in aid of The Prince's Trust, one of Charles's pet charities. The magnificent rug which covers most of the floor area was rolled back and Diana persuaded some of the talented guests to play the grand Broadwood piano. Elton John, who never needs any persuading to play at a party, gave a rendering of some of his hits and even Labi Siffre did a turn. Diana, who is a good player herself (her grandmother, Lady Fermoy, was a concert pianist), was too shy to take part. She did, however, give a small recital during their 1988 visit to Australia when a wily old professor of music encouraged her to play a few bars of Rachmaninov's Piano Concerto number 2.

'All my side of the family are very music-orientated,' Diana says, 'and that's where I picked it up. I love it.'

It was also in this room, under the large tapestry, that the royal couple gave their television interview to Sir Alastair Burnet – something that is unlikely ever to be repeated. Charles and Diana were disappointed with the results of the two separate films that were made and shown all over the world and Charles found the television cameras, which followed them for a year, too intrusive.

The bedroom suite on the first floor is the most private area in the house. Here Charles and Diana have a large bedroom with a four-poster bed, brought from Charles's old quarters at Buckingham Palace, and a separate dressing room and bathroom each. Charles also has a uniform room where his valet Ken Stronach keeps the many uniforms, and a brushing room where minor repairs are made. Diana's dressing room and bathroom are smart but functional with floor-length mirrors, an antique chest of drawers, and, of course, the huge walk-in cupboards that house her wardrobe.

Above the bedroom is the nursery suite – William and Harry's little kingdom. There is a day nursery or playroom and a night nursery with bedrooms for the

boys and a bathroom. All the furniture is scaled-down
and the nursery is very smart with a beige and red
carpet. Childlike drawings, together with cowboy hats
(souvenirs from foreign trips), decorate the walls and
Diana insists that all the toys are neatly stored away in
cupboards or on the bright red toy-racks at the side of
the room. Charles is most particular about the nursery
and has fond memories of his own when at Buckingham Palace.

A few months before he met Diana, Charles was
horrified to discover that Andrew had re-decorated the
wonderful old nursery in Buckingham Palace with its
open fire. 'Why did you have to do that?' he exclaimed
in horror. 'Why not?' Andrew retorted. 'You won't be
needing it.' As it happened Andrew didn't need it
either because shortly afterwards Charles got married
and moved out of his quarters, vacating them for
Andrew. 'Such a waste,' Charles kept muttering.

Charles insists on dealing with the running of Kensington Palace, leaving Diana only to supervise meals
or any re-decoration. Charles communicates with his
staff and neighbours by memo. Princess Michael, who
lives next door, has been the recipient of many a short
note, signed with a curt 'C'. Her outgoing nature was
once offended when he asked her to stop interfering
with his staff – she had admonished the then butler
Alan Fisher for the bad language he had used in front
of her two children – and Fisher had gone to Charles
and complained.

'Why doesn't she complain to me?' Charles said to
Fisher.

'Why doesn't he pick up the telephone and complain
to me if I have done something to upset him instead of
sending me a memo,' replied Princess Michael. 'I didn't
think it worth bothering the Prince of Wales with a

minor complaint about his staff, but in future I will,' she added defiantly.

The relationship between the two, never one of much respect since the time Charles told his then girlfriend Anna Wallace, 'not to curtsy to that woman,' worsened when he entertained Robert Maxwell in the walled garden of his apartment. Maxwell's newspaper, the *Daily Mirror*, had been responsible for exposing the story that Princess Michael's father had been a member of the Nazi party, causing her great distress. She couldn't understand why Charles, of all people, should choose to entertain the man right next door!

The truth of the matter was that Maxwell was presenting a large cheque to a charity parachute jump performed by the crack parachute team, The Red Devils, and Prince Charles, ever anxious to perform his Robin Hood act and extract money from the rich, had agreed that they could make the presentation in his garden. So Prince Michael's pleas, on behalf of his wife, not to entertain Maxwell, fell on deaf ears.

Diana's relationship with the flamboyant Princess is much better. She has even persuaded Charles that Marie Christine is simply someone who says what she thinks and, therefore, rather refreshing to have about. In the early days things weren't quite so good, however.

One morning Princess Michael woke up to see a group of noisy schoolchildren outside her bedroom window. Horrified, as she had no idea how they got there or what they were doing, she telephoned the sentry at the gate to find out. Several more telephone calls ensued before she discovered that they were there specially to sing 'Happy Birthday' on Diana's twenty-first. By the time Princess Michael had discovered this the word was about that she was complaining again and even Princess Michael's attempts to put things right by sending round by hand a present for Diana, did little to improve relationships.

Prince Charles has a few other things that provoke his memos. He can't abide plumbing that gurgles in the night, and over-heated rooms. If a member of his staff turns up a radiator or the central heating they will receive a curt note, telling them to please leave the heating alone, signed 'C'. He also can't stand smoking and even has the ashtrays removed from his car. And woe betide anyone that should smoke in Kensington Palace. His staff say he can smell smoke 'a mile off' and if he does so, this provokes yet another memo.

It is probably Charles's dislike of cities that promotes his irritation when he is resident at Kensington Palace. 'I am a countryman at heart,' he says, and can't wait to leave the confines of Kensington Palace for some peace and quiet in the countryside. Prince Charles has, however, found a new interest at Kensington Palace. He has played a crucial role in the drawing up of designs for a new £780,000 block in the Palace grounds to house his ever-increasing staff, and will follow the construction through. He has insisted the design should be in harmony with the rest of the 300-year-old Christopher Wren original and all the materials must be hand-made multi-stock bricks, green Cumberland slates and stone sills. Each of the eight staff flats will have access to its own private garden and there is a delightful clocktower in the centre to harmonize with the one already there. The Kensington Palace staff, who are at present housed on the nursery floor where they have to be careful not to make too much noise as the Prince and Princess's bedroom is directly below, are naturally delighted. They will be able to smoke, drink and make merry with their friends without fear of being disturbed. It is also a bonus to their meagre salaries – even butler Harold

Brown has to make extra money by 'moonlighting' at cocktail parties to supplement his wages.

The practice of 'moonlighting' is not uncommon among royal staff and the Queen has often been confronted with one of her footmen at some grand house or other. She doesn't mind at all, she likes to see a friendly face and it usually means she will get better service.

Besides Highgrove, the Waleses have other country retreats: Tamarisk, a tiny house on the Scilly Isles is one and Craigowan, a five-bedroom house on the Balmoral estate is another. When the Queen Mother dies they will probably inherit Royal Lodge at Windsor and Clarence House in The Mall, but naturally Charles can't even bear to think of such a thing, although he once remarked that he thought Clarence House would be 'far too expensive to run'.

Tamarisk belongs to the Duchy of Cornwall and is a tiny house with only two main bedrooms, overlooking the sea. As it is rather small for Charles, Diana and their children, let alone the staff necessary to look after them, they hardly use it – although they did spend a few days there before William was born. Instead Charles lends it to various staff and every summer Freddie and Ella, Prince and Princess Michael of Kent's two children, spend a week there accompanied by their nanny.

Although Craigowan does not belong to Prince Charles, he still uses it for the odd weekend and it was here that he and Diana spent the Scottish part of their honeymoon, so it has fond memories. The younger members of the Royal Family, Andrew and Fergie and Prince Edward have first call on it these days as it is far more cosy than the draughty castle.

Nowadays, when Charles and Diana are in Scotland,

they usually stay at the Queen Mother's house, Birkhall, which she has left to them in her will. Not long ago she had the entire kitchen re-done, at no small cost. But the Queen Mother will spare no expense when it comes to her home comforts. Prince Charles adores his grandmother and throughout his life has turned to her when things have got difficult. He doesn't expect her to take sides – she won't, always sitting on the fence – but she offers great comfort and solace. 'She has seen everything before,' he says.

In spite of the many houses available to them, Highgrove is the place that Charles and Diana consider their real home. Diana echoes that sentiment. 'There's no place like Home,' reads the cushion she embroidered herself.

8
Motherhood – part 1

In her effort to be a thoroughly modern mother, Diana
has broken away from generations of royal tradition.
When Buckingham Palace announced that she was
pregnant for the first time on 5 November 1981, it was
assumed the baby would be born within the privacy of
a royal home – either Kensington Palace or Buckingham Palace.

There were good grounds for this supposition. Diana
had not been born in hospital, but at Park House and
in the same bedroom as her mother, twenty-five years
before. And Charles, Andrew, and Edward had all been
born at Buckingham Palace, although Anne was born
at Clarence House. In the late fifties and sixties it was
not unusual for women to have babies at home,
especially if they belonged to rich upper-class families
where there were plenty of staff to assist.

Diana had plenty of staff, but she also had a slavish
devotion to the wisdom of her doctor, 57-year-old
George Pinker, Surgeon-Gynaecologist to the Queen.
Pinker has a certain reputation as a high-tech doctor
and draws the line at home deliveries – even with
someone like Diana who was both young and healthy,
as the announcement that November morning
confirmed:

'The Princess is in excellent health,' it read. 'Her
doctor during the pregnancy will be Mr George Pinker,
Surgeon-Gynaecologist to the Queen. The Princess
hopes to continue to undertake some public engagements but regrets any disappointment which may be

caused by any curtailment of her planned programme. The baby will be second in line to the throne.'

It was the last line of the announcement which served as a reminder that this was no ordinary birth, and the Spencer family, the Royal Family and especially the Queen assumed the baby would be born at home. But right from the start Diana knew this would never be the case. She implored Pinker to explain the situation to the Queen, of whom she was highly nervous. Apart from the medical problems she couldn't imagine anything worse than the prospect of having her baby in Buckingham Palace, with its ornate furniture and acres of red carpet, and Kensington Palace was not yet finished – they did not move in until 17 May 1982, a little more than a month before the birth.

No, she would have her baby in St Mary's Hospital, Paddington, where George Pinker kept his National Health patients and where his private patients had their babies on the fourth floor of the Lindo Wing. It was the first time an Heir Presumptive was to be born in a public hospital, albeit in the private sector.

On Sunday evening of 20 June 1982, former nurse and midwife Betty Parsons received a call from Diana.

'My contractions have begun,' she said.

Betty Parsons, who was with the Queen when Prince Edward was born, has assisted almost every Duchess within the pages of *Debrett*'s with her philosophy of childbirth. She claims that there is no such thing as an unnatural birth and teaches relaxation by breathing – with different breathing for each stage of labour.

Diana knew what to expect. She had attended Betty's classes on relaxation and had her come to Kensington Palace regularly in the last month. Prince Charles, who had been devouring the pages of books on natural childbirth, was also a pupil of Betty's. He read her amusing guide, *The Expectant Father* which told him to help and encourage his wife. She explained all the medical equipment which would be used to monitor the baby's heartbeat and Diana's contractions. And she answered a host of intelligent questions the Prince posed.

'I think it's a very good thing for a husband to be with a mother when she is expecting a baby,' he told well-wishers at the beginning of Diana's pregnancy. He had no intention of being left out now and when Diana's contractions became more acute he leapt out of bed, helped her dress and, with a detective in the back of his car, drove her to St Mary's.

They arrived at 5 A.M. on the Monday morning, entered through a side door and took the lift to the top floor of the Lindo Wing. Everything was in readiness for the Princess. The adjacent three rooms had been cleared of any patients, a screen put up by Diana's room, which was at the end of a corridor at the back, and a private telephone line installed by her bed.

For a future Queen, the surroundings were not impressive. Her room, with its metal hospital bed, small standing wardrobe, fridge, television and wash basin, was functional rather than pretty. Although it is the largest in the maternity wing, it only measures about 12 feet by 14 feet and would easily have fitted in her dressing room at Kensington Palace. It has no private bathroom, but a screen was placed outside the door and the shared bathroom opposite, with its two baths and two loos, was made exclusively available for Diana during her brief stay.

Diana didn't care. She hardly noticed the ugly floral wallpaper or the pink curtains with their tatty fringes. She knew she was in the best hands and in the best place to have her baby. Above all, she felt safe. She had total confidence in her doctor, George Pinker, the Welsh Sister, Delphine Stevens – who would rush off down the corridor for a smoke, much to Diana's amusement – and the nursing sisters, Sister Kirwin and Sister Suarez. She also had Betty Parsons to help her with the contractions.

'Pick up your surf board and ride it like a whale,' Betty told her when she started the contractions, and then later on, 'doggy, doggy, candle, candle', (pant, pant, blow, blow). Prince Charles was present throughout the day, holding her hand and whispering words of encouragement. After several hours Diana was given an epidural injection to relieve the pain – she had wanted to try and have the baby without, but swiftly changed her mind when the pain became too intense. Betty Parsons's opinion that, 'There is no such thing as an unnatural childbirth,' was being given medicinal proof.

At 9.03 that evening Diana delivered a baby son. He weighed 7lb 1oz, and had 'a wisp of fair hair, sort of blondish, and blue eyes.' Motherhood, for the Princess of Wales, had begun.

Diana had definite ideas on how any child of hers was to be raised and she took charge right from the start. Determined to breast-feed her baby she also vetoed the suggestion that he might be circumcised – although there is no official record if he was or wasn't. The only record of that kind that exists is for Prince Charles, who was circumcised five days after he was born.

Diana also insisted, less than twenty-four hours after the birth, she was ready to go home. Even for someone with as many staff to help her as she had, this was somewhat unusual with a first child. After such a long labour her doctor knew what a big effort it would be

for Diana to walk and move with ease. But Mr Pinker
made a statement to the effect he was perfectly happy
with the arrangement, concealing any doubts he might
have had.

Charles was thrilled with his baby son. He was
delighted with his wife. In the choice of godparents,
however, tradition and Charles's wishes reigned. When
William was christened in the Music Room at Buckingham Palace on the Queen Mother's eighty-second
birthday, 4 August 1982, the only godparent of Diana's
age was the Duchess of Westminster, known as 'Tally'.
A couple of years older than Diana, she married the
Duke of Westminster, Britain's richest landowner, in
1978. 'Tally' had a baby daughter, Lady Tamara, and
she and Diana had long telephone conversations about
the merits of breast-feeding and childbirth (she had
also been a pupil of Betty Parsons and had had her
baby in the Lindo Wing under the care of George
Pinker). Today Diana claims Tally is 'too grand', and
prefers the company of her more risqué friends, but six
years ago Diana was new to the scene and she was
pleased to have at least one of her contemporaries
represented. The other two female godparents, Princess Alexandra, nicknamed 'Pud' by the Royal Family,
and Lady Susan Hussey, one of the Queen's senior
Ladies-in-Waiting, were both close to Diana – Susan
Hussey having shown her the royal ropes in those
lonely early days at Buckingham Palace and Princess
Alexandra being the light relief at the many family
gatherings. They were, however, both much older. So
was the most surprising choice of all, author and
philosopher Sir Laurens Van der Post, who was
seventy-six at the time, a mere six years younger than
the Queen Mother. Sir Laurens comes from a wealthy
South African family and during the war survived three

years in a Japanese POW camp. He met Prince Charles through the late Earl Mountbatten of Burma and has remained his friend and mentor since the Earl's untimely death in 1979. Charles has been greatly influenced by the ideas and example of Van der Post and later explained in an interview why he had chosen him as a godparent.

'His thoughts and experiences mean a great deal to me,' Charles said. 'One of the reasons I asked him to be a godfather to my son was because he is one of the best story-tellers I have ever come across. I want my son to be able to sit at his godfather's knee and listen to his wonderful stories. That's really the best way to learn, through story-telling. It was the ancient way, through stories handed down from generation to generation. We've lost the art today. All the mystery and excitement, romance and imaginativeness have gone – mainly, I think, because of television.'

It wasn't Sir Laurens's stories that silenced William Arthur Philip Louis that day in the Music Room at Buckingham Palace, but the comfort of sucking his mother's finger. He cried noisily and resisted any attempts to stop him by the Queen, Charles or either of the two other godparents, former King Constantine of Greece or Lord Mountbatten's grandson Lord Romsey, a Gordonstoun contemporary of Charles. No, it was his mother's finger he wanted, and Diana, who hates the use of plastic dummies, provided it.

When Diana returned to Kensington Palace after the birth of William, she immediately put into practice all the things she had been taught, read and done herself. She was used to children, having looked after her young brother Charles when he was a baby, helped with her two sisters' children and, of course, had her experience as a nursery school teacher. When Diana was a baby she had a succession of nannies who only stayed a few years each. The nursery was very much their domain and the children only saw their parents for short periods during the day.

This was not going to be the case with any child of hers. Both she and Charles agreed that their first-born must have 'as normal a life as is possible,' and they wanted their children brought up in a close family unit where the parents involved themselves with all the aspects of bringing up a baby, including changing nappies. Nanny was there merely to assist, not to take charge. But it was for that very reason that Diana and Charles had their first disagreement about the upbringing of their son. Diana was terrified of employing one of the 'dyed in the wool' traditional royal nannies, who are used to having servants to cater for them, while their duties revolve solely around the care of the child. She wanted a modern, more progressive nanny that she could control. Charles disagreed. He thought a royal nanny should know the royal ropes. He wanted to employ his old nanny, Mabel Anderson, who looked after him for most of his young life and to whom he was extremely attached.

Mabel Anderson joined the royal nurseries soon after Charles's christening along with another Scottish nanny, Helen Lightbody. Helen had been nanny to the Duchess of Gloucester's two boys, William and Richard, and Mabel had answered an advertisement in the 'situations vacant' column of a nursing magazine only to discover to her amazement that her application was answered by Buckingham Palace.

Their nursery duties followed a regular pattern. They would wake the children (Charles and his sister Anne) at 7 A.M., dress them and give them breakfast in the nursery. Then at 9 A.M., Nanny Lightbody would take them downstairs to play with their mother for half-an-hour before going for their morning walk.

When the Queen and Prince Philip left on a six-month tour of the Commonwealth in 1953, the two Scottish nannies were left in sole charge of the two royal children. Naturally, they became closer to their nannies than their parents, and, until the day she died at the age of seventy-nine last year, Charles would pay regular visits to Nanny Lightbody at her grace-and-favour flat in Kennington. On the day of her funeral Charles sent a hand-written note on a wreath which read: 'For Nana, in loving memory of early childhood – Charles.'

Nanny Lightbody left royal service in 1956 and Mabel continued to look after the Queen's children – Anne, Andrew and Edward. In 1977 she went to Gatcombe Park to take charge of Anne's first child, Peter Phillips. But life at Gatcombe was nothing like the days at Buckingham Palace when Mabel had the nursery floor to herself. Although Mabel didn't wear a uniform – she stuck to a blue blouse and skirt, a white cardigan and flat sensible shoes – she was in every respect the epitome of the traditional royal nanny. She had an assistant, nursery maid, chauffeur and two nursery footmen, and shared the duties of looking after the children with governess Miss Peebles, known to her young charges as 'Mipsy'.

Unable to adapt to the informality of Gatcombe Park, Mabel eventually left to be replaced by a less formal nanny, Pat Moss.

'No way,' Diana thought, would she fit in any home of hers and firmly put her foot down. Mabel wasn't coming. Charles swallowed his disappointment. He had to. Diana would not have allowed him the 'quiet life' he craved if he had insisted on Nanny Anderson.

Instead the job went to the daughter of a forestry worker, 42-year-old Barbara Barnes, who found herself the first royal nanny to a probable heir not to have two footmen and two housemaids to help her. She did, however, have a nursery maid, Mrs Olga Powell, an experienced nurse in her late fifties to assist her and all the comforts of the nursery suite at Kensington Palace with its scaled-down furniture, open fireplace and tasteful decoration, inspired by Dudley Poplak. The Highgrove nursery is equally attractive and Diana went to the trouble of having some characters out of nursery rhymes painted on the walls as a mural only to discover, to her horror, they looked far too frightening for children and so had them painted over again.

Barbara Barnes, whose informal manner and no-nonsense approach seemed just what Diana was looking for, was a far cry from the stiff and starchy sort who used to reign supreme. She didn't wear a uniform, have any formal training or regard the royal nursery as her private domain and herself as a mother substitute. 'I'm here to help the Princess, not take over,' she said. But her methods of bringing up the children, which had delighted her former employer Lord Glenconner, husband of Princess Margaret's Lady-in-Waiting, Lady Glenconner, did not meet with quite such the same enthusiasm from Prince Charles who believes in 'simple old-fashioned values for survival,' not in the changing fashions in child rearing.

'There were some experts who were very certain about how you should bring up children,' he says. 'But then, after twenty years, they turned round and said they'd been wrong. Well, think of all the people who followed their suggestions!' One of those experts is Dr Benjamin Spock – a distant relation of Diana's.

At the beginning, however, Charles was quite happy

with the set-up. Lord Glenconner's praise of Nanny Barnes seemed quite justified.

'She has a natural way with children,' Glenconner said. 'She has a genius for bringing out the best in them. They are never bored. She has all the traditional values to the highest degree, but is perfectly up to date.'

She was indeed up to date and very careful not to interfere with Diana's upbringing of baby William. They did things together such as walking in nearby Kensington Gardens or shopping for baby clothes (not that William needed anything – but Diana could never resist a shop). Barbara knew it was fun for Diana to go shopping for her new baby.

Diana became so involved with the baby she thought of little else. Her husband, as husbands often do in these circumstances, found that he was no longer the centre of his wife's attention. But Charles, who Diana sometimes thought was 'rather stuffy', took a delight in bathing his son and heir and helping change his nappies. Diana was forever worrying about William's health and listened carefully to his breathing at night.

'Is he all right, Baba?' she would say, looking anxiously down at his recumbent form in the cot. 'Is he breathing properly?' Both Barbara and Prince Charles understood her natural anxiety and had friends who had suffered from the tragic occurrence of 'cot deaths' – when the baby stops breathing and dies for no apparent reason.

It was not William's health that should have worried Diana at this time, but her own. She had lost a huge amount of weight very soon after the birth and seemed unable to get any enthusiasm for anything. Charles was worried and consulted several expert doctors. They assured him she did not have the slimmers' disease anorexia nervosa, as her sister Sarah once had, but was suffering from a form of post-natal depression. She was thoroughly exhausted. Giving birth can be a huge strain on a woman's body and it can take up to a year to return to normal, so the doctors assured him. It was not the pressures of her own home, or the baby, Diana insisted, but the outside world that bothered her. She had been under the microscope of public scrutiny for almost two years and instead of letting up it appeared to be getting more intense.

Barbara Barnes suggested that she be allowed to take over more of the responsibilities of looking after William but Diana was adamant. 'A mother's arms are so much more comforting,' she said. 'He comes first . . . always.'

He came first on the night Charles and Diana were both expected at the Annual Festival of Remembrance at the Royal Albert Hall, two minutes' drive from Kensington Palace. Diana was exhausted from her sleepless nights and didn't want to go. Charles insisted and they had a heated row. He finally arrived alone and flustered.

'Diana's not well,' he told the rest of the family gathering. She wasn't: she was unhappy, fraught and depressed.

'I'm exhausted,' she told her hairdresser Kevin Shanley, 'but how can I let people down?'

She decided she couldn't and finally went to the Albert Hall – arriving fifteen minutes late and after the Queen, which is against royal protocol. The royal party ignored the obvious coolness between the couple and when they got home later that evening Charles decided that Diana needed a holiday, not Balmoral, not the Scilly Islands, but somewhere abroad.

In January 1983 they had that long-awaited vacation, as guests of Prince Franz Joseph of Liechtenstein in his

castle perched high on the cliffs. It was not a success.
There wasn't enough snow locally so the royal couple
were forced to travel to different venues every day and
failed in their attempts to thwart the attendant press.
Diana was miserable at leaving William, miserable with
the weather and thoroughly fed up with the photographers, so much so that she refused to pose for them.

'Please darling, just one picture,' Charles pleaded.
She refused and was close to tears. It was the last thing
she needed at this stage. Charles hoped that if Diana
agreed to pose then the photographers would leave
them alone – they didn't.

It was a difficult time for Diana, but she had made
her choice. She had married the Prince of Wales and
she had to put up with what went with it. She would
have to cope as best she could.

It was for this reason the Queen agreed with Diana's
suggestion that William should accompany her and
Charles on their six-week tour of Australia and New
Zealand. She felt, quite rightly, that Diana was close to
breaking point and that the presence of her baby, even
if he was not with her the entire time, would have a
stabilizing effect on the Princess, both mentally and
physically. She also knew it would present the
troubled couple in a happy light to the Australian
people and help make their trip a success.

Diana had broken another royal tradition – never
before had a member of the royal family undertaken an
overseas tour with such a young child. If Diana wanted
something badly enough she always got her own way –
even with the Queen.

When they arrived in Australia, Nanny Barnes, complete with nappies, clothing and special food sup-
plements, fluoride drops and multi-vitamins for
William, headed for their temporary home in the tiny

town of Woomargama. Diana and Charles returned there every few days, to break their trip and be with him. Apart from his routine and sleeping pattern being disturbed, William, the experts agreed, was far better off to be close to his mother than if he had been left at home in the Kensington Palace nursery.

The experiment was a success. But not to be repeated: when Charles and Diana went to Canada two months later, they left William behind – missing his first birthday. She didn't enjoy the trip nearly as much as Australia and claimed, on her twenty-second birthday ten days after William's, 'My perfect birthday present is going home. I can't wait to see William.'

It wasn't just Diana who missed William. So did Charles. Having devoured dozens of books on child rearing and baby care he became an authority on the subject, which prompted Diana to remark in irritation, 'Charles knows so much about babies – he can have the next one.' But they both agreed all the attention they lavished on William was worth it. 'Babies like being talked to,' Diana said. She and Charles believe a baby left alone in his cot without lots of kisses and cuddles can become bored and may well turn out to be a slow developer, something William certainly wasn't. When he was just over a year old and Nanny Barnes had left him unattended for a few minutes in the Balmoral nursery, his natural curiosity got the better of him, and he pushed a button on the wall, unwittingly sending a direct signal to the police headquarters in Aberdeen, some fifty miles away. The police raced to Balmoral and sealed off the grounds, before it was discovered William was the culprit. A couple of months later he toddled through an infra-red alarm beam in the walled garden of Kensington Palace and brought another couple of dozen policemen on to the scene. Nanny

Barnes was highly embarrassed and the Prince had to apologize to the amused policemen for his son's mobility.

'You couldn't take your eyes off him for a second,' Diana's former hairdresser, Kevin Shanley, remembers. 'He was into everything.' Not only was William into everything, but he broke everything and developed an original habit of flushing anything he could lay his hands on down the loo – including his toys and his father's shoes. Diana nicknamed him her 'mini tornado' and delighted in telling the people she met during her official duties little snippets about her son. She told how Prince Charles encouraged William to get used to the bath by getting in the tub with him and one night when they were both due to go out for an important engagement she couldn't find Charles anywhere. She discovered him in the bath with William.

'They were having a great time,' she said. 'There was soap and water everywhere.'

9

Motherhood – part 2

'One of the most important roles any woman could ever perform is to be a mother,' Prince Charles said. Diana had fulfilled this role for her husband with great success and when she discovered she was pregnant for the second time in January 1984 Charles was delighted. Just before the official announcement was made, Diana flew to Norway on her first official solo trip. She returned to a love note written by her husband, which read, 'We were so proud of you,' and was signed 'Willie Wombat and I' (the nickname Charles gave to his son at the time). For whatever reasons of State Charles may have married, affection had now developed into something much stronger. The man whose position had ensured him centre stage of his own universe, had adjusted to having a wife and child to care for. He was enjoying the change in his routine and was taking a pleasure in the new responsibilities.

Prince William was twenty months old and Charles felt that by the time the new baby was born he would be ready to accept the new addition to the family without jealousy. Diana was not quite so sure. William was used to being the centre of attraction and had toddled into the limelight at the age of eighteen months in the garden of Kensington Palace, to speak that time-honoured word, 'Daddy'. Six months later he was again in the walled garden, this time to celebrate his second birthday with an increased vocabulary. The media noted he weighed twenty-eight pounds and was three feet tall. Diana noted he loved their attentions and was fascinated by the lens of a television camera. Photographer John Scott remembers Charles at the same age. 'He was precocious too,' he says, 'and when he was hardly three years old he could pronounce my Yugoslavian name, Colonel Voynovich, as well as if he'd been brought up in Belgrade.'

Diana was worried he was developing too fast, but circumstances were overtaking her and her inquisitive self-possessed little child. She hoped the new arrival would teach him to share, not only his possessions, but his position at centre-stage. Although Diana loved children and babies, being pregnant did not suit her. Again she suffered from morning sickness and complained of feeling rotten 'since day one'. She joked with friends about Charles's excitement and added, 'If men had babies, they would only have one each.'

During the long months of her pregnancy, Diana did her best to remain cheerful. The only time she let her feelings show was when Prince Charles left on a two-week tour of Africa when photographs show her looking thoroughly miserable. She was tired, William was still teething and her nights were often disturbed with his cries. Nanny Barnes was experiencing problems as Diana refused to allow her to do very much, but she hoped the arrival of the second child would allow her more control. From her very first trip without Prince Charles at her side, immediately before her pregnancy was announced on St Valentine's Day, Diana continued with her public engagements, the last of which was, fittingly enough, to open the Birthright Centre at King's College Hospital in London.

On Saturday morning, 15 September Diana's contractions began. This time she really knew what to expect. Her suitcase was already packed with a cotton nightgown, ear plugs, lipsyl, water spray and all the other

things Betty Parsons recommends expectant mothers to
take to hospital. Diana wanted everything done with as
little fuss as possible. It was – almost. Outside the
Lindo Wing the police had already erected the crash
barriers to hold back the crowds and inside the screens
were up and the room next to Diana's had been con-
verted into an office, complete with a telephone and a
lady-in-waiting in attendance. Positioned in the corridor outside Diana's room was one of her two personal
detectives, who had been alerted that the Princess was
on her way. At 7.30 A.M. Charles and Diana arrived and
the hospital staff sprang into action.

At 4.20 P.M. on Saturday, Diana gave birth to a second
son. And when Prince Charles emerged from the hospital a couple of hours later he told the waiting crowd,
'My wife is very well. The delivery couldn't have been
better. It was much quicker this time.' It was, however,
a full nine hours and he admitted, 'She's very tired. I
reckoned it was time she was left alone to recuperate.'
He then added, 'As for me, what I think I need is a
celebration drink.'

Throughout the nine-hour labour Charles had, once
again, been at Diana's side. When she was thirsty he
gave her ice-cubes to suck and held her hand when she
needed comfort. He admitted he had fallen asleep
briefly while waiting for the birth, but said it was only
a 'little doze'. Once again Diana was determined to
leave the hospital as soon as possible, but first she
insisted William must visit his baby brother to estab-
lish an all-important bond between the two children.
Diana had already told friends that she wanted William
to take a keen interest in the baby and would do
everything to ensure that he was included in the
celebrations. She did and on the Sunday morning

William was driven to the hospital with Prince Charles and Nanny Barnes.

There was so much excitement inside the hospital that Diana's bodyguard knocked over the screen outside her door with a resounding crash. A few seconds later William and Charles arrived in the lift and William ran down the corridor looking for Mummy. Diana heard the commotion and popped her head around her door, scooping William into her arms so that she was holding him when he first saw his baby brother. Meanwhile Nanny Barnes was waiting politely outside in the corridor, anxious that the family should be left alone, but after a couple of minutes Charles beckoned her in to see Harry before she took William back to Kensington Palace.

At 2.30 P.M. Diana left the hospital, less than twenty-four hours after the birth. This time she was prepared for the crowds that awaited her and had taken care with her hair and dressed in a smart red coat. Charles drove her back to Kensington Palace and then drove to Smiths Lawn polo ground, Windsor, where he had a friendly polo match organized to mark the big event. Sipping champagne, which he rarely ever touches, he held an impromptu party, using the back of a Land Rover as a makeshift bar. His polo-playing pals drank many toasts to the baby, already named Prince Henry Charles Albert David, to be known as Harry. Back at Kensington Palace Diana was sleeping, the tiny baby in the care of Sister Anne Wallace, who looked after William for the first weeks of his life. She was happy, she had no problems with breast feeding and, above all, William was delighted with his little brother.

Indeed William was so delighted with the baby that he wanted to play with him and hold him at every opportunity and when Harry was christened in

Above: The Spencer sisters
return to their old school,
West Heath, and pose on the
steps with former headmistress, Miss Rudge. Left to
right: Lady Jane Fellowes,
Miss Rudge, the Princess of
Wales and Lady Sarah
McCorquodale.
Right: Frances Shand-Kydd,
Diana's elegant mother, who
separated from her husband,
wallpaper heir, Peter, in early
1988. It is from her mother
that Diana inherited her
sense of style and colour and
she helped the Princess
decorate both her homes.

Diana's stepmother, Raine Spencer, holds tightly on to Earl Spencer's hand, in their gift shop at Althorp. The house is open to the public and they have a thriving business selling china and small luxury items to visiting American and Japanese tourists.

Above: A pensive Diana with Prince Philip as they watch a polo match.

Left: The Duchess of York shielding Diana and Prince William from the typical British summer weather with a large umbrella. Polo matches are much more fun for Diana when she has Fergie for company and to lend a helping hand with the two boys.

Diana at the wheel of the family Range Rover during a shooting party at Sandringham. Diana is careful never to be seen with a gun in her hand and although she has a very stylish shooting suit, restricts her activities to following the guns and transporting the ladies to the lunch, often held at one of the lodges on the Sandringham estate.

Horses are not Diana's favourite animals, but being a member of the British Royal Family means they are unavoidable. Here she makes friends with one of the polo ponies, while spending yet another afternoon watching Prince Charles play.

Left: After a social day at Royal Ascot, Diana watches her husband play polo at Smith's Lawn, Windsor, from the bonnet of his Aston Martin. When she realized that photographers were getting more than their fair share of her shapely legs she quickly leapt off and Prince Charles teased her, claiming she had made a dent in his beloved car. She hadn't, of course, but went along with the joke. *Below:* Before the tragic skiing accident which killed one of their friends, Major Hugh Lindsay, Sarah and Diana enjoy their annual visit to Klosters.

Right: While on holiday at King Juan Carlos's summer palace in Majorca, Diana, the loving mother, helps Prince Harry put on his shoe.

Left: Easter Sunday means church. Here Diana takes William by one hand while Peter Phillips (Princess Anne's son) takes him by the other. Diana and William's identical blue coats are made by Catherine Walker.

Left: Prince Charles plays his part in looking after the children and here he is on the banks of the River Dee in Scotland, watching them while they throw stones into the river.

Below: Not quite so experienced a rider as his elder brother, Prince Harry feels safer when his mummy's holding his tiny pony's head.

Above: Diana, who feels nervous on horseback, goes out riding with the Queen and Prince Edward during the long winter break at Sandringham.

Below: Another bit of fun during the New Year's holiday at Sandringham is playing on the old fire-engine in the grounds. William, Harry and Peter Phillips try on the antique helmets for the benefit of the photographers, who promised if they had one picture they would leave the Queen and her family alone to enjoy their holiday.

Right: Schooldays can be fun. Prince Harry, dressed as a goblin, accompanied by his friend the wolf, sets out for his first acting performance.

Left: Behind the scenes at Buckingham Palace on the Duke and Duchess of York's wedding day. Diana cheers up an over-tired, over-exhausted Prince William as members of the Palace Household and Royal Family go to the gates to see Fergie and Andrew off on their honeymoon. (The lady in white next to Diana is the Duchess of Kent.)

Above: The Princess shows off her newly acquired ability with sign language in her role as Patron of The British Deaf Association.

Below: Caring and thoughtful, the Princess chats with old folks at a Help the Aged centre during the cold winter of 1987.

Diana often presents the prizes at polo matches, and always gives her husband a kiss. On this occasion he was hot and sweaty and Diana got the giggles when his wet face brushed hers.

The many faces of Diana:

Left: Anxious – as she waits for Charles while visiting the flood victims of Wales. It was the first time she had seen her husband for some weeks and as soon as the visit was over he returned to Scotland fuelling speculation that their marriage was in trouble. *Below:* Beautiful – in Thailand with her hair adorned with orchids, carefully pinned in place and colour co-ordinated by her hairdresser.

Right: Serious – as she looks over her shoulder during a highly successful visit to France with Charles in November 1988.
Below: Childlike – as she pulls a face of mock horror at the Bute Highland Games.

The glamorous Princess of Wales standing next to her husband at a reception in Germany. Diana is wearing a deep-blue velvet dress designed by Victor Edelstein, the Spencer tiara she wore on her wedding day, and thousands of pounds worth of jewellery round her neck and wrist – a gift from the Sultan of Oman.

Movie star – Diana at her very best arriving at a film première in London. Her stunning gown is designed by Murray Arbeid and Diana has added her personal touches of one black and one red glove.

Diana poses happily in the rock garden of her Gloucestershire home – Highgrove. Princes William and Harry are dressed in their best shirts and ties from their father's outfitters, Turnbull and Asser.

St George's Chapel, Windsor, on 21 December, he couldn't understand why he wasn't allowed to hold him as he had done during Lord Snowdon's photographic session some six weeks before. But the delicate christening robe, which had survived for 143 years, would have been shredded if William had got his hands on it, so Diana turned to Lord Snowdon, who was taking the official photographs, for help. Snowdon came up with the perfect solution to keep William in the picture and out of mischief – an antique bird cage, which held the excited little boy's attention just long enough for Snowdon and his assistant to shoot the pictures. His assistant remembers being surprised with the attention William was getting from the assembled godparents and the Royal Family: 'Every time he did something naughty they roared with laughter, no one admonished him and he was being a thorough pest.'

His antics were, however, something of a relief to the Royal Family: formal photographic sessions have a habit of being very stilted and William provided the distraction they all needed. The christening celebration was televised and shown as part of the Queen's Christmas broadcast that year. Naturally enough Prince William's antics, including chasing his cousin Zara Phillips round the legs of the Archbishop of Canterbury, stole the show. In one sequence Diana is shown explaining to young William how many generations of the Royal Family had worn the valuable christening gown.

'Great Granny was christened in it,' she said, causing Charles to give her one of his quizzical looks and add, 'And I was christened in it.' Diana had slipped up on her history as palace officials explained later, 'Great Granny's *husband* was christened in it. Great Granny wasn't.'Great Granny is the Queen Mother who married the Duke of York, later King George VI, and it was he who wore the robe as a baby.

By her own admission Diana is no scholar and often tells jokes against herself to explain her lack of knowledge. 'I'm as thick as a plank,' she admitted to a group of youngsters, and on knocking her head when passing through a low doorway during a visit to Italy, quipped, 'Don't worry, there's nothing in it'. Empty-headed or not, she did have a little more say in the choice of godparents for Harry than she did for William. Her former flatmate, Carolyn Pride, married to brewery heir William Bartholomew who runs Juliana's Discotheques, was one and Lady Sarah Armstrong Jones, who had invited her on board *Britannia* almost five years before, was another. Lady Cece Vesty, second wife of meat baron Lord Sam Vesty, Prince Andrew, artist Brian Organ, whose informal portrait of Diana was vandalized in 1981, and Old Etonian farmer Gerald Ward completed the group. Her sister-in-law Princess Anne was not there. Her sister Lady Jane Fellowes was.

Jane was especially supportive. Her two older children, Laura and Alexander, are playmates of William and Harry, who often walk down the drive with their detective to have tea at Jane's house.

Having three children of her own and a husband who was in a senior position within the royal household, Jane's proximity and sensible advice has proved invaluable to Diana, who was already thinking of possible schools for William. She considered having a governess like she and Charles did at an early age. They both agreed, however, it would be better for William if he were to mix with ordinary children rather than remain in the hallowed atmosphere of Kensington Palace with a few carefully chosen playmates. The problem was brought home to Diana when she started looking at nursery schools and visited the school where she herself once taught, Young England Kindergarten in St George's Square, Pimlico. While she was chatting with the headmistress, Prince William, never one to sit on his laurels, joined in with the other children's game. 'Prince William couldn't do galloping horses,' one of the tiny pupils explained to her mother when she returned home. 'Why?' Galloping horses is a simple, child's game, which involves putting one foot in front of the other like a horse and galloping round the room. William's inability to play was merely because he had never mixed with any large numbers of children in a classroom and didn't know the popular games. Diana discussed the incident with Charles that evening and convinced him, no matter what, that William would benefit from mixing with ordinary children of his own age. But which school?

Young England, the Montessori-based kindergarten, renowned for its wonderful school plays, was a bit too far away and all the children ranging from two-and-a-half to five were taught in a large hall. After much deliberation and discussion with her husband, her sister and girlfriends, Diana found the solution: Mrs Mynors's school in nearby Chepstow Villas, a quiet tree-lined street near London's Notting Hill Gate. Several of Diana's friends had children there, including Charles's newly appointed private secretary, Sir John Riddell.

Remembering the fuss which ensued when Prince Charles arrived at Hill House School in Knightsbridge, twenty-eight years earlier, Charles and Diana composed a joint letter to be sent to all the Fleet Street editors. The letter politely requested that after the initial photo call William should be left alone. Mrs Mynors did her bit too and knocked on all her neighbours' doors to inform them that the little Prince was coming to her school and would they be very kind and give him some privacy. She also spoke to the parents who had children at the £200-a-term kindergarten and explained that under no circumstances were any of them to speak to the press.

On a warm day in September 1985, 150 reporters and photographers, many of whom had set up their ladders hours earlier to ensure a good position, waited behind the crash barriers for the three-year-old Prince to arrive on his first day at school. William was used to cameras as he had been paraded in front of batteries of photographers on many occasions. But even for so sophisticated a youngster, the whirr of the motordrives that sunny day was a bit much and he seemed surprised. Diana confessed later, she was far more nervous than William, who was terribly excited and longing to make some new playmates. To ensure he smiled for the cameras Diana let William choose what he wanted to wear – a pair of red shorts and a checked shirt. 'It's best to let him do that if you want him to smile,' she said, and he did.

Throughout his three short years, media attention had become commonplace to William, and during his time at Mrs Mynors's, his classmates became as blasé as their rambunctious new friend and took little notice when banks of photographers stood outside while they rehearsed their school play.

'His classmates hardly know who he is,' Mrs Mynors commented. 'Sadly that won't be the case at the next school he goes to.'

Mrs Mynors was not entirely right and Wills had discovered how a bit of pulling rank enabled him to get what he wanted. 'My Daddy can beat up your Daddy,' he is reputed to have said. 'My Daddy's a real Prince.' His detective, always present in the classroom and as unobtrusive as possible, accompanied him to school and kept a watchful eye on his charge. If there was any tears or pushing in the playground, he soon sorted it out gently but firmly. 'Come on, William,' he would say, 'that's not a very nice way to behave.' Both Charles and Diana insist that good manners are the most important aspect of their children's education. But any punishments doled out have to be administered by themselves, not a detective. They also insist that the detectives who watch over William and Harry should work on a rota system, to ensure that neither child becomes too attached to any one of them.

It was impossible to prevent a few tales of William's high-spirited behaviour filtering out of the classroom from time to time and he was nicknamed 'basher Wills'. Some parents insisted these stories were untrue. 'He's a charming little boy, and the most destructive thing he ever does is paint his face instead of the paper.' Others claimed he was 'rather a confused child, not unhappy, but increasingly aware he was in some way different from the others – something children hate'.

This was the very thing Charles and Diana wanted to avoid. They insisted the policemen assigned to the Royal Protection Squad called William by his first name and made no reference to his title; the same rule applied to Mrs Mynors and his classmates and if anything went wrong at school, or William misbehaved, Diana insisted she was informed immediately. She liked to deal with problems herself, however trivial, rather than letting Barbara Barnes dish out the discipline. Although both Barbara and Diana agreed that the nursery rule was no raised voices and no spanking unless absolutely necessary, she often took William's or Harry's side against Nanny.

'I'll always listen to both sides of an argument, then

make my decision,' she says, so each point of discipline was decided by a sort of committee. This often delayed any immediate action and William had already forgotten what he had done wrong by the time the punishment was decided.

A few years ago at Highgrove William caused a major scare. One minute he was playing happily and the next minute he was nowhere to be seen. Diana ran around the house shouting for him and instructed her detectives to search the garden, but to no avail. William was eventually discovered in the walk-in larder drinking from a large bottle of cherry pop, most of which had gone all over him. Diana was so delighted to find her little rascal that instead of telling him off she grabbed the bottle and read the label. She was horrified to read the additive ingredients in the fizzy drink and requested the staff to remove all the carbonated drinks from the larder. She has always been a champion of additive-free food for her children, believing they can cause hyper-activity. Even when William was taken to Australia in 1983, she insisted that special additive-free baby foods be taken along.

The desire of Diana's to be the perfect mother was contributory to the departure of Nanny Barbara Barnes in February 1987. In spite of rumours to the contrary, all Diana's friends insist, 'there is nothing pretentious about her, she is considerate, kind and patient with everyone – especially her staff'. But Diana has one overriding characteristic, which she finds hard to control – jealousy. Try as she might to organize her day around the children, her official engagements prevented her from spending as much time with them as she wanted to. Charles had the same problem, but he was in a better position to do as he wished and it wasn't until his father, Prince Philip, pointed out he

was neglecting his duties, that Charles tore himself
away from the nursery. Relations between the two
became very strained following the birth of Prince
Harry when Charles had just a dozen engagements in a
four-month period and Prince Philip felt his son was
not living up to his responsibilities – Philip made his
feelings public by failing to visit Prince Harry until he
was almost five weeks old.

Diana, who hated becoming embroiled in family
rows, kept in the background. Instead, her irritation
began to manifest itself against 'Darling Baba'. She felt
guilty resenting her, but couldn't control the pangs of
jealousy she felt when William ran to Papa or Baba,
instead of to her; worse still he played up in her
company, making her exasperated and irritable. She
experienced no such problems with Harry. He was
gentle, quieter than his elder brother and satisfied just
to watch. He worshipped William and roared with
laughter at everything he did, his eyes never leaving
his elder brother's cheeky face. When William was at
school in the mornings he slept and Nanny Barnes got
him up in time to have lunch with his brother when he
returned at midday.

Diana tried hard to organize her official engagements
around her children's schedule, but it wasn't always
possible and some days she would leave early in the
morning, return briefly in the late afternoon, only to
have a bath, change and go out again. She did everything she could to avoid this clash of schedules; she
felt the most important time to be with her children
was at bath- and bed-time and even if she was going to
a film première or early evening engagement she would
try and be the one to read them their bedtime story or
sing nursery rhymes, rather than leave it to Nanny or
Charles.

Another of Diana's pleasures is shopping for the children. In the early days she chose smocked romper suits from the White House in Bond Street, and William wore a frilly blouse that once belonged to Prince Charles for a photo session with Lord Snowdon, shortly after Harry's birth. But these traditional old-fashioned children's clothes are reserved for special occasions and Diana likes to see her young boys in practical up-to-the-minute outfits. Striped T-shirts by Jean Bourget from Harrods, sweatshirts and corduroy trousers from Benetton 0–12 and Osh Kosh dungarees form part of their wardrobe and although Harry has some of William's hand-me-downs, they are often dressed in identical outfits. For a photo session at Sandringham in January 1988 they both wore their smart pale-blue coats, trimmed with white and fastened with mother-of-pearl buttons. Diana had one the same, copied for her by Catherine Walker. It was one of her less inspired fashion decisions: when she and William appeared one day in the 'his and hers' outfits, the world laughed.

Diana also patronizes fashionable children's boutiques such as Anthea Moore Ede's in Launceston Place, opposite one of her favourite restaurants, and is not averse to sending one of her staff into Marks and Spencer children's department for an assortment of T-shirts and shorts.

In spite of the huge number of toys and other gifts presented to Diana for her children, she still loves to buy them herself. Educational toys from the Early Learning Centre in Kensington High Street, or something musical from Toddler Toys off Sloane Street. Then there are those special Christmas visits to Harrods toy department at 8.30 in the morning when they have the whole store to themselves for half an hour. They enter by the side entrance in Hans Crescent where they are greeted by the manager, who escorts them to the escalator, which takes them straight up to the toy department. William and Harry then spend half an hour of bliss running from one counter to another squealing with delight. Diana ensures they have a hand in choosing gifts for their friends as well as deciding what they want themselves while she, with the ability of the seasoned shopper, selects toys for her sister's children and the other junior members of the Royal Family. Diana, unlike her husband, is very generous and derives great pleasure from choosing expensive presents to give to her family and friends. She is also very organized and admits, apart from last-minute purchases, 'I do all my Christmas shopping in October.'

By the time he was three William was well versed in the niceties of royal etiquette. He had mastered the Windsor wave, learnt to shake hands and punctuate his conversation with plenty of 'please's and 'thank-you's. But still Diana felt his public appearances should be kept to a minimum. Traditionally, royal offspring are trusted to behave themselves from an early age, but William's mounting indiscretions, harmless enough for any ordinary child, weighed heavily against him. She was forced to slap his bottom in public on more than one occasion and when he crept into a policeman's car at Highgrove to play with the radio telephone, Diana was very annoyed, gave him a sharp spank and made him apologize to the policeman for playing in his car while he was on duty.

In 1986 he had his first of many outings to watch polo at Smiths Lawn, but from the moment he arrived he demanded attention. 'Where's Papa? Can I have a drink? I want an ice cream.' Diana, who had arrived alone, found William's whining impossible and was forced to bundle him into the car and take him straight

back to Windsor Castle and the attentive arms of
Nanny.

It was later that summer, after the excitement of
Sarah and Andrew's wedding, where William juggled,
fiddled and was thoroughly entertaining as a sailor-
suited page, that Nanny Barnes decided her role as the
royal nanny was not working out as she had hoped.
She was very fond of her little charges, especially
William. But she was accustomed to living as one of
the family and after the initial excitement of living as
the premier royal nanny, missed the more intimate
atmosphere of a more cosy environment. She decided
working for the Prince and Princess of Wales was not a
'forever' situation and she would wait for a suitable
moment to leave. In December 1986 she attended her
former boss, Lord Glenconner's birthday party on the
Caribbean island of Mustique, hobnobbing with the
likes of Princess Margaret, Raquel Welch and Jerry
Hall. When Barbara Barnes was spotted in the group
photograph, people were intrigued: why was Diana's
nanny at this élite bash, when she was supposed to
be in charge of the heir to the heir? Diana asked
herself the same question. She knew Barbara had been
anxious to attend, but she didn't like the idea of a
member of her staff, however close, socializing with
her circle of friends. Some would consider Diana's
attitude a snobbish one, but she simply believed that
this was not the order of things, she wasn't used to it.
Her nanny would never have done such a thing. It
would have been unthinkable for Mabel Anderson,
Charles's old nanny, to mix with the 'upstairs' set
socially. Clearly, having a 'young, modern nanny' had
its problems.

When Barbara returned to the calm of Kensington
Palace with her West Indies tan, she was aware of a

certain coolness between herself and her employers. William had completed fifteen months at the nursery school and was ready for his next step, pre-prep school, where he would remain until he was eight. It was, she thought, a good moment to give in her notice. She could wait until her darling 'Wills' started school and retreat quietly into the background. Harry would still have Olga Powell to look after him and Barbara could stay on until a suitable replacement had been found.

Immediately after the New Year when Diana returned to London from Sandringham, Barbara discussed the situation with her. They both agreed that William's first day at school, 15 January 1987, would be an ideal date to announce her impending departure. 'I thought no one would notice,' Diana confessed later, 'but I was wrong, wasn't I?' Just how wrong she had been was revealed the day after William's arrival at his new school. The front pages of most newspapers were devoted to Nanny Barnes and the inside pages to William's first day at Wetherby, his new school in Pembridge Square. Buckingham Palace refused to throw any light on the situation and merely stated that the move had been under discussion for ten days, and that Miss Barnes had no job to go to and that no replacement had been found.

No replacement had been found, but the feelers on the nanny network were already out and the Waleses' staff at Buckingham Palace were preparing a list of possible applicants. Prince Charles, who hadn't joined Diana for William's first day at school – he was stuck in a blizzard at Sandringham – was not too concerned. He felt Wills needed more discipline, something he hoped Wetherby would provide quite successfully. One of the reasons Charles and Diana had chosen the

£785-a-term school was that the headmistress, Frederika
Blair Turner, who was educated at Diana's old prep
school, Riddlesworth Hall, placed great emphasis on
manners.

Diana and Charles had given William's future education a great deal of thought. 'We're still learning the
tricks of the trade,' Diana admitted, and having drawn
up a list of schools within a one-mile radius of Kensington Palace, narrowed the choice down to less than
half a dozen. It was not easy. Within a five-minute
drive from the gates of Kensington Palace, there were
three excellent schools: Wetherby, Faulkner House and
Norland Place. Security, of course, played a part in
their considerations. William had to be driven to
school every day accompanied by a detective and a
back-up car, in case anything went wrong. Police also
had to be positioned outside the school, so the nearer
he was to home the easier it was for the Royal Protection Squad to do their job properly. This was something
the Queen was most anxious for Charles and Diana to
take into account.

'We're open minded about William and his education,' Charles said. 'I would like to try and bring up our
children to be well mannered, to think of other people,
to put themselves in other people's positions. That
way, even if they turn out not very bright or very
qualified, at least if they have reasonable manners they
will get so much further in life than if they did not
have any at all.'

Wetherby, with its 120 boy pupils ranging from four-
and-a-half to nine, and its smart grey uniform with red
trim (available only from Harrods), fitted the bill
perfectly.

Lord Freddie Windsor, the son of Prince and Princess
Michael of Kent, had attended Wetherby and had been

extremely happy. He had sung in the choir, done well in exams and, above all, according to other mothers, 'had the most perfect manners'. More important to Charles than Princess Michael's son was that his close friend, Andrew Parker-Bowles's nephews, Luke and Sam, had also been educated at Wetherby. Parker-Bowles, Silver Stick-in-Waiting to the Queen and Commander of the Household Cavalry, was full of praise for the school, its educational merits and its headmistress, Miss Blair Turner.

Most of the parents are affluent, upper-crust and live locally, returning to their country houses on Friday afternoons when school finishes at lunchtime. William would not feel out of place in such company, although his Monday essays on what he did at the weekend would make far more interesting reading.

When William arrived at Wetherby on a snowy January morning in 1987, he was greeted on the steps by Miss Blair Turner. Six-foot tall and dressed entirely in blue with her long fair hair in a plait, she looked more like a Nordic figurehead than a schoolmistress and it was all Diana could do to suppress her giggles – she told friends later she wanted to die laughing, but wouldn't have dared do so in front of William and so many pressmen. On his first day William left before lunch but a staff member confirmed, 'he had fitted in immediately,' with his form mistress, Miss Jane Ritchie, and his twenty classmates.

Diana, who had several official engagements to fulfil that day told some old folks she was visiting in Islington she had no trouble packing William off to school and thought he looked sweet in his school uniform. She also revealed proudly that her son was developing into a perfect little gentleman.

'He's already opening doors for ladies,' she said, 'and he's calling men sir.'

Barbara Barnes publicly agreed. She felt she was leaving behind a young prince who, as she says, 'is a perfect little gentleman.'

Bob Geldof was not so enthusiastic. When the dishevelled Irishman called at Kensington Palace to discuss the famine problems in Africa with Charles, he was met by father and son.

'Why do you talk to that man?' William inquired, pointing to Geldof, attired as usual in jeans and sneakers, his face covered by his regulation designer stubble.

'Because we have work to do,' Prince Charles replied.

'He's all dirty,' William insisted. 'He's got scruffy hair and wet shoes.'

Geldof, true to form, retorted: 'Shut up, you horrible little boy. Your hair's scruffy too.'

To which the cheeky William replied: 'No it's not, my mummy brushed it.'

Mummy looked set to do her fair share of hair brushing, for finding a new nanny was proving a problem. Several applicants were interviewed, but there was always something wrong. One girl was on the point of accepting the job. But when she was questioned about her religious beliefs she admitted she was a Roman Catholic. A polite letter arrived from Buckingham Palace informing her that her application had been unsuccessful. 'I never thought about religion,' she told her current employer, who had been unaware of the secret interviews that had taken place. 'How could a man, who is one day going to be head of the Church of England, employ a Catholic nanny?' her employer told her. 'Of course you wouldn't get the job.'

There were no such problems for forty-year-old Ruth Wallace, who finally took the sought-after job. She was working for Princess Michael of Kent on a freelance basis, looking after her two children, Lord Frederick and Lady Gabriella Windsor, and had often come across William and Harry within the confines of Kensington Palace. She had also spent some time working for William's godfather, ex-King Constantine of Greece, a relative of the Royal Family, who lives in exile in London. Ruth, a State Registered Nurse trained at St Bartholomew's Hospital in central London, was experienced with children and had worked as a freelance nanny since 1980.

On 2 March 1987, she started her new job, assisted by sixty-year-old Olga Powell, who was happy to teach her the ropes. Princess Michael, her former employer and next-door neighbour, was not quite so happy. This time Princess Michael decided there was no point in making a fuss. She was upset, but felt Diana needed all the support she could get and anything she said would do little to change the situation. 'Ruth is highly competent,' she said, 'and who can blame her for wanting to work for the Princess of Wales.'

It wasn't all work, as Ruth Wallace discovered. She had very comfortable quarters on the top floor of Kensington Palace, the use of a car, a chauffeur and the invaluable assistance of Olga Powell. Before she accepted the job she had a long talk with the Prince and Princess on how they wanted and expected their children to behave. They agreed when it came to discipline, the parents have the final say, but assured Ruth they weren't averse to her slapping the children if necessary. The practical experience of parenthood was changing the Waleses' views. Charles reiterated his desire for the children to be kept out of the public eye as much as possible and explained that from now on they should all travel separately. This was not practical when they were flying to Majorca for their annual summer visit to King Juan Carlos's palace outside Palma, but was a rule of thumb when going to Balmoral. Ruth would share weekend duties with Olga Powell so they both had some time off. Television was to be limited to certain programmes and, above all, Charles explained, Ruth must be discreet.

'They're normal little boys,' Charles said, 'who are unlucky enough to create an abnormal amount of attention.'

According to child psychologists, Prince Charles is quite correct. 'Prince William appears to be going through a phase common in four- to five-year-olds. Their intelligence is developing rapidly at this age and they need a lot of stimulation. Going to school full-time usually sorts them out; it occupies their growing mental and physical energies.'

Attending school full-time certainly occupies a great deal of William's energy. Besides his ordinary lessons he takes weekly 'Fun with Music' lessons at a cost of £50 per term. Every Wednesday he attends classes in a North London church hall, where teacher Ann Rachlin spins stories round the classical music. And when he's not taking extra lessons, playing football or swimming, he attends numerous children's tea parties, accompanied inevitably by Nanny and his detective. It was during one of these parties he was reputed to have thrown his food on the floor, screaming he hated the sandwiches, jelly and ice cream on offer. When one of the other nannies made him clear up the mess, he shouted:

'When I'm King I'm going to send my knights round to kill you.'

Tears of rage and frustration are natural and William, like any other child, likes to get his own way, and whatever Charles and Diana may wish, it would be impossible for him to be completely unaware of who he is. Both Ruth and Olga are sensitive to this situation and try to deal out the discipline fairly, remembering the little boys are at a great disadvantage. Anything they do is newsworthy and anything they say can be misquoted. Charles and Diana were particularly upset to hear of reports that William had been bossing around the guardsmen at Balmoral during the summer holiday of 1987 and decided he should not attend the annual Highland Games at Braemar.

Only a few weeks earlier William had encouraged Harry to join in his pranks and they hid in a horsebox at Highgrove. As the box was being driven out of the stable yard, taking one of Charles's horses to trainer Nick Gaselee's Lambourn stables, it was stopped and the two little Princes were discovered giggling in the back. Again Diana gave them a stern ticking off, for fear they might do it again and not be discovered.

Prince Harry, like many younger brothers is an altogether gentler character than William. 'Number two skates in quite nicely,' Prince Charles said and he did. In September 1987 he followed in William's footsteps and started at Mrs Mynors's kindergarten. On his first day he was accompanied by his brother who was not due to return to school until a couple of days later. William was only too keen to show him his old classroom and almost ignored the photographers in his haste to drag Harry down the basement steps.

The previous day Harry had celebrated his third birthday with a visit to London Zoo in Regent's Park and he couldn't wait to tell his classmates about all the animals he had seen. Diana cut short an official engagement opening a dairy to dash back to Kensington Palace to meet her son when he returned shortly after midday.

'I was upset about leaving Harry,' she said. 'But now I'm going to meet him I can't wait.'

Harry, shy of the assembled photographers, covered his face with a home-made pair of binoculars as he left the school just before lunch. He had enjoyed his morning and been far less upset than his parents. Prince Charles admitted it had been a wrench to leave their gentle youngest son behind.

'It made me feel very sad,' he said. 'I had a bit of a lump in my throat when we left Harry.'

Leaving children behind is part of royal life and Diana and Charles are accustomed to missing small milestones in their children's lives. They do try though to be around for sports day – Diana and Charles attended William's at the end of June 1987 and Diana won the mother's 200-yard race, and they sat in front-row seats at Christmas to watch Wills perform as The Little Drummer Boy in St Mary Abbots church, Kensington. Not to be outdone, Prince Harry took the part of a goblin in his Christmas play. And unlike his brother, who burst into tears when he saw his parents in the audience when he was at Mrs Mynors's, acted his part well. Harry was so excited before the performance he couldn't resist sticking his tongue out at waiting cameramen.

Harry's first few terms at Mrs Mynors's élite nursery school proved he was quite a different character from William. He hid shyly at breaktime and refused to join in the playground games that his elder brother had so often instigated. At first he was embarrassed about using the two toilets and wouldn't put his hand up to be 'excused' and he felt overshadowed by the ever present competition with his brother. Psychologists explain this is quite normal with a younger child, who is dominated by an elder brother and in order to avoid failure the child avoids doing anything at all. But eventually Harry settled in and wasn't always longing to go home at the end of the morning.

Diana paid particular attention to Harry and tried to have lunch with him whenever she could, rushing back from her engagements in time for a plate of spaghetti or fish fingers in the nursery. At weekends she accompanied groom Marion Cox when she gave the two boys riding lessons on their little ponies, taking the leading rein of Harry's pony, while William rushed on ahead. When Charles played polo and the boys came to watch, he showed Harry how to feed the ponies sugar by holding the lump in the flattened palm of his hand. Harry's love of animals encouraged his parents to give him a pony and at the age of almost four he was competent enough to do without the leading rein.

Diana and Charles's fervent wish for their children to have as normal an upbringing as possible has not been entirely unsuccessful. During their school holidays their activities are carefully planned to be as diverse as possible. They make unexpected trips to a North London playgroup, where they mix with children from working families, as well as their normal visits to the Queen at Balmoral, Sandringham or Windsor, and their annual summer holiday to Majorca to stay with the King of Spain. They have plenty of friends, as Diana explains:

'I have two sisters who have five children between them, and have lots of friends who have children.' Since both boys have started school Diana's circle of friends has widened to include the mothers of those children whom William and Harry have befriended. Flicky Playdell Bouverie, whose son Nicholas was a pal of William's at Mrs Mynors's and is following him to Wetherby, is one such person. Flicky is over ten years older than Diana, but the Princess sometimes used to pop into her Holland Park house to collect William after tea. Diana's friendly disposition endears her to everyone she meets and they are very protective of her and the children.

'The things you read about William being badly behaved are simply not true,' one young mother says. 'He's a charming little boy with an inquisitive nature and the natural boundless energy of any child his age.'

'He's just like me,' Diana says, but Buckingham Palace staff, on the other hand, find him more reminiscent of his Uncle Andrew. Andrew was so naughty and cheeky he drove staff to distraction and they sometimes belted him when no-one was looking. His pranks were also well documented – he tied the laces of the guardsmen together, poured bubble bath into the swimming pool and teased the corgis (William got a walloping from Nanny Wallace for teasing the gundogs at Sandringham last November). Harry could also be compared to Edward as a child. He was quieter than his older brother and far better behaved.

Norman Myers, who as Uncle Myers and his assistant, Monty the monkey, have entertained two generations of royal children, agrees:

'William's like Andrew, extrovert and a bit cheeky. But a happy person and utterly delightful. Harry's more like Edward, more shy and introverted.'

At children's parties Myers leads his young charges through Pass the Parcel and Simon Says and games of Musical Bumps (the winner is whoever sits down on the floor fastest when the music stops). 'William and Harry don't get singled out for special treatment,' he says. 'They love all the same sort of things as other kids.' And they were always, he insisted, on good behaviour.

But however well they might behave at parties there are occasions when, as Diana has remarked, they appear to have 'grown into a couple of little thugs'. And they can be exhausting. She gets a break from them when she goes to 'work', but tries to organize her life around them as much as possible. When they are unwell they climb into her bed, not Nanny's, and although she may not be able to sleep that is the way she wants it. If she has another child, which she obviously wants, she would very much like a girl.

'I don't think I'd like to have three boys,' she said, 'but I'd love a girl.' Even Diana cannot control nature but the other day at a party she told a friend who has two girls: 'If I have another son and you have another daughter, we'll swop.'

10
Working Life

There is a routine to the life of the Prince and Princess of Wales. It is a routine of rush. It is a lifestyle very different from that enjoyed by their royal predecessors. In former days their life was very much their own, to be enjoyed in their own way, simply or extravagantly, but always self-indulgently. But the role of the Royal Family has changed. Today there is work to do. Life, as Charles says, is a job. And their job is their life.

Says John Merton, the society artist who painted a triptych portrait of Diana, 'I saw her engagement book, which is a terrifying thing. Every hour of the day is booked up for nine months ahead.' Diana's engagement book is not really a book but a series of neatly printed pages in an embossed folder, one day to a page and one line for every hour. These are neatly filled in by her lady-in-waiting – appointments every fifteen to twenty minutes and a strict timetable for official engagements. Evenings and weekends are also inked in with a line through the page to denote holidays. John Merton and other portrait painters are allotted a certain number of sittings – he had five, one at Kensington Palace and four more at his studio near Marlborough in Wiltshire. Otherwise they work from photographs, and there are plenty of those available. It all takes careful organization and rules out too many of the impromptu gatherings of which the Princess is so fond.

'Imagine having to go to a wedding every day of your life – as the bride – well that's a bit what it's like,'

Diana confides, and because her day is so busy she has to start early.

The day will begin when butler Harold Brown knocks on the bedroom door, never later than 7.30 A.M., bearing a tray of weak coffee for Diana and Lapsang Souchong tea for Charles – he never touches coffee or sugar, preferring to sweeten his drinks with large spoonfuls of honey, which he takes with him everywhere. The breakfast china has a delicate pattern of butterflies and leaves – very much Diana's taste – she loves pretty feminine things. Depending on her schedule for the day she will don a tracksuit and head for the front door. Her detective is already waiting in the car with the engine running and they make the short drive to Buckingham Palace in record time, avoiding all the rush-hour traffic, for her early morning swim. If Diana has an early engagement or one of her children is unwell, she will sacrifice the dip and do a few stretching exercises instead before sitting down to a frugal breakfast of pink grapefruit, muesli and a piece of toast while glancing through the *Daily Mail* and the *Daily Express* gossip columns to see what her friends have been up to. She avoids reading stories about herself as she finds them too upsetting. But she knows what is being said: either her postbag of letters will tell her, or her friends.

'If anyone mentions that story to me again, I will go mad,' she says, referring to her fit of giggles at the Sovereign's Parade at the Royal Military Academy, Sandhurst, where she represented the Queen. When she met the journalist responsible for the 'giggling' part of the story, the *Daily Mirror*'s James Whitaker, she told him she had a bone to pick with him. Whitaker, who invented the job of royal watcher and followed Diana's romance with Charles right from the start, was

concerned; he hated the idea of being blamed personally by the Princess for upsetting her. She then
informed him she had not read his report, but had
received dozens of letters referring to his story in the
Daily Mirror, so she knew he was to blame. Their
conversation was very good natured and Whitaker
questioned her as to why she had giggled in the first
place – as a Princess, he observed, she should be used
to such things.

'I was nervous, and when I'm nervous I always
giggle,' Diana said, and then added endearingly, 'There
were so many Princes and Princesses there.' [There
were two Kings, four Princes and eight Princesses –
from the Jordanian, Greek and Danish royal families.]
'It made me even more scared.'

Diana's nerves are a real hazard when it comes to
speech making and she revealed that her 'rude' royal
relatives often tease her about her faltering attempts.
Her own family are her worst critics. Yet she still hasn't
learnt to adjust her voice tones and it all sounds rather
flat as she reads from her notes.

In January 1987 she gave her first-ever interview to
Independent Radio News court correspondent, Dickie
Arbiter, who is now one of the Palace press secretaries.
It was during a particularly cold snap and the Princess
was visiting the headquarters of Help the Aged, of which
she is Patron, to see if there was anything she could do to
help their plight. Dickie, an experienced interviewer,
requested a few words with the Princess and much to his
surprise and delight he was invited to Buckingham
Palace later in the afternoon to talk to her. He immediately put her at ease and assured her he was only going
to ask her a few simple questions, but as soon as the tape
was turned on she tensed up and her answers came back
in the emotionless voice she adopts when nervous:

'I certainly feel that since I've come into public life I perhaps need a little more guidance,' Diana said. 'I know that my grandmother has got all the answers, purely because she's been through some of the experiences herself and it's so important to listen to someone older. We, the younger ones, always think we know better, but we don't – we have to go through experiences to learn the ups and downs of life and it's an enormous help to have a grandparent around who will say it in the nicest way.'

Dickie was very pleased with the interview. Besides giving her views on the plight of the aged, Diana had added her own personal touch by mentioning the advice she received from her grandmother, Lady Fermoy. It was not rehearsed or pre-planned (normally it takes several letters and a lot of patience to get an interview with a member of the Royal Family, and the only interview Diana had ever done before was a written reply to prepared questions about the charity, Birthright). But he felt if Diana was willing to speak when she visited her charities, people would take far less interest in her clothes and appearance and concentrate instead on what she said.

Even recording a prepared speech on to a mini tape machine and then playing it through the earphones of her Sony Walkman hasn't helped much. It was a method she tried before her maiden speech at the Guildhall in July 1987. It was not a notable success but she did raise a laugh when she took a swipe at her critics who had labelled her a 'boozer' after reports that she went on drinking binges with her friend Fergie.

'Contrary to recent reports,' she said, 'I have not been drinking and I am not, I can assure you, about to become an alcoholic.'

When these stories start up the people who work for

her close ranks. Particularly protective is her hair-dresser, Richard Dalton. He sees her every working day, and passes on the news to keep her amused.

He usually arrives at Kensington Palace at around 9 A.M. to style her hair in the pastel-green-walled dressing room with its kidney-shaped dressing table. He seldom sees Charles. The Prince of Wales, who likes to sleep in total darkness, is an early riser who listens to the farming report on Radio 4 at 6.10 A.M. Recently he has acquired the disconcerting habit of being in his study and on the telephone, a breakfast tray of bran flakes and honey on his desk, before 8.00 A.M. He will read the papers, though newspaper games, it can be said, do confuse him.

One morning he lost his entry card for *The Times* Portfolio game.

'Find it for me quickly,' he instructed the butler.

'Don't worry, sir, I'll get you another,' the butler replied.

'No, you can't do that – I must have mine,' the Prince insisted, in the mistaken belief that the card had been specially made for him.

As Charles wrestles with the sometimes unfamiliar ways of the modern world, Diana will be getting on with her own day. As a mother she is a light sleeper and may have had her night disturbed by that perennial cry for a glass of water or complaint of a stomach ache. The boys will always crawl into bed on Diana's side if they are frightened or unwell and Charles seldom wakes up. But whatever Charles and Diana are doing during the day they always kiss the boys goodbye before they go off to school in the mornings. William has acquired an endearing habit of saluting his father by the front door, imitating some of the soldiers and officials, who do the same. And amidst much giggling

Harry will copy his elder brother. If Diana doesn't have any pressing appointments she will accompany the detective and the children to school in their Ford Granada estate car. She doesn't pick them up, but tries to organize her day so she can be around in the early evening to read to them before they go to bed. She is most particular about this and feels it is her duty as a mother, in spite of the large number of staff she and Charles employ at Kensington Palace – between sixteen and twenty, including two valets for Charles, two dressers for Diana, two cooks, two chauffeurs, a butler, a housekeeper, an army orderly and a host of daily cleaners, plus the two nannies.

Diana is on first-name terms with all her staff at Kensington Palace, but is not over familiar with them as she was in the early days of her marriage. She remembers their birthdays and at Christmas chooses gifts with great care, having everything wrapped, tagged and hidden well before the middle of December. Charles is happy to leave that 'chore' to his wife, just as before his marriage he left it up to his valet to do all his shopping – with the minimum of expense! Diana also never forgets how her royal life consumes that of her staff (the Royal Family never refer to their staff as servants), and if they have been working particularly long hours she always thanks them, often with a personal note written in her large rounded handwriting. But being a perfectionist herself she gets irritated if things are left untidy or dirty and won't hesitate to inform them if she is displeased. At Highgrove one of the maids once left some dirty fingermarks on the paintwork and Diana, who was feeling tetchy anyway, threw an angry fit. Normally, however, she is never haughty or bossy and asks for things to be done in the nicest possible way:

'Would it be possible to do this for me?' she says
with a smile.

In their seven years of living at Kensington Palace,
the Waleses have had a rapid turnover of staff. Diana is
very sensitive about being blamed for this and even
took the trouble privately to defend herself, explaining
she was not responsible for sacking any of her staff.
She did feel insecure, however, in the early days,
surrounded by people who had known the Prince
throughout his bachelor days. She considered them a
bunch of 'fuddy duddies' and resented their interfering
in her new life with Charles. 'It was as if he was
married to them, not me,' she told one of her girlfriends, 'and they are so patronizing it drives me mad!'

Diana also found it very hard to adjust to having a
member of the Royal Protection Squad with her wherever she went, and in the early days resented it for a
long time. However, she succeeded in making a few
late-night forays on her own – once being chased by a
carload of Arabs who recognized her. The story came
out in 1987. It was true, but had happened several
years before. Diana would never attempt to do anything
like that these days. More to the point her detectives
would not allow her to and she, for her part, has grown
accustomed to the shadowy figures that follow her
everywhere – if she goes out to dinner they come too,
sitting in an adjoining room until the Princess is ready
to leave.

The lot of a Royal Protection Officer is not an easy
one. They have to be prepared to leave their families
behind for long periods, work unsociable hours and
dress and act as courtiers while remembering their real
role is that of an armed guard employed to ensure the
safety of their charges. They dislike being referred to as
bodyguards or detectives, but most people find Royal

Protection Officer a bit of a mouthful, so they have to put up with it. Diana's senior detective is stern-faced Inspector Graham Smith who keeps up the twenty-four-hour security by dividing his time with Inspector Tony Parker and Inspector Allan Peters and a couple of others, who also look after the royal children. They call the little Princes by their Christian names, as requested by Prince Charles, and refer to Diana as 'Your Royal Highness' and then 'Ma'am'. She calls them by their Christian names or in some cases a nickname – Graham Smith is known as 'Smudger'.

For a short period when Prince William started his pre-prep school, he was assigned a female detective, but she didn't last long. 'She found the hours interfered with her social life,' a member of the household said. It was not surprising as the women in the royal employ find their social lives curtailed to such an extent that their job, like their employers', becomes their life.

Diana's chief lady-in-waiting, Anne Beckwith-Smith, is one such person. For seven years she has held one of the most demanding posts in the Waleses' household. She joined Diana in September 1981 on the recommendation of the Queen Mother, who knew her father, Major Peter Beckwith-Smith, who is the clerk of the course at Epsom where the Derby is run. Friendly and with sparkling blue eyes, Anne came with impeccable cultural and family references. She was educated at West Heath (the same school as Diana and her sisters) and Queen's Gate and went on to study art in Paris and Florence. That had led to a job in the English Picture Department of Sotheby's. But far more important than her connections and education, was her personality. She had an exacting task in front of her, becoming an advisor and friend and general factotum to a young girl who barely knew what her own job was, let alone

Anne's. But Anne, a mature 28-year-old when she took the job, handled it with easy grace. She successfully remained in the background, while encouraging Princess Diana to accept the foreground, which would always be hers.

'Absolute discretion at all times is the most important requirement for the job of lady-in-waiting,' says the Queen's assistant press secretary, John Haslem. 'They will never discuss their role with outsiders.'

The role of a modern lady-in-waiting is difficult. They have to be prepared to chat to anyone from a factory worker to a visiting monarch, provide an extra pair of hands to help with bouquets of flowers and gifts and if they see a member of the public holding the royal attention for too long, persuade them to move along and give others a chance to meet them. They are paid very little; the part-time ones receive only out-of-pocket expenses, although the full-time ones, such as Anne, receive a proper salary. They also write hundreds of thank-you letters, which often means working late into the night.

Because of Diana's increased workload – she carried out 175 official engagements in 1987, excluding overseas tours – she has five ladies-in-waiting, who work on a rota system. After the twice-yearly programme meetings, now held in the Waleses' larger offices in St James's Palace, they decide between themselves who should do what and when. Of the married ladies-in-waiting, Mrs George West, wife of the Comptroller of the Lord Chamberlain's office, lives in London so is readily accessible, while the Countess Campden, who has an eleven-year-old son, is not – she lives in Rutland where her husband runs the family estate, and prefers to work during the term-time. Baronet's daughter,

Vivien Baring, who has three children, and Diana's old schoolfriend Alexandra Loyd complete the élite group.

Alexandra, who is the youngest and newest of Diana's ladies-in-waiting, is the daughter of the Sandringham land agent, Julian Loyd, and lived virtually next door to Diana when they were children. She went to the same school, Silfield in King's Lynn near both their homes and they have remained friends ever since.

'To be a lady-in-waiting you do not have to be a friend,' one of them remarked, 'but once you start working for the Princess, it is impossible not to become attached to her.'

Anne Beckwith-Smith is very attached to the Princess, and the feeling is mutual. Diana calls Anne 'Darling' and sees almost more of her than anyone else in her household. Anne deals with Diana's many designers, setting up appointments and advising them on how much they can and can't say.

'Her guidelines are very simple,' Jacques Azagury explains. 'We can claim an outfit that we designed, but never volunteer anything personal.'

Anne also orders many of Diana's smaller items, such as tights, over the telephone and if she is very busy might send a driver to collect them. One of Diana's favourite shops for tights, Fogal in Bond Street, often receives calls from Anne. They inform her what they have in stock and if there is anything new the Princess might like. Anne has struck up such a good relationship with Diana's designers that she often buys their clothes for herself – at reduced rates, taking care to ensure they are neither too flashy nor too obvious.

Ordering clothes and liaising with designers is, however, a small part of Anne's job. Her most important role is to assist Diana with her official engagements. The day before such an engagement, Anne and Diana's equerry, Lieutenant-Commander Jephson RN will arrive at Kensington Palace to brief the Princess, having already briefed the people she is due to visit, informing them of her likes and dislikes if she is lunching, on how to address her and – as vital to a princess as anybody else – checking on the availability of lavatories. It is a rule that the Queen and members of her family should have a special separate loo provided for their visit. This can cause all kinds of problems and new loos are often quickly installed, sometimes to no avail as the royal visitor might not feel any pressing need to use them. If they do, the lady-in-waiting will stand outside the door 'on guard' to prevent any possible embarrassing intruders. Diana finds this very amusing and is far more embarrassed by the possibility of a new loo being installed especially for her, than the possibility of someone else wanting to use it at the same time.

When all this planning is complete, the timetable is reduced to pocket size to enable everyone to have a copy in their pocket or handbag. Everyone except Diana, that is, who will have done her homework the night before and be well-versed on who she is going to meet and what part they have played. When Diana attends a charity ball or film première, the charity will submit to her office in St James's a list of those people they wish to present to the Princess. The people accorded this honour have usually put a great deal of time and effort into ensuring that the evening is both a social and financial success.

This work brings her into contact with a wide and eclectic range of people. Some are interesting and intelligent, others, inevitably, are not. But they all want to shake her hand, and on her visit to Australia in 1988 she almost wilted away with the heat and the seemingly endless number of hands she had to clasp. And many of them sticky. It is a problem all members of the 'Firm' have to face and Diana admits she sometimes doesn't know what to do as she can't very well wipe her hand on the back of her dress – and she hates wearing long white cotton gloves as the Queen does to overcome this problem.

Sticky hands are the least of Diana's problems with children. She hates having to deal with too many of them at once, explaining she doesn't have a chance to do anything beneficial if faced with a whole classroom. She prefers to meet each child individually or talk to them in small groups so she can walk from one to another. She experiences the same problems anyone would when faced with terribly handicapped children and often has to bite her lip to prevent the tears from running down her cheeks.

On one occasion she was presented with an angelic-looking child who was both deaf and blind. The child had been told, through sophisticated methods of touch, that Princess Diana was coming to see him. But when Diana saw the child she was so overcome with shock at his sad plight that she literally froze and couldn't touch him. When she returned home later in the day she ran to her bedroom, shut the door and wept, confused and upset by her inability to cope with the situation.

She experiences the same kind of emotion when visiting hospices, when she knows the patients she is talking to might be dead within a few weeks or months, and comes home drained physically and mentally, rushing up to the nursery to hug her own children.

'I'm so lucky,' she says, 'to have two healthy strong boys. I don't know how I could cope if I had a child who was physically or mentally handicapped in some way.'

A great deal of Diana's work is involved with children of all kinds and as Patron of the British Deaf Association she has taken the trouble to learn a number of words in sign language. The Association sent her a video and after a couple of weeks she mastered and performed her new-found skills in front of a crowd of people. To honour her, children at an East End school for the deaf invented a special sign for her name: you run your hand from the front of your hair to the back – which refers to her famous swept-back hairstyle.

So conscious is Diana of trying to project her image as that of a hard worker, not an empty-headed fashion plate, that she goes to extraordinary lengths to do her homework and understand the complicated methods by which certain diseases or disabilities are treated. Her former equerry, Richard Aylard, writes all her briefs, but the Princess does a lot of her own research and refuses to be merely a figurehead to the charities of which she is Patron.

'I think it's important to show you're interested and that you're not just breezing in and out, having seen them for a morning,' she explains. 'I don't just want to be a name on a letterhead.'

The pursuit of royal patronage for the many thousands of registered charities needs time, effort and patience. First a letter has to be sent to the private secretary, in Diana's case Sir John Riddell, who has been with the Prince and Princess since 1985, replacing Edward Adeane. He will acknowledge immediately, either with a 'no', or if there is a chance of Diana being interested, the request will be put on hold in a large file, along with hundreds of others. When Diana's love of dancing and childhood yearning to become a professional dancer became public news, she was inundated with requests from ballet companies anxious to benefit from her royal patronage. The London City Ballet, after many letters, were finally rewarded:

'We got the usual letter of acknowledgement, so we wrote several more times to let her know what we were doing,' a member of the company explained. 'We were delighted when she agreed to become our Patron and now she often pops in informally to watch us rehearsing.' In spite of Diana's patronage and interest the London City Ballet are in serious financial difficulties and like many other small dance companies might be forced to close down if they fail to raise substantial sums of money soon.

Larger charities such as Dr Barnardo's and Birthright have raised thousands of pounds from just one appearance by the Princess at a ball or film première, but her appearance alone will not raise the money. A huge amount of organization has to go into the efficient running of the charity. Diana takes care not to be only associated with the glamorous side of things, and visits the charity offices and chats with the staff at least twice a year. During the cold spell in January 1987 she made several pleas on behalf of Help the Aged, another of her special interests.

To watch Diana 'work a room' is to witness a remarkable performance. There is something almost mystical in the way even the very ill respond to her presence. Eyes open, young and old forget their pain for a moment and smile.

In primitive societies Kings and Queens were believed to be blessed with magic powers and it took the Civil War, three centuries ago, to dispense with the Divine Right of Kings to rule. But the arrival of the

Princess of Wales at a hospital or hospice can stir those atavistic folk memories. And even the more worldly amongst us rarely fail to respond to Diana's very natural charm, and I include myself here.

She is an expert in the art of small talk and always looks directly into the eye of whomever she is talking to. She is very quick witted, with an ability to respond to a question with a snappy reply, which always stands her in good stead. I have seen hardened journalists walk away after speaking to her with a bemused look on their faces, muttering, 'She's wonderful, so beautiful – and so much more intelligent than I thought.' The old magic of royalty can still work its spell.

It can be employed for the best of reasons. The photograph of Diana holding the hand of a young man dying of Aids in the Middlesex Hospital in April 1987 flashed all the way around the world.

'She was remarkable,' Professor Semple said afterwards, 'calm, dignified and courageous. Her visit will now dispel all the hysteria that surrounds Aids.'

Both Diana and Charles play a valuable role with hysterical scares such as Aids and national disasters such as the IRA's Remembrance Day bombing of Enniskillen in Ireland. They were criticized for not arriving on the scene immediately, but there was a very real personal danger to themselves, which they chose to ignore.

'If your name is on the bullet there is nothing you can do,' Prince Charles said, no doubt thinking once again of the death of his beloved Uncle Dickie at the hands of the IRA bombers. So their visit to Enniskillen in November 1987, a week after the disaster, went ahead amidst intense security – their Wessex helicopter of the Queen's Flight was escorted by four other helicopters, and when they appeared out of the skies it was like a scene from the movie *Apocalypse Now*. They were then taken in an armour-plated car to the Erne hospital in Ulster to meet seven of the victims injured in the explosion. Mr Gordon Wilson, whose twenty-year-old daughter had been killed in the explosion, slipped his arms out of his bandages to shake hands with the Prince.

'Their visit has helped me enormously,' he said later. 'Princess Diana is a really lovely girl.'

It is a sentiment echoed by everyone she meets.

Almost every year for the seven years of their marriage the Prince and Princess have embarked on several overseas royal tours. For Diana, whose travelling had been limited to a few European resorts and one trip to Australia to see her mother, it was very exciting. But her first Commonwealth tour to Australia and New Zealand in 1983, she admitted, was something of a shock:

'It was like a baptism of fire,' she said, 'but by the time I left I felt I'd actually been able to achieve something.'

Tours may look glamorous, but they are very hard work and during their most recent visit to Australia the Princess confessed to friends later she felt exhausted most of the time and was longing to lie in the sun, instead of standing in a smart frock shaking hands. She suffers badly from jet-lag and that combined with the heat wiped her out.

'Although you are tired you just have to get on with the job,' she says, and helped by her hard-working staff, that is exactly what she does.

Weeks of preparation are necessary to ensure everything runs smoothly, and Diana, helped by her two dressers Fay Marshalsea and Evelyn Dagley, selects a wardrobe she hopes will be suitable for every eventuality. The dressers lay out all her clothes with colour-coordinated bags and shoes to match and when Diana has made her selection, often with the assistance of her hairdresser Richard Dalton, who has an uncanny eye for accessories, they pack them into special trunks, all carefully labelled. Diana has a good relationship with both her dressers and attended the wedding of Fay Marshalsea in 1987. But behind Fay's smiles on her wedding day was a tragic secret: she had recently learnt she had cancer and could die. Only her husband-to-be, Steven Appleby, who is in the RAF, their immediate families and the Princess knew. Fay continued to work for Diana after the wedding until she became too weak and was forced to stop work. Diana insisted she keep her flat in Kensington Palace as it would be easier for her to get the necessary treatment than if she had to travel from the home she shared with her husband at RAF Benson in Oxfordshire. Throughout Fay's illness Diana was deeply concerned and on one occasion even accompanied Fay to hospital for her daily treatment. The genuine concern and support Fay received from the Princess helped speed her recovery and although she is still not out of danger, she is back at work with nothing but praise for her employer:

'She knew of my illness virtually from the start,' Fay said in an interview with the *Sunday Express*. 'She is very close to me and I wanted to tell her. She gave me encouragement to carry on. She is a lovely person to work for and very special to me.'

Diana is very caring with her personal staff and nothing is too much trouble for her if something goes wrong in their lives. She also loves a romance within her household – as long as it's between two parties of the opposite sex. When Diana first appeared on the royal scene she was shocked when she realized how many gays there were in royal service. But she has now come to terms with the 'gay mafia' in royal service realizing it isn't such a wonderful job for someone with a wife and family they seldom see.

Diana, too, faces the problem of long separations and although she speaks to William and Harry on the telephone from wherever she is in the world, she can't wait to get home after a strenuous tour. And although she does not have time to do much personal shopping she is always presented with hundreds of things for herself, Charles and the children by her hosts. A diamond and sapphire suite of jewellery from the Sultan of Oman, reputed to be worth millions, is one of the most spectacular gifts. Anxious they shouldn't become too spoilt she rations the children's presents and hides most of them away in a high top cupboard – William would be bound to discover any treasure chest of goodies if it were at his level. Diana is fortunate that her ladies-in-waiting keep up with the 'thank you' letters along the route and her dressers unpack all her clothes and send them to the cleaners after a tour, so she is left to relax. It is, however, rarely more than a short respite.

'We're never alone,' Diana frequently complains to Charles, and her moans are quite justified. When she is free he is often busy, and if she is not visiting friends she spends quiet evenings in her sitting room catching up on the TV programmes she might have missed – she leaves a list with the butler, Harold Brown, of the programmes she wants to see and he organizes for them to be recorded. Soap-operas like 'Dallas', 'Dynasty' and 'EastEnders' are favourites and she saw 'Woman of Substance' starring Jenny Seagrove and 'The Thornbirds' with Richard Chamberlain, but she doesn't always find time to watch the whole of the many current mini-series showing on television. Sometimes Diana will curl up with a book, but finds it easier to read intellectually untaxing ones such as Danielle Steel, Colleen McCullough and Barbara Taylor Bradford romances.

'My husband doesn't approve of the books I read,' she admits, but she finds trashy novels easy to pick up and put down and there are usually a couple included in her luggage.

Packing and unpacking, entertaining and being entertained are all part of Diana's everyday life. In 1987 she attended 25 receptions, 7 official lunches, 19 film premières, 108 general visits and performed 16 State duties (garden parties, state banquets etc). She also spent 17 days abroad on official duties. Yet in spite of this quite considerable work load Diana still harbours a feeling of being unfulfilled. As Princess of Wales she has to maintain a degree of dignity and there are certain things Charles feels she should and should not do. He wasn't at all annoyed by her and Fergie's pranks at Royal Ascot last year and even offered to give her a piggy-back ride over a puddle himself, which she wisely declined. But when it came to a discussion as to whether or not she should be included in the royal 'It's A Knockout' team, he put his foot down – quite correctly as it transpired. Prince Edward was annoyed. He saw his sister-in-law as a major pulling power to persuade Hollywood stars to take part. But Charles was adamant and a family row ensued. The Princess Royal accused Charles of being 'a stick-in-the-mud' and Diana felt, once again, she was missing all the fun. When the show came to be screened she was secretly relieved she had not been allowed to take part; although she

thought it a 'jolly good giggle', she realized she would
have not come out of it at all well.

A few years ago Diana confessed in an interview
with Sir Alastair Burnet, 'My husband's taught me
everything I know.' He has indeed taught her a great
deal, one of the most significant things being a desire
for more knowledge – and if being the Princess of
Wales is a job in itself, Diana wants more – and in the
years to come the Spencer determination will ensure
that she gets it.

11
Fashion

The woman who, almost single-handed, has made the British fashion industry a multi-million-pound export business stands 5 feet 10 inches tall. Her long, slim feet take a size 7AA. Her bust and hips measure 35 inches, whilst her waist regularly expands to a boyish, rather than anorexic, 29 inches. She wears a size 10 or 12, depending on the designer. Hers is not a conventional shape by any means. But put it all together and the effect is stunning.

As Princess Michael of Kent once remarked to me, 'Princess Diana has such a beautiful figure she would look good in a sack.'

Fortunately it has never come down to that for this demure Sloane. She has grown up to be one of the most elegant princesses in the world, and she has certainly come a long way from the little girl in her family's photograph album, in which she is pictured wearing a pair of old curtains.

'She has always loved dressing up,' her father explains. It is a love affair that turned into a way of life, one which Diana now recognizes almost consumed her. Unlike the Princess Royal, whom she admires greatly, Diana is not judged by what she does, but by what she wears. Her true personality is lost in a swirl of silks and chiffons, and lace and brocades. And that has depressed her for some time.

'My clothes are not my priority,' Diana insisted in a television interview a couple of years ago. 'I enjoy bright colours and my husband likes to see me look smart, presentable, but fashion isn't my big thing at all.'

When Diana first became engaged to Prince Charles and wore that blue off-the-peg suit from Harrods – chosen with her mother – fashion certainly *wasn't* her big thing. She has, however, always been interested in clothes and even at Althorp where there was a number of staff to take care of such things as laundry, did her own washing and ironing, but couldn't afford the highest fashion, not in those early days. The £310 she paid for the engagement suit, designed by Cojana, seemed a fortune, but now Diana would pay that sum just for a handbag. When her new royal role took her from her life as a Sloane Ranger shopping at Laura Ashley, Miss Selfridge or Peter Jones, into the circuit of haute couture, she used it as a crutch. She wasn't allowed to say anything or do anything apart from smile and look pretty. Her freedom had been snatched, her personality engulfed. She began to express herself in the only available way – through her clothes and the newly opened coffers of her husband.

Diana was right when she said her husband liked to see her looking smart. 'It was one of the first things I noticed about her,' he admitted. But being no great expert on womankind, he had no idea of the extent of this growing obsession or the reasons it came about.

Anxious, trapped and insecure within the gloomy confines of Buckingham Palace, Diana was determined her future husband was going to continue to notice her, so she started shopping. It was also something to do.

Her sister, Lady Jane Fellowes, who had contact with *Vogue* magazine where she once worked as an editorial assistant, gave her some guidance. The two girls decided that it would be an excellent idea if they approached Jane's chums and entered the fashion

world through the back door. It literally *was* the back
door through which they entered into the offices of
Vogue in London's Hanover Square. Diana was always
being followed by a posse of photographers and back
doors were becoming an everyday event.

At the time Beatrix Miller was editor of *Vogue* and
she thought that the softly-spoken Anna Harvey, assistant fashion editor, and beauty editor Felicity Clark,
were the most suitable members of her team to help
Diana create an appropriate image. They did an excellent job. While Diana was rummaging through the rails
in the *Vogue* offices looking at some clothes that were
being used for a shoot, she came across a blouse
designed by a young couple hardly heard of outside
the fashion world – The Emanuels.

Diana liked it and got it, thus formulating the love-
hate relationship she has had with that husband and
wife team ever since. Recently they have been right
back in favour and have even designed the odd frock
for Fergie (the black-and-white outfit she wore in
Mauritius, for example). Immediately after the wedding, however, they were right out. 'We'll see about
them,' Diana remarked, referring to what she considered their cashing in on the publicity surrounding
the famous wedding dress. She was still disgruntled
when they presented her with the photograph album,
showing the stages of making the dress and the final
product. As she flicked through the album moodily she
felt like tearing out all the photographs and using the
white leather book for something else. But Diana
doesn't bear grudges for long. It is not in her nature
and besides she likes their clothes. She considers them
'dramatic'.

From the black taffeta evening gown, which was so
low-cut it caused a sensation when Diana wore it to the
Goldsmiths' Hall in March 1981, to the 'crumpled'

wedding dress whose hem they failed to weight down, to the vivid-green check coat worn in Venice that reminded onlookers of a horse blanket, the Emanuels have been an important part of the Diana style. But they are not cheap. An off-the-peg ball-gown can cost over £1000 and some of the fabrics they use can retail at over £100 a metre – with all the beading or sequins sewn on by hand.

The Emanuels, Victor Edelstein, Bruce Oldfield, Murray Arbeid, Jacques Azagury, Catherine Walker – the list is endless – all have a great deal to thank Anna Harvey for. 'She just went round and round,' a fashion assistant said, 'until she found the right clothes for Diana.' Anna herself is understandably too reticent to speak about the part she played in dressing the most famous figure in the world and refuses to take any credit for turning Sloane Diana into mannequin Diana.

'She [Anna] claims she just happened to be there at the time,' a member of the *Vogue* staff says. 'She's not at all pushy, she's very professional and very discreet.'

It is Anna's discretion that has enabled her to remain friends with the Princess of Wales and besides her job as fashion director of *Vogue* she plays a very active part in charity work, especially for Birthright, whose Patron is, of course, Diana. Always busy, Anna divides her time between her terraced house in Wandsworth, which she shares with her stockbroker husband Jonathan (they have three children), and the *Vogue* offices in Hanover Square. Slim, smart and dark-haired, Anna was recently offered the job as top fashion buyer for Harrods, but preferred to continue her work at *Vogue*.

Not all the Princess's clothes come from the British designers that Anna and *Vogue* introduced her to. From the early years of her marriage when she was pregnant with Prince William and suffered from morning sickness and bouts of dizziness all day, she has shopped by catalogue.

Harrods send her books from Laurel and Mondi – both German companies – and anything that takes her fancy is then ordered by her chief lady-in-waiting Anne Beckwith-Smith. Her distinctive spotted skirt worn with matching ankle socks at a polo match a couple of years ago, was a Mondi outfit, although Diana delighted the assistants in the separates department on the first floor of Harrods by purchasing this one herself. For the Highland Games at Braemar in 1986 her ensemble of a pink and green tartan skirt with colour-coordinated Tam O'Shanter was straight out of the Laurel catalogue – ordered by telephone.

The cost of the Princess's wardrobe is not, therefore, as much as has been wildly estimated and there have been some wild estimates.

In April 1985 it was suggested that Diana had spent a staggering £80,000 on a new wardrobe for her Italian trip. She reacted by appearing at a gala evening at La Scala theatre in Milan – the centre of the Italian fashion industry – in an evening dress she had worn two years before in Canada.

The 'old' dress – albeit a beautiful pink chiffon creation by designer Victor Edelstein – had the desired effect and the ensuing criticism satisfied Diana's desire for revenge, although it must be said that for the remainder of the trip she produced some stunning new creations which did, it must also be said, cost a considerable amount of money. However, when the Waleses are on royal tours and therefore representing the Monarch and their country, the cost of their official wardrobe is borne by the Keeper of the Privy Purse and Treasurer to the Queen, Shane Blewitt. The clothes are paid for, I can disclose, out of a special fund which constitutes part of the Civil List – the only funds they take from the List.

The Prince of Wales's income is derived from his Duchy of Cornwall estates, which make him a very rich man indeed. Before he married in 1981, Charles took fifty per cent of the net revenue from the Duchy and gave the other half to the Treasury in lieu of income tax. But once his bachelor days were over and he had the additional expense of two main residences, a wife and two children, he made arrangements to take three-quarters of the revenue and pay a quarter instead of a half back to the Treasury. As the annual income from the Duchy returns an income in excess of £1 million, this leaves the Prince of Wales with at least £750,000 for his family and household needs.

'I have never heard them discuss the cost of her clothes,' a member of their staff says. This might, of course, be partly to do with the fact that Charles seldom sees a bill.

Bills from designers and shops are signed by the lady-in-waiting and sent to the Waleses' office, now in St James's Palace, or they are paid for immediately by a Duchy of Cornwall American Express card. Along with the elegant shopping bags and parcels both Diana's lady-in-waiting and detective carry these American Express cards. Some cash is carried for smaller items, but the Coutts cheques, where Diana has an account, are seldom used because people have a habit of not cashing them, but keeping them as souvenirs, which only confuses the household books.

Even before those handy and practical Duchy of Cornwall credit cards, Charles rarely saw bills and as a consequence had little idea of the cost of anything. He still doesn't and can kick up a terrible fuss if he thinks he is being overcharged, which he rarely is. Diana has tried to break her husband of this tedious habit. More generous, she is always buying him pairs of socks, ties, handkerchiefs and sweaters.

Charles does not always reciprocate in quite the way Diana would like. At a dinner party she asked a girlfriend who had just had a baby what her husband had given her. Before the friend could answer, Diana said, 'Mine only gave me a boring old picture.'

But then Charles does not have quite Diana's passion for shopping. Indeed, it is not unusual for Diana to park her Jaguar on the double yellow lines outside shops like Night Owls in London's Fulham Road and rush into the store with her lady-in-waiting.

Sometimes a shop is cleared, but more often than not Diana will just browse through the racks with the other would-be purchasers. One young woman was flabbergasted when she spotted Diana in a boutique changing room with the curtain drawn aside so that she could ask the opinion of her lady-in-waiting who was standing in the shop. The grey silk underwear and the length of the Princess's legs reduced the surprised shopper to near paralysis. 'I realized I was staring,' she said, 'but the Princess didn't seem to mind, she just looked at me and smiled.'

Although Diana makes many forays into the boutiques she patronizes, when it comes to trying on clothes she usually has them sent to her or else takes them home. This can have some unfortunate results. Once when shopping at the popular Benetton chain she purchased a garment in the wrong size. Returning a couple of days later to change it, she was told by an assistant that she couldn't have a refund without a receipt!

As the uncrowned Queen of British fashion, Diana

takes her role of ambassador very seriously. When she is at home she can wear Valentino, Ungaro, Chanel or Saint Laurent, but when she is doing official duties Diana seldom lets the side down. However, underneath all her British fashion she allows herself to splash out on extravagant Italian or French underwear. Courtenay's in Brook Street stock the Italian range La Perla of which she is very fond. Their silk knickers are exquisite and very expensive, as is their nightwear. When it gets cold Diana wears thermal underwear by Damart because it enables her to wear dresses and thin coats in the middle of winter when most people might be protected by a fur or, at least, a fur-lined coat.

No furs are the order of the day and however much Diana might yearn to wear a beautiful fox or mink coat, she would not dream of doing so. She has not appeared in fur in public since the early days of her marriage when she wore a creamy fur jacket to a film première. Even on skiing holidays Diana has to make do with a woolly headband instead of the popular fur headband that Fergie favours. If it's fur, it's fake, and Diana has a swagger coat designed by Arabella Pollen with a fake beaver collar and cuffs.

Attractive Bella Pollen is one of the youngest designers to have worked for the Princess and has come a long way since Diana picked out some outfits from her winter collection in 1982. Bella started business when Nicholas Coleridge, now editor of the glossy fashion magazine *Harpers and Queen*, spotted her potential and introduced her to publisher and entrepreneur Naim Attallah, with a suggestion that Naim might finance her. He did so for a short time and I was employed to assist Bella with a public relations image. Knowing nothing about fashion public relations I didn't do a very good job, but Bella was far too talented to be held back and has, after many set-backs, found her niche alongside many top fashion designers.

Bella isn't the only one to thank the Princess for putting them on the international map. Established designers, such as Caroline Charles and Donald Campbell, Gina Fratini, David Neil and Benny Ong, to name but a few, became household names when the Princess wore their designs in the early days of her marriage.

Even with the assistance of the *Vogue* team, Diana still made mistakes. But she was getting used to the restrictions the royal dress code placed upon her and was not secure enough to be as daring as she is today.

Hats were a problem. They were simply something that Diana had only previously worn to weddings or for the occasional day at the races. Wind was another problem – it ruffled her carefully coiffured hair and had a habit of blowing up her skirts. In fact, in those early days, as much fun as it was, everything was a problem.

'It's like getting dressed to go to a wedding every day,' she moaned to a friend at the time, 'and when you see yourself photographed in black and white, all the little mistakes show.'

Diana is, by her own admission, a perfectionist. If something isn't exactly right she feels unhappy and uncomfortable until it is. Normally punctual by nature, she has been known to stand for hours in front of her full-length mirrors discarding outfit after outfit because some detail was wrong. An exasperated Prince Charles would be waiting downstairs, pacing the floor, as the minutes ticked away.

Nowadays this happens very seldom. Her two dressers, Fay Marshalsea and Evelyn Dagley, are in charge of the vast and ever increasing wardrobe. In 1987 it was estimated to contain 80-odd suits; over 60 evening dresses; 50-plus day dresses, many made up in the same style with different fabrics; 72-odd hats and numerous blouses, sweaters, skirts and trousers and over 100 pair of earrings!

Her clothes are stored in vast walk-in wardrobes in her dressing room, hung on padded hangers and protected by plastic dressing bags from Eximious in London's Halkin Street who hold a Royal Warrant. The Royal Family are great hoarders – at Buckingham Palace there are cupboards full of ancient clothing belonging to family members long dead – and Diana has relegated the clothes she seldom wears to a room downstairs at Kensington Palace.

Whenever possible, Diana asks her designers to revamp her clothes. A hemline altered, a pleat taken out or a sleeve re-made can make the outfit last for another season. She sometimes gives clothes to her sister Lady Jane Fellowes, who is a similar shape, but as Diana's clothes are so recognizable Jane is reluctant to take anything too dramatic.

Just before Fergie's engagement was made public, Diana lent her one of her old coats – a black-and-white check – which Fergie wore when she visited Andrew's ship HMS *Brazen*. It wasn't long before everyone noticed it was one of Diana's cast-offs and that useful idea had to be terminated. They do, however, swop sweaters and designers. For her trip to Thailand Diana wore several Alistair Blair outfits and has privately borrowed some of Fergie's pre-pregnancy Yves Saint Laurent couture frocks.

Diana loves looking for new clothes but as her workload increases, her forays outside her royal world decrease. She still finds time to go shopping, to play tennis or have lunch, but one of the things she most enjoyed – visiting the showrooms of her designers – has almost come to a halt.

Anne Beckwith-Smith would accompany the Princess on these visits and as they entered the showroom (usually in the back-streets of London's West End), she would keep a wary eye on the time as the designer produced a selection of garments for Diana to try on.

'The Princess likes looking at people's collections in the showroom if possible, but if there is not time we will go to her,' Jan Vanvelden says. The designer, whether it's Victor Edelstein, Catherine Walker, Rifat Ozbek or Murray Arbeid, will make an early appointment at Kensington Palace – usually around 9 A.M. – park their car in the gravel courtyard and walk through the side entrance, under the old stone archway to the Waleses' back door where butler Harold Brown will let them in. He takes them to the Princess's sitting room on the first floor where they will wait until she is ready.

In the early days Diana could happily spend a morning, even a day, sifting through materials and discussing designs. No longer. As milliner John Boyd says: 'She knows exactly what she wants.'

And her designers know exactly what her clothing problems are. Says the Princess, 'You'd be amazed what one has to worry about, from the obvious things like the wind – because there is always a gale wherever we go and the wind is my enemy, there's no doubt about that.'

Her solution to that, ever since the day in Bristol a couple of years ago when the wind won, has been to weight her hemlines with lead.

'Then,' she continues, 'you've got to put your arm up to get some flowers and you can't have anything too revealing. And you can't have hems too short because when you bend over there are six children looking up your skirt.

'Clothes are for the job. They've got to be practical. Sometimes I can be a little outrageous, which is nice, but only sometimes.'

If she can't be too outrageous, Diana will sometimes make a statement – one black glove and one red glove for instance (at the suggestion of her hairdresser Richard Dalton), or pick a vivid colour such as Rifat Ozbek's turquoise suit with gold embroidery, worn in Spain, or the cheeky 'Sergeant Pepper' white suit, designed by Catherine Walker and worn to greet the King of Saudi Arabia.

The restraints of royal dress code don't have to be spelt out to her designers. They know her taste and they know what she can or cannot wear, so the meetings at Kensington Palace are very professional. The Princess is on first-name terms with all her designers and they in turn are fond of her, but are always careful to remember to address her as 'Ma'am' (to rhyme with ham).

At Christmas time she sends them cards – usually a colour photograph of the family on thick card with the Prince of Wales crest on the outside. In 1985 the photograph, taken by Prince Andrew, was one of them all at Highgrove. The following year it was a reproduction of a thirteenth-century map, found hidden among the possessions of the Duchy of Cornwall estate. But whatever the picture, Diana always includes a personal note such as, 'Thank you for designing my dresses,' signed, simply, 'Diana'.

'The Princess is so friendly that it is sometimes hard to remember that you are not chatting to an old friend,' one of her team says. 'We have a good giggle about all the rubbish that is written about her clothes – although nowadays she seldom reads what is written about her.'

Meanwhile, the clock set up on the table is ticking away the allotted twenty minutes and Diana grimaces as she realizes she will have to go to her next appointment. Anne Beckwith-Smith will then finalize all the arrangements and organize the outfits to be picked up or delivered and further fittings booked.

Shoes are also often brought to Diana at home. The sample range from Charles Jordan and, more recently, the traditional court cobblers, Raine, will be shown to her and she will order what she wants. She prefers classic shapes with medium-height heels but might not like the colour. If she wants some shoes that are only produced in red leather she can have them in purple satin – as long as she orders in time. She pays wholesale prices for these, but any shoes she might just see in a shop window such as Pied à Terre, Midas or Footloose, she will pay full price for.

By paying wholesale prices (the cost of the fabric, labour and expenses like light and heat), Diana manages to reduce the expenditure on the large number of outfits she needs. She also gets most of her clothes direct from the designer, which cuts out the mark-up the store is making, reducing the total cost to less than a quarter of the retail price. It is a mutually beneficial arrangement and one that designers have with many of those favoured clients, who generate publicity. And there is no better publicity than having your clothes worn by the Princess of Wales.

These reductions, of course, only apply when Diana is organized about her shopping. An unexpected little foray into small boutiques or shops will result in the Princess having to pay the full price. It doesn't bother her. There is hardly a shop within the square mile of

Kensington and Chelsea that hasn't had the excitement of the Princess of Wales walking through the door, either to buy something for herself or for a friend, and, more often than not, these little shopping trips get reported.

'I can't win,' Diana tells her friends. 'They either accuse me of spending too much on my clothes or of wearing the same outfit all the time. I wish everyone would stop talking about my clothes, they are not my priority.'

Seven years ago they had to be her priority.

'I had to buy endless new things,' Diana explained. 'Clothes for the job and, of course, the essential complement to royal dressing – the hat.'

It was Diana's mother, Mrs Frances Shand-Kydd, who introduced her daughter to her first real milliner, John Boyd. A few days after the engagement had been announced they both went to Boyd's London base – a tiny shop in the Brompton Arcade at the time – and bought a sensible felt hat for Diana to wear to an event in the country. While she was browsing through Boyd's collection Diana spotted a hat she loved – small with a curvy brim and a flowing ostrich feather. She asked him to reserve it for her, which he did, removing it from his summer collection, and Diana wore it on her wedding day as the finishing touch to her pink Belville Sassoon going-away outfit. The whole world saw that hat and Boyd was firmly on the map.

Boyd remained discreet and faithful to his new royal client and was rewarded by being asked to make the hats for her first trip to Australia. However, the climatic conditions were not exactly what the royal party had expected and Diana only had a limited number of warmer clothes with her, so more dresses, suits and hats had to be quickly made and sent out to the

Princess by plane. Boyd played his part by creating
hats with only sketches and small swatches of material
to match them to. It was a challenge, but one which he
relished.

'It was hectic, but exciting to be able to see hats so
quickly,' he says.

Nowadays Boyd seldom makes hats for Diana, but
the other milliners Diana patronizes – Graham Smith,
David Shilling, and Philip Sommerville – usually find
themselves invited to the Palace rather than having the
pleasure of Diana popping into their shops. They are
shown a selection of designs which their hats are meant
to complement and must try to assess what the Princess
will be doing when wearing them. Milliners often
complain that Diana wears their hats the wrong way
round, at the wrong angle, or even with the wrong
outfit. But she, however, remains silent if she doesn't
like a particular hat.

'The Princess never says if she doesn't like something, but I always know,' says Boyd. She just won't
wear it or she will have the offending creation returned
by one of her ladies-in-waiting. 'No-one wants to make
Diana something she doesn't like,' says another milliner, 'so we make sure we try and interpret her latest
look.'

'Hats give me confidence,' Diana now says. And
although she does not feel the necessity to wear them
as much as she used to, they are still part of her style –
the style which has given such a boost to the British
fashion industry and created a look which is copied by
millions of women around the world.

Fashions change, but a sense of style does not and
Diana's is part of her. It's not just her clothes, the way
she wears them, but in her personality as a whole.

That same sense of style is apparent in her jewellery.

Since her marriage Diana has acquired a fantastic collection. She also has access to the Queen's, but she often prefers to wear costume jewellery.

'If it looks right, I don't think it matters whether its real or fake,' she says. A sentiment also proffered by the late Duchess of Windsor.

Prince Charles was in the bidding for a piece of the Duchess's jewellery in the Geneva sale two years ago. The piece, a fantastic brooch of diamonds set in the shape of the Prince of Wales feathers, finally went to Elizabeth Taylor for $567,000 or £350,000. Certainly far more than Prince Charles would have wished to pay for any piece of jewellery, let alone something that, if his late uncle were still alive, he might surely have given to him.

It was the jewellers Wartski who gave Diana the 'Mary Queen of Scots' cross she wore in the autumn of 1987. It was the time when speculation as to the state of the Waleses' marriage was at its height and Diana declared that she wanted a cross. Garrard's didn't have one. Wartski's did, and they lent it to her. She wore it, rather to Garrard's consternation, to Garrard's charity evening in aid of Birthright. The effect of the cross and the Renaissance-style dress with its high collar especially made for *Harpers and Queen* by Catherine Walker and lent to Diana, was dramatic. If Diana was trying to make a theatrical point by inviting a comparison to that tragic Scottish queen then she certainly succeeded.

Normally, of course, Diana will wear her own 'rocks'. And ever since that memorable Sunday night at Windsor when Diana was shown a large tray of engagement rings and 'picked the biggest one', a sapphire surrounded by diamonds – the jewellery has been amassing. Charles bought her an Art Deco emerald and diamond bracelet as a wedding present. The Queen gave her an emerald necklace.

It is not only Charles and the Queen who have given Diana such gifts. The Queen Mother presented Diana with an enormous sapphire brooch, surrounded by diamonds. It was so heavy that Diana found when she pinned it on a dress that, even with the supportive backing specially sewn inside the dress material, it dragged the front down.

'Wear it as a choker,' Princess Michael of Kent advised her. 'It will look much prettier that way.'

Diana took her advice and was seen wearing it fastened on to a six-pearl choker for the Reagans' White House dinner in November 1985. Diana had never looked so lovely. In a midnight-blue velvet off-the-shoulder dress, designed by Victor Edelstein, with the choker glimmering round her neck, she had the devastating effect of making every other woman in the room appear badly dressed. The Washington élite, including a large number of imported movie stars, were suitably impressed. And when John Travolta took to the floor with the Princess, you could hear a pin drop. While the band played a medley of Travolta music the couple did a series of spins and twirls. Travolta, later 'door-stepped' by the British press, admitted that Diana was a good dancer and then added with relish, 'My greatest moment was when I put my arm around her waist – she's so tiny.'

That night Diana didn't wear a tiara, and avoids doing so whenever possible. They are difficult to hold in place and the family heirloom – the Spencer tiara – falls forward over her head. On her wedding day her former hairdresser, Kevin Shanley, admitted it did just that, creating the effect of an even fuller fringe. 'It was a humid day and the style dropped completely,' he said.

The bow-knot pearl and diamond tiara, which the Queen gave to Diana as the formal gift that marked her entry into the Royal Family, is mounted on a velvet Alice band and gives her a headache. Diana caused a sensation by wearing the emerald and diamond necklace, another family heirloom given to her by the Queen, as a headband in place of a tiara while in Australia in 1986. But, it turns out, this was not because she wanted to avoid a headache, but for the simpler and more worrying reason was that the tiara had been mislaid in the luggage!

Besides gifts from her immediate family, Diana has received some of her most spectacular jewellery from the Arab sheiks. The pieces are often too flashy for her liking, but Diana, out of politeness, is obliged to wear them and without usually having them re-mounted or re-set. She does, however, add her individual stamp. A suite of sapphires – a wedding gift from the Crown Prince of Saudi Arabia – was given the Diana touch when she wore the bracelet as a choker on a narrow velvet ribbon around her neck.

During a visit to Germany last year, she displayed another spectacular gift – a suite of diamonds and sapphires in a modern setting – this time a gift from the Sultan of Oman.

As the Princess of Wales, Diana will continue to receive heirlooms and gifts but one of her most treasured is something quite simple: a watered silk ribbon pinned to which is a miniature painting of the Queen surrounded by diamonds. This is the Queen's Family Order and it is not given to all the royal ladies, so when Diana received it a year after her marriage she knew it was a very special honour.

Sometimes she is even tempted to buy her own jewellery. She was very taken by a £16,000 Cartier watch she saw in Zales. Then she exclaimed, 'Oh, it hasn't got any numbers – I couldn't manage a watch without numbers.'

She also, like many people, is worried about the stones she wears. 'I don't particularly like expensive jewellery because I am frightened of losing it,' she says. It is for this reason that she often wears costume jewellery.

Butler and Wilson, who have shops in London's Fulham and the West End, are her favourites. Earrings, brooches in the shapes of large lizards or stars, set with diamanté, often adorn her person. She likes to mix a frankly fake brooch or pair of earrings with her most elegant ballgown – it works. It's part of the Diana style.

Although Diana no longer has to call on the assistance of the *Vogue* team to advise her, and knows all the designers personally, she is not averse to accepting a little advice. That advice comes from one of the people she spends a great deal of time with, her hairdresser Richard Dalton.

A softly-spoken Scot in his early thirties, Dalton used to work at Headlines with Kevin Shanley. But when Shanley broke the royal rule and talked to a newspaper about his life as the Princess's hairdresser, Diana turned to Dalton to tend her locks. Dalton, whose loyalty to his illustrious client is unswerving, decided that he could no longer continue to work with Shanley and left to work freelance. He has recently opened his own salon in Claridge's.

Dalton has the complete trust of the Princess. And, besides doing her hair most days, accompanies her on royal tours and acts as unofficial advisor to the royal wardrobe. It was Dalton who suggested that Diana wear the chiffon scarf slung round her neck, à la Grace Kelly, when she attended the Cannes Film Festival last year.

It was Dalton who suggested it might be fun to wear one black and one red glove – thus setting a fashion trend. And it is Dalton who gives the Princess that little bit of encouragement when she decides to wear something just a little more daring than usual.

Dalton also has fixed ideas about the Princess's designers. He can spot the ones who are good and professional and is scathing of those who he considers charge far too much money and produce substandard goods. The old favourites like Bruce Oldfield, Jasper Conran and Victor Edelstein have never failed the Princess and she continues to support the newer designers like Rifat Ozbek, but it is Catherine Walker, who works from a small shop in Chelsea, the Chelsea Design Company, who now produces the majority of Diana's clothes. Catherine, an elegant dark-haired Frenchwoman in her early forties is quiet and unassuming. She started the Chelsea Design Company in 1977 after she had painstakingly taught herself to sew as therapy after the death of her husband. From a hobby she built up a thriving business and now has over forty people working for her. Her clothes range from £500 to £5,000 for her special couture range, and are beautifully designed and made.

A couple of years ago Diana was introduced to Catherine by Anna Harvey and has patronized her little shop ever since. Diana is inclined to buy clothes she likes when she sees them and not with a particular occasion in mind, Catherine claims, although she designed the white suit with the gold thread especially for Diana's visit to the Military Academy at Sandhurst – only to find Diana wore it somewhere else first.

Diana is not the only member of the Royal Family to wear Catherine's creations. Fergie has called into her Chelsea boutique and the Duchess of Kent often arrives demanding outfits identical to Diana's – down to the last button. This can be awkward and Catherine has to dissuade her – pointing out it would be most odd if she turned up to an official function wearing something exactly the same as Diana.

Everybody, it seems, even other members of the Royal Family, want to copy Diana's style.

'She has the best image we could possibly hope to have for this country,' says David Sassoon, who has made well over fifty outfits for the Princess, including her pink 'going away' suit.

'We are very lucky to have someone as glamorous and as pretty as she is. For us she is a miracle worker.'

Having the body of a top model is a great help of course and Diana, the most famous clotheshorse in the world, is fascinated by the possibility. During a photographic session with fashion photographer Terence Donovan, Diana asked, 'How much would a girl earn if she was sitting here like me being photographed by you?'

'Oh, 'bout £800 an hour, luv,' the Cockney snapper replied. Diana giggled and asked, 'I wonder how much I could earn?'

Donovan's reply is not recorded. But *Life* magazine photographer Harry Benson, when asked to consider the question, replied, 'She could retire after a day.'

Mention fashion to Prince Charles and he will assume you are referring to his wife. No oversize tie-knot or extravagant checks will ever carry his name, for this Prince of Wales, unlike his late great-uncle, is happier discussing coloured cabbage than coloured socks. Before Diana arrived on the scene he never noticed fashion fads, hated bright sweaters, slip-on shoes and anything that was what he considered 'too loud'.

'I could never get him to wear yellow,' Stephen Barry once said grumpily. 'Then along came the Princess and the next moment I see him in a yellow sweater!'

During their courtship Diana delighted in giving Charles little gifts and his clothing was an area she thought she could certainly improve. She knew he wouldn't accept any immediate radical changes and gently persuaded him to try wearing loafers – bought from the Jermyn Street cobblers, Trickers, recommended by her brother, Viscount Althorp. At first he wore them just to please her, but now seldom wears anything else and has several pairs in black and navy.

The Prince of Wales's newly awakened fashion sense is not entirely due to his wife. He has always had his own style and although the Menswear Association claimed his clothes were 'dull and boring', they are traditionally English: expensively tailored suits, crisp cotton shirts and Burberry raincoats. He seldom wears an overcoat, but if he does, sports a coloured handkerchief in the lapel pocket. That handkerchief – always just visible – is as much his trade mark as his shirts from Turnbull and Asser, the Jermyn Street shirtmakers who hold his Royal Warrant.

It was the late Earl Mountbatten of Burma who introduced the Prince to Turnbull and Asser and their 'brother' shop Hawes and Curtis, where Charles occasionally buys suits. Charles never goes into a London shop, even a Savile Row one – the shop comes to him.

Mr Johns of Johns and Pegg, the Clifford Street tailors, remembers several trips to the Palace, but admits, 'We haven't made a suit for the Prince for some time.' They have, however, made most of his military ceremonial uniforms including the naval uniform he wore on his wedding day and the casual blazer with the Welsh Guards leek-motif buttons he wears after a game of polo.

Charles now favours the ultimately discreet and very expensive Anderson and Sheppard of Savile Row. Their soft, loose look is the most distinctive cut in British tailoring and very fashionable, which pleases Diana. She used to complain about his seemingly ill-fitting suits and tease him about the way he walked with his hands behind his back like his father – something he has done ever since he was a small boy.

'It's not a genetic trait,' he once said during a speech. 'It is because we both have the same tailor and he makes the sleeves so tight we can't get our hands in front.'

When Charles decides it is time for him to have a new suit, his valet will telephone the tailor and various materials will be delivered to Kensington Palace. When the Prince, assisted by Diana, has made his choice the tailor will appear and discuss the style – narrow lapels, long sleeves and double vents at the back, with big pockets to accommodate his hands. Once the style – never radical of course – has been decided the tailor returns for fittings. He will sometimes run up a few pairs of casual trousers, but although the Prince is slim his muscular shape is not ideal for the trendy front-pleated trousers.

'I've got a long body and short legs,' he says, but wears them anyway – 'to please the wife.'

Paul Cuss, the holder of the Royal Warrant for Turnbull and Asser, also goes to Kensington Palace with a large selection of materials. If Diana isn't there to offer expert advice the Prince will always pick the ones with the small discreet patterns, subtle stripes and checks. The rest will be returned. 'He hasn't changed shape at all,' says Paul Cuss. 'He has the same collar he designed himself, which is less extravagant with a smaller space for the tie.'

Diana is not averse to borrowing Charles's Turnbull and Asser shirts herself and uses them for casual wear. She also once borrowed one of his dinner jackets, wearing it to a pop concert, before she had one of her own made.

Like most men, even if he doesn't show it, the Prince has a touch of vanity. He is proud of his collection of uniforms and has so many – over a hundred at the last count – that he has a special room for them in his Kensington Palace apartment. Shortly before his marriage he took the key of the room, situated in Buckingham Palace at the time, and showed the startled Lady Diana the braided collection. A princely version of 'Come up and see my etchings.'

It is the job of valet Ken Stronach and his assistant Michael Fawcett to look after this vast array of uniforms, ceremonial robes and civilian clothes. Stronach does not occupy quite the same position as the late Stephen Barry, who used to run the Prince's life, but he does lay out his clothes and help him dress if he is wearing a complicated uniform. He makes sure his shoes are shined to that high gloss favoured by the Royal Family, his suits are pressed with a knife edge crease and that all his shirt buttons are secure. He is also responsible for packing and unpacking, supervising the laundry and keeping an eye on the weekly list of engagements in case any special items of clothing are required. One form of dress Charles can't stand is the white tie and tails worn for State Banquets.

'Must we?' he would ask his valet. 'It's so uncomfortable.'

Comfort is all important to Charles and if he doesn't enjoy shopping for those smaller items that have

spruced up his wardrobe, Diana certainly does. She
sometimes buys his socks in Fogal of Bond Street
where she gets her tights and was once spotted by a
delighted American customer in the elegant downstairs
room at Turnbull and Asser. The customer was seated
at the adjoining table to hers and thought he recognized
the attractive girl next to him, who was selecting
striped boxer shorts. When he realized it was 'Lady Di'
and she was buying underpants for her husband he
was so anxious to get back to his hotel and tell his wife,
he forgot to pay the bill and had to return the following
day suitably red-faced.

According to Diana the changes in her husband's
wardrobe are nothing dramatic. For instance, she hasn't
been able to persuade him out of the formal suits he
wears for pop concerts, and the only time he wears
jeans is when he is practising polo before a match. He
hates personal jewellery, especially anything with a
designer's motif, and apart from watches and a signet
ring, wears none. Charles does however sometimes
allow himself a little bit of flamboyance – when he is
wearing a uniform.

'If you've got it, wear it,' was one of his late Uncle
Dickie's favourite sayings. And when Prince Charles
was getting dressed to go to Earl Mountbatten's funeral,
he declared:

'I'm going to wear every decoration I'm permitted –
Mountbatten would have liked that.'

Diana likes to see her husband in uniform too, and
thinks it makes him look very dashing. She has tried –
and failed – to encourage him to wear trendy clothes,
although after a game of polo at weekends he will
sometimes wear the blue leather jacket she gave him.
But he still prefers his blazer.

'Let my wife do the dressing up,' he says. 'She does it better than I do.' He is right, of course, and Diana realizes she will never change him. He is traditional and will always remain so.

12

Beauty, Diet and Exercise

As a teenager Diana was never part of the high-living set. She was too unsophisticated to relish wild nights on the town, druggy parties or anything more daring than the odd bottle of wine. She hated smoking and was not born of the age that thought it smart and clever. And in those days she could eat as much as she liked without putting on the pounds. She also had a perfect English complexion, her only problem being the occasional spot and a tendency towards high colouring when she was excited or nervous.

Nerves were, and still are, a problem for Diana. She is highly strung and sensitive and if she feels people are hostile towards her, will 'freeze them out' rather than have a direct confrontation. Still insecure about her looks, she worries about her weight, which since the birth of William has fluctuated dramatically. So much so that during the early years there were even suggestions that she had the slimmers' disease anorexia nervosa, something her own sister, Lady Sarah McCorquodale, suffered during the time of her romance with Prince Charles.

The restrictions of Diana's new life were, however, making her increasingly tense. In her bachelor days she had always been the one to do the washing up, empty ashtrays and water the plants, and when she first moved into Buckingham Palace she had no domestic distractions to occupy her time and energy, so she decided to renew her love affair with dancing and took tap dancing lessons in the Music Room, ruining the parquet floor.

Royal dance teacher, 77-year-old Lily Snipp came to the Palace twice a week with Diana's teacher, Wendy Vickers. Together they took the young Lady Diana through energetic hour-long sessions.

'She just lived for ballet and was completely dedicated,' Miss Snipp said. 'The two days a week we taught her were the times she most enjoyed, her lessons helped her get away from the pressures of being a member of the Royal Family.'

When the two teachers arrived at Buckingham Palace they were shown to the Music Room by a footman, who informed Diana they were waiting. Diana, dressed in a black leotard, always insisted they start the music straight away. First it was ballet, and then ten minutes of tap dancing in the circular mirrored room. One morning when they arrived Diana was upset: her new tap shoes with studded heels had marked the floor. An official from the Department of the Environment, responsible for the upkeep of all the official royal residences, was sent for, but seemed unperturbed.

'Don't worry,' he said, 'we have another room and the floor in there doesn't matter.' He then showed them into the Throne Room where the Queen does all her investitures. The Throne Room has a balcony at one end where there is an upright piano.

'It was a wonderful setting for a ballet lesson,' Miss Snipp remembered, 'but I wasn't too keen on playing an upright piano – so the official simply ordered some footmen to manhandle a grand piano into position. So we had our lessons in the Throne Room.'

As a schoolgirl Diana would never miss a dancing class and was 'mad keen' on ballet. Her name was always at the top of the list for school outings to the ballet and she saw all the favourites like 'Swan Lake' and 'Sleeping Beauty' several times and used to wait outside the stage door to get the dancers' autographs. When she met the Russian ballet star, Mikail Baryshnikov, at the White House in 1985 she confessed to him she had once been one of the eager fans waiting outside Covent Garden after his performance.

Nowadays, as Patron of the London City Ballet, Diana goes to rehearsals to watch the dancers and chat to them about their work and their exercise routines, some of which she follows herself at home. The thirty-strong company is underfunded with no local or Arts Council grant and Diana sees herself as something of a fairy godmother to them. The company's spokeswoman, Marian St Claire, explains Diana's personal involvement:

'She certainly loves her dancing. She really enjoys the nitty gritty of the rehearsal studio. She's always asking what it feels like to be lifted high into the air. What thrills us is how relaxed she is with us. She has fits of giggles when we tell her about our dressing room picnics. She's more than our mascot – she's one of us.'

As much as the Princess might have liked to have been one of the young dancers, she readily admits:

'I actually wanted to be a dancer, but overshot the height by a long way.'

Instead Diana concentrated on being a teacher. She didn't concentrate hard enough, however, and after a term at Miss Vacini's School of Dancing, where she taught two-year-olds and upwards to dance to nursery rhymes, abandoned the idea, but persisted with evening classes in Latin American, jazz and tap. Today those classes are transferred to the sitting room at Kensington Palace.

'I do it once or twice a week,' Diana says. 'It's a

combination of tap, jazz and ballet.' The Princess also attends outside classes with other dancers and in 1983 arranged six weeks of lessons at the South London studio of Royal Ballet director, Merle Park. And, before her surprising début on stage at the Royal Opera House, Covent Garden in December 1985, she took lessons from dancer Wayne Sleep – over the telephone.

No one was more surprised than 39-year-old Wayne Sleep when he received a call from the Princess of Wales suggesting that they both do a dance routine for the Friends of Covent Garden Gala on the day before Christmas Eve. They had discussed the possibility of her dancing on stage when they had met through Wayne's company, London City Ballet, but because of her position he hadn't taken it seriously.

'It was all her idea,' Wayne explained. 'For her the excitement of doing it was to keep it from her husband more than anything else. Our biggest problem was going to be rehearsing in complete secrecy.'

Diana sent Wayne a tape of her current favourite record, 'Uptown Girl' by Billy Joel, and he went round to Kensington Palace to choreograph the number. In track suits they both danced around the sitting room, with Diana collapsing into giggles when she thought of how Prince Charles would look when he saw them on stage. But Wayne was impressed with her genuine ability:

'She has rhythm, she can do high kicks, and she has a real feel for jazz dancing which was great, so the rehearsal was amazing.'

As both Wayne Sleep and Diana were very busy they continued their lessons over the telephone, Diana speaking in a breathless whisper in case anyone overheard her and told Charles. Their second and last rehearsal was on the day of the Gala when Diana

arrived at the Opera House in the morning, for two
hours of rehearsals – she even practised her curtsy to
the Royal Box, and the idea of Diana bowing to her
own husband caused Wayne great amusement.

Throughout the performance that evening Charles
suspected nothing and hardly noticed Diana leaving
his side two numbers before the end. She dashed
backstage, changed into a flimsy dress and calmly
waited in the wings until Wayne beckoned her on
stage.

The sophisticated, elegant audience at Covent
Garden could not believe what they were witnessing
when the Princess came on and they let out a multiple
gasp of amazement. 'The only time I've had a reaction
like that is when I've fallen over on stage,' Wayne said.
'It was astonishing.'

There was no one more astonished than the Prince
of Wales as he watched his wife of just over four years
do her routine, which went from classical steps to the
Charleston. They were called back eight times, before a
still-nervous Wayne Sleep noticed Prince Charles
laughing and clapping with delight as Diana turned for
the carefully practised curtsy to the Royal Box. He was
greatly relieved to see this reaction and when he came
face to face with Charles at the party afterwards, had a
short chat with him.

Charles admitted he had been 'absolutely amazed'
when he saw his wife appear on stage with Wayne and
had known nothing about it. As for Diana – she was so
thrilled with the reaction from the Covent Garden
audience, her original thrill of surprising her husband
was almost forgotten.

Unlike Diana, Charles dreads what he calls the 'awful
exhibition' they are obliged to make of themselves as a
royal couple, when they start the dancing during the

many gala dinner-dances they attend. Diana enjoys it and she has had some very glamorous and powerful partners. At the White House dinner in 1985 Diana started the dancing with Ronald Reagan and after a couple of minutes John Travolta, the star of *Saturday Night Fever*, tapped him on the shoulder and asked if he could dance with Diana.

'Mrs Reagan told me,' Travolta recalls, 'that when the President was finished dancing with Diana, I should go over and ask her to dance. I was worried it wasn't appropriate, but she assured me it was.'

Travolta and Diana jived for eight minutes to a medley of songs from *Saturday Night Fever* and *Stayin' Alive*, while the other guests retreated from the floor to watch the spectacle. Diana confided to Travolta she was suffering from jet-lag and might not be at her best. Travolta assured her she was terrific, and said, 'My cure is exercise and sleep and based on my theory, this is the beginning of your cure.'

Dancing is one area where Diana knows she can excel, but according to a former flatmate, Caroline Bartholomew, swimming is another.

'Diana was an excellent swimmer at school and won the diving cup three years running. She was also a very good dancer and a superb tap dancer.'

Dancing and swimming are not Diana's only forms of exercise, but they consume a large amount of her nervous energy. In those early days at Buckingham Palace she was able to avail herself of the heated indoor swimming pool, something she still does today. This is usually in the early mornings when there is no one else around. Princess Margaret, the other regular swimmer, rarely gets up before noon and does not use it until later in the day.

'I'm quite disciplined,' Diana says. 'I swim regularly

– once a day if possible.' Diana finds these sessions so
therapeutic that during royal tours a swimming pool is
always made available for her use. Few of the Embassies where the Prince and Princess stay have a pool of
their own, so the nearest possible one is made available. Accompanied only by her detective, Diana will
go to the pool, swim her regulation twenty lengths, dry
off and head back to base – in time to have her hair
done and get ready for the day ahead.

One of the best things about royal tours, Diana
admits, is having Richard Dalton around to do her hair
whenever she needs him. Dalton visits Kensington
Palace most mornings when the Princess has an official
engagement and, depending on the timing, she sometimes washes her own hair in the shower and is ready
in her dressing room listening to Capital Radio before
he arrives. If they have very little time, he will brush
her hair through and re-style it with curling tongs. As
it is lightly permed on the top Diana's hair holds a
style well and doesn't need to be washed every day,
unless she has been swimming. Whenever necessary
Dalton streaks her naturally fair hair and they sometimes experiment with new styles – nothing too outlan-
dish – just a change in the length and nowadays Diana
reserves the more outrageous hairstyles she longs to
have, for private photo sessions.

When the Princess is on holiday she finds her hair a
problem. The heat and damp frizzes it, so she often
wears a scarf or just pins it back. Both William and
Harry have their hair cut by Dalton and if Prince
Charles is around he will have his thinning thatch
shaped too. Diana admits, 'lots of lacquer' helps keep
her hair in place between sessions, but she is not very
good at handling it herself, hence her relief on royal
tours when she has Dalton on hand. Then he will also

do the lady-in-waiting's hair – Anne Beckwith-Smith has a hairstyle suspiciously like her employer's.

During Ascot week in the summer and big shooting weekends in the winter, Dalton will spend a couple of nights at Windsor or Sandringham, to ensure Diana's hair is perfect. Then the entire party – apart from the Queen who has her own hairdresser, Charles Martin – can benefit from Dalton's expertise and have their hair done before the evening's entertainment. It is hard work for him, but he readily admits the advantages far outweigh the disadvantages.

'I once dreamt of being Elizabeth Taylor's hairdresser,' he said, 'but I never thought I would end up doing the hair of the future Queen.'

Ever since Grace Coddington, the Beauty Without Cruelty cosmetics champion and her team at *Vogue* introduced her to Barbara Daly, Diana has remained with Britain's top make-up artist. Barbara did Diana's make-up for the wedding and, until she became adept at it herself, for important engagements. When Diana first saw the effect the television cameras had on her simple make-up, she implored Barbara to help her. It was, however, impractical for her to do Diana's make-up all the time so the Princess, through trial and error, devised her own methods. Sometimes she got it wrong and wore too much but increasingly got it right. She has learned to accentuate her startling blue eyes with liner drawn just inside the lower lid and to combat her high colouring by using peach, not pink, blusher, and has literally hundreds of different cosmetic brushes to blend colour on every part of her face. Many of the products she uses are allergy-tested such as Clinique or from Daly's extensive 'Colourings' or 'Body Shop' range.

'I'm a fan of Body Shop,' Diana says. (She even

insists her husband uses their shampoo.) She likes experimenting with different-coloured eyeshadows and wears Christian Dior's 'Sailboat Blue' mascara. A couple of years ago she was brave enough to wear body glitter and sprayed it on her hair and shoulders for the British Fashion Banquet, where she knew it wouldn't cause any comment. To combat the small blemishes she gets on her cheek she uses a concealer stick from the 'Colourings' range. She also uses their leg make-up in the summer, though not always as expertly applied as she might wish. It does, however, have the effect of making slightly tanned legs look 'holiday brown' and saves the necessity of wearing tights.

'Tights are great,' Diana says, 'but I hate them in the summer and prefer tanned legs.' So much so that during a Buckingham Palace garden party in the early part of the marriage Diana turned up with bare legs, shocking the Establishment who considered it 'undressed' to appear without tights or stockings.

The pencil-slim suntanned Diana is almost a thing of yesteryear. No longer desperate to stretch out by the pool or rush up on to the roof garden at Kensington Palace the moment the sun appears, Diana has opted for a paler, though still athletic look. In 1987, when holidaying with King Juan Carlos and his family in Majorca, a snapshot revealed Diana's considerable stomach and sparked rumours of another pregnancy. Nothing could have been further from the truth. It was as a result of her pregnancies that Diana had gained her stomach – her abdominal muscles had collapsed, doctors explained, due to lack of postnatal exercise. It wasn't simple laziness (she is after all a very athletic woman). But she had lost weight easily after the birth of Harry and did not feel the pressing necessity to embark on a special exercise programme. She has now installed an exercise machine in Kensington Palace to combat the problem.

Although she still tucks into her favourite sweets or any form of chocolate, because she finds it gives her energy, Diana, partly under the influence of her husband, is obsessed with healthy eating. All their vegetables are organically grown at Highgrove and transported to London on Monday mornings. Charles has been an advocate of the low-fat, high-fibre diet for ten years, sparked off by a visit to an agricultural centre in 1978. He was disturbed by the environment in which the pigs were kept to produce maximum output.

'I shall become a vegetarian,' he declared. 'I'm glad I'm not a pig.' Both Charles and Diana admit they feel much better if they don't eat much meat, so their meals consist mainly of fish, chicken, eggs and fresh vegetables. Despite having taken a cordon bleu cooking course, Diana still only describes herself as an 'average cook'.

She loves to tuck into pasta, home-made soups and quiches. 'I'm so busy,' she says, 'I never put on an ounce and I can eat as much as I like.'

When their former butler, Alan Fisher, who once worked for Bing Crosby in Hollywood, was employed by the Prince and Princess of Wales he complained they never entertained and his duties included almost everything except looking after the dining room.

'If Charles was out, I would take a tray of simple food to the Princess in her sitting room,' he said. 'Once I found her sitting there in her nightdress, all ready to go to bed. I was most embarrassed to find her like this and tried to make a hasty retreat from the room, while putting the tray down at the same time.

"Don't be silly, Alan," she said, calling me back into the room, "but look, this plate has a chip in it!" Fisher recalls his added embarrassment at the idea of the kitchen staff producing a plate that was chipped when so many dinner services lay unused in the kitchen, and cheekily suggested the royal couple ought to entertain, if only to utilize the china.

Nowadays Charles and Diana entertain far more, although Diana complains finding a date to suit them both is difficult. So if Charles is busy she will have her own friends over for informal dinners. As in all royal households, the chef will consult with the lady of the house about the week's menus. Diana is careful to stick to one or two simple courses as Charles loathes any kind of waste. When she first dined at Highgrove, surrounded by packing cases, Diana was astounded at Charles's 'Scottish meanness' when she was served with one of his egg meals with left-over summer pudding. It was not what she expected, but she was obliged to eat it with as much grace as she could muster.

Prince Charles has also educated his wife to believe in the Kurt Hahn (the founder of Gordonstoun) philosophy of the 'platonic ideal' of a healthy mind in a healthy body. He feels the pressures of living in the 'royal goldfish bowl' can generate problems which directly affect the body: stress, loneliness, anger and frustration – all regular features of royal life.

'I'm a great believer in having friends to whom you can talk about anything that bothers you,' Charles says. 'I'm against bottling it up. If you haven't got someone to talk to, it's vital to get rid of what's bothering you in some way or another.'

His way, along with other members of the family, is regular exercise, and when Sarah Ferguson first arrived on the scene as a serious girlfriend to his brother Andrew, he was delighted. At last Diana would have

someone inside the family of her own age to talk to.
Sarah's arrival also boosted Diana's morale. She opti-
mistically hoped it would ease the pressure on herself.
Diana was wrong, of course – she is still centre stage,
but she now has a friend to share the burden.

'It's nice for Diana to have a friend to talk to that
really understands what it's like to be watched whenever she sneezes or coughs,' says former Highgrove
housekeeper Joan Boardman. 'I don't think she's jealous that a new face on the scene will steal the limelight
from her. In fact I am sure she is quite glad to have
someone to share it.'

Diana was, and she started to mix with Fergie's
friends, some of whom seemed much more fun than
her own. They played tennis at the exclusive Vanderbilt Racquet Club in London's Shepherd's Bush – Diana
had always been a good player, but started to improve
rapidly under the tuition of the club's managing director, Charles Swallow. Always conscious of her legs –
as a schoolgirl she found them too thin, too fat or too
knobbly – Diana was annoyed at discovering photographs of herself in a tennis dress in the press, but it
didn't stop her enjoyment of the game and afterwards
she would cool off in the cocktail bar with a glass of
orange juice. It was exactly the kind of physical and
mental therapy Charles was talking about and he was
pleased to see Diana enjoying her twice-weekly sessions on the tennis court.

To please the Queen, Diana also went riding,
although she has never liked horses or the horsey set.
Talk of the day's eventing or hunting and analysis of
the merits of various horses bored her to tears. But as
many of the Royal Family circle are of that ilk, she was
obliged to put up with it. The royals feel at ease in the
company of horsey folk, they share a common ground

where class, money and breeding are all superseded by their knowledge of horseflesh.

Diana has never felt happy on a horse. She is too nervous and she had that minor fall from her pony, Romany, at the age of eight and used that as an excuse to avoid riding whenever she could. Such excuses simply don't hold up however, when confronted with a request from the Queen. She didn't pressurize Diana into going riding, merely suggested she might give her some lessons and get her confidence back. Diana could hardly refuse. But in spite of this encouragement and further help from Fergie during the long summer and winter breaks at Balmoral and Sandringham, Diana looks as uncomfortable as ever on horseback.

It was therefore all the more surprising when in 1987 she went out hunting. Encouraged this time by her sister Lady Sarah McCorquodale, with whom she was staying on her Lincolnshire farm, she followed the hounds with the Belvoir, reputed to be one of the toughest hunts in Britain. Although Diana only went at a gentle pace on her sister's horse and didn't tackle any large fences, she was obviously making an effort to please Charles, who is mad keen on hunting and loves everyone to indulge in the sports he enjoys. She might have pleased Charles, but she didn't please the League Against Cruel Sports and was predictably criticized for her action.

A similar outcry had occurred when Diana was accused of shooting and wounding a stag during her honeymoon in October 1980. She was livid when the story appeared in the press and Charles could do nothing to appease her. He spent the following day on the telephone to his London office, deciding what course of action to take. Finally, as is the usual royal way, he did nothing and hoped the story would just fade away. It did, but Diana remained thoroughly miserable. It was not her first taste of unpleasant press – she had also been accused of spending a night with Charles on the royal train before their marriage – and it certainly wasn't going to be her last. At the time, however, she couldn't understand why her husband didn't do something, and felt let down. Not that Diana minds shooting. The Royal Family have been stalking deer at Balmoral since Queen Victoria purchased the place in 1848 and Diana first went stalking in Scotland in her early teens. She is a good shot and a ghillie from the Balmoral estate clearly remembers 'blooding' Diana after she had shot her first stag there. Blooding is the traditional, if barbaric, practice of smearing the blood of a dead stag on the face of the man or woman who has killed it.

Diana cannot win. If she refuses to join the traditional stalking parties – the Queen shot her first stag at sixteen, but no longer shoots – she would appear rude, but if she goes, she runs the risk of unwelcome publicity from animal campaigners. However, although Diana joins the royal shooting parties for pheasant, partridge and grouse, she has never been spotted with a gun. She has even been credited with persuading Prince Charles to give up shooting for a short period.

In fact, Charles was simply going through one of his phases, as when he turned vegetarian for a short time. He felt that killing anything, especially the over-fed pheasants at Sandringham, was not good sport and he gave his priceless pair of Purdy guns to his brother Andrew. After some pressure from Prince Philip, who rightly pointed out that Charles was the mainstay of shooting parties on the royal estates, he started again.

It is eight years since Diana was first spotted with

Prince Charles on the banks of the River Dee in Scotland and it appeared she might have had the makings of a keen fisherwoman. It was not to be. In spite of fly-fishing lessons from her mother in the Highlands of Scotland and instructions from one of the Balmoral ghillies, Charles Knight, Diana never took to her husband's favourite pastime. She even had to put up with him fishing on the River Test on the first evening of their honeymoon at Broadlands. Charles still goes fishing and most years joins his friends Lord and Lady Tryon at their fishing lodge in Iceland. Charles goes alone. Diana will sail with him, ski with him, but fishing is something she has abandoned.

As a child Diana spent many skiing holidays in Switzerland, and improved her skill when attending the finishing school there. Subsequent chalet parties with her contemporaries have left her an adept skier, but she never likes skiing furiously down the black runs like Prince Charles or the Duchess of York. And she hates skiing when it is very cold. Charles and Diana are still fussy about their diet and chalet girls are dispatched to all the neighbouring villages to find fish, vegetables and fruit suitable for the royal palates. And when Charles is off powder skiing with the Duchess of York and a guide, Diana is quite happy to give her rusty cooking skills a whirl while she waits for the more adventurous in the party to return.

This lack of bravery on the pistes does have a medical justification. She enjoys good health which is just as well for one who says, 'I don't like needles or drips.' But she did once break her leg skiing and she suffers from a painful back. Physiotherapists have little doubt that her problem stems from her habit of holding her children on her hip, thus causing her back muscles injury. When they play up she has a physiotherapist visit her at home to give her treatment. Standing for long intervals in high heels doesn't help, and Diana admits to getting 'backache not tired feet'. When her back is bad the only exercise she does is walking. With her Sony Walkman clamped firmly to her head she goes for long solitary strolls.

'I'm a great believer in having music wherever I go,' she says. 'And it's just a big treat to go out for a walk with music still coming with me.' Diana also has a specially hard mattress to help her back. She is a very light sleeper and, unlike her husband, 'who can sleep through anything,' is wakened by the slightest sound. A pair of earplugs were once found next to her side of the bed by an amused member of staff who found it strange to think of Diana sitting through ear-shattering rock concerts, but going to bed with a pair of earplugs. (She does, however, also take them to concerts!)

Like her husband and most members of the Royal Family, including the Queen and Queen Mother, Diana has become a champion of alternative medicine, using whenever possible herbal remedies as cures rather than the antibiotics of modern medicine. It was not always so. When she was being courted by the Prince she didn't know what the word homeopathic meant. A friend pointed out:

'If you're going to become the daughter-in-law of the Queen, you'd better find out.'

She went away and tried a homeopathic cure for the flu she was suffering from. It worked for twenty-four hours. 'But when the effect wore off I think my cold was worse than ever,' she reported. But encouraged by Charles her faith has increased and she tries herbal remedies such as diluted traces of arsenic for stomach complaints, deadly nightshade for sore throats and feverfew plant, a type of chrysanthemum, to relieve symptoms of migraine.

If either of them is really unwell, they will consult a doctor, but for a cold or headache Charles finds a game of polo just as good.

'If I have a game of polo,' he says, 'I feel five hundred times better.'

Because the children pick up all types of childhood ailments at school including colds and flu, Charles and Diana suffer during the winter. If Charles has a cold he will sleep in another room to try and avoid infecting Diana and keeping her awake with his coughing. All the Royal Family avoid each other when they have colds – an illness might mean a cancelled engagement and disappointing hundreds of people. Even during the uncomfortable times of her pregnancies when the Princess was suffering from morning sickness which went on all day, Diana seldom cancelled an appointment, preferring to suffer the discomfort rather than the guilt she felt at letting so many people down.

Diana couldn't bear the extra weight she gained whilst carrying William and was determined to lose it as quickly as possible. 'I want to fit into my jeans,' she said, and did the vigorous aerobics made fashionable by Jane Fonda at the time. She didn't do them after the birth of Harry, however, which led to another bout of rumour. But then there are always rumours about Diana's weight gain and loss.

In 1986 she is supposed to have visited the clinic of Swedish homeopath Gudrun Jonsson, and undergone sessions encased in a white plastic barrel, which electronically neutralizes the harmful ions which build up in the body. Gudrun, whose treatment – a mixture of homeopathy, reflexology and biopathy – is designed to bring the body back to its correct balance, has many society patients – including the Duchess of York – but has never treated the Princess. The rumour started because Diana, who gets slightly claustrophobic in large crowds, suffered a dizzy spell during a tour of Expo '86 in Vancouver and appeared to faint. (Gudrun's treatment, so the story goes, was designed to counteract Diana's fainting spells.)

These stories annoy Diana because they involve not only her, but many other innocent parties and each story draws the net around her a little tighter. In Australia in January 1988 Diana decided to make it perfectly clear why she appeared to be wilting and needed to ask for a glass of water.

'I'm a real Pom,' she said, 'the heat is getting me down.'

Diana, who doesn't have very good circulation, suffers from extremes of temperature and jet-lag. Unlike her husband, who has the ability to 'cat-nap' anywhere and has even been known to fall asleep over dinner and wake ten minutes later, refreshed, Diana will lie down for a rest only to discover she is unable to sleep. Combating jet-lag with plenty of water and very little food has not helped and she now resigns herself to staring at the ceiling or half-watching any programme on television, while she tries to relax. The breathing exercises that Betty Parsons taught her during her pregnancies sometimes help, but they don't put her to sleep and she dislikes sleeping pills.

Even the most seasoned travellers suffer such discomfort of course. But Diana, because of her exhausting schedules, does have to take care. She doesn't always take enough. When she is very busy her eating habits become erratic and her weight starts fluctuating. She was suspected of having bulimia (a slimmers' illness where the sufferer eats like a pig when no one is

watching, then makes themself sick to compensate for
the vast amount of calories they have consumed) when
she was spied in the kitchens at Windsor Castle by a
footman, just as she was cramming a feast of meat pie
into her mouth. And one story has it that she consumed
an entire chicken meant for a dinner party. Diana's
friends deny all this. Diana, they say, eats normally but
she still does not like official banquets. Says Kevin
Shanley, 'Diana told me how she cuts up her food,
moves it around her plate and brings her fork to her
mouth a couple of times without taking a mouthful.'

She takes the same precautions with alcohol, realizing that if she drank all the booze offered to her at
official functions Prince Charles would have to carry
her home on his back. To make up for this calorie
deficiency, Diana will grab a sandwich or a piece of
chocolate afterwards. She does not throw up. Nor does
she binge.

'I'm a perfectionist with myself,' she says. And as a
perfectionist she always wants to look and be at her
best.

13
Fergie

When Prince Andrew became engaged to Sarah
Ferguson, Diana drew an almost audible sigh of relief.

'You don't need me any more,' she told waiting
newsmen. 'Now you've got Fergie.'

That will never be quite true. The Duchess of York is
vibrant, adventurous and without stuffiness. And as
the newest daughter-in-law of the Queen, she has
inevitably attracted the flock of photographers and
reporters who make their living following the Royal
Family.

But Diana will one day be Queen, a status Fergie –
the wife of a younger son – will never attain. For all
the attention she now attracts, her life will always be
played out in the shadow of the younger woman.

In a very real way, however, Sarah's arrival has eased
the pressure on Diana. And, most importantly, Diana
now has a real friend she can confide in. For no matter
how outgoing and informal she may be – and Diana is
both – there is always the barrier of her royalty between
her and even her oldest friends.

For it is a royal rule, and one emphasized over and
over again by her husband who is constantly warning
her to be on her guard against people whose motives
for courting her friendship may not be unconnected to
the fact that she is the Princess of Wales, that problems
are never discussed outside the immediate family.

With Fergie that regal precept does not apply. The
two have been friends ever since they met at polo ('And
doesn't everyone meet at polo?' as Fergie's mother,

Mrs Susan Barrantes, exclaimed from the ivory tower of her own interests), when Diana first started walking out with Charles. 'Look after her for me,' Charles told the friendly redhead. And she did.

It was a natural friendship that drew on a common background. Both had spent their childhoods in the company of the royal circle. Diana grew up calling Andrew and Edward by their first names.

Fergie has also known the Queen's younger sons for almost as long as she can remember. But not in quite the same way. Her father, Major Ronald Ferguson, had once commanded the Sovereign's Escort, the cavalry detachment that accompanies the Monarch on ceremonial occasions. It brought him into close contact with the Queen and Prince Philip. A fine horseman and a finer polo player who had acted as military advisor on the film *Charge of the Light Brigade*, the Major remained a close friend of Prince Philip. They played polo together and socialized within the élite polo crowd.

When Philip was forced to give up the game because of arthritis of the wrists, Ferguson was placed in charge of Prince Charles's polo interests.

'It just sort of happened,' the Major says. 'When Philip was playing, the Chairman of the Guards Polo Club was Colonel Gerald Leigh – he looked after Philip's affairs and organized his matches. As Deputy Chairman I do much the same thing for Charles.

'I'm not employed by the Prince of Wales. I do it as an act of friendship and it's worked terribly well. I don't have to refer to anybody except him.'

It is a role that puts him on first-name terms with the future king. But only in the environment of that tough, hard, equestrian sport. Away from the polo field, he says, 'I don't see very much of the Royal Family.'

And nor did his daughter Sarah.

There were, it is true, the occasional picnics at polo which Fergie was invited to. But that was really as far as it went. An independent young woman, Fergie had set off at an early age to make her own life and her own set of friends.

While Diana's pre-marital experiences were confined to a spell working as a cleaning lady for her friends and, on one occasion, for her sister in Chelsea, and a few months as a daily help at a nursery school in London's Pimlico, Fergie had pursued a much more worldly path.

After school where, like Diana, she had not exactly distinguished herself academically (though unlike Diana she did manage to garner which gave her the British equivalent of junior high school graduation), she had taken a bus ride through South America down to Argentina where her mother now lives.

She had had two serious love affairs, one with Kim Smith Bingham and one with Paddy McNally, a motor racing entrepreneur almost old enough to be her father, and with whom she had stayed in the Swiss ski resort of Verbier.

And while Diana had a family trust to fall back on, Fergie had had to work for a living.

The Fergusons own an 800-acre estate called Dummer Down in Hampshire. But as a retired army officer from a family of army officers and without any great family fortune behind him, Major Ferguson was not able to give his daughter more than a small private income – 'And when I say small, I mean small,' he insists.

For all those differences – and as slight as they may seem to the untutored eye, they constitute the finer nuances that make up the class divides in Britain – the two women hit it off immediately.

There was, for instance, the similarity in their childhoods. When Diana was six years old her mother Frances (who, by one of those ironic coincidences not uncommon in the small, claustrophobic world of Society, had once been proposed to by Ronald Ferguson) had left the marital home and moved in with wallpaper heir Peter Shand-Kydd.

When Fergie was thirteen, her mother Susan had done likewise and run off with the Argentine polo player Hector Barrantes.

'It was a trauma,' for both Sarah and her sister Jane, as their father recalls.

It would be stretching the psychological truth, however, to say that these early upsets provided the foundation of the empathy Fergie and Diana felt for each other. Rather it was the way each had reacted to the upheavals in their lives that opened the way to a friendship which has changed the face of the Royal Family for ever.

The departure of her mother had left Diana diffident and insecure; a woman whose shyness had only been emphasized by her entry into the most isolated family in the world.

Fergie, on the other hand, had responded to the change in her domestic circumstances by developing into a buoyant, outgoing personality, always willing to join in and always eager to please. In Verbier she had always made it her duty to ensure that everyone who came to McNally's 'castle' – the sixteen-room chalet up the hill from the notorious Farm Club he retreats to for weekends and school holidays – was put at their ease: no mean feat in the acerbic, conversationally savage McNally set.

It was this quality Fergie brought into her relationship with Diana. She knew how to put the Princess at her ease. She had been accustomed to talking to royalty and courtiers since she was a child. She had refined that ability to draw the best out of people without losing sight of her own personality in the hard school of jet-setters she had mixed with in Switzerland, the south of France and on the holiday island of Ibiza.

She was outgoing and friendly and she made Diana laugh and they giggled together at some of the characters they observed on the polo scene.

Also, and more importantly, Fergie represented no threat. For in those early days of her marriage Diana was noticeably on her guard if any attractive 'rival' ventured into the vicinity of her husband; Lady Tryon and Camilla Parker-Bowles, for instance, quickly found themselves on the outside of the royal circle they had once been so close to the centre of.

No one was surprised when Diana asked Fergie to her wedding at St Paul's Cathedral. And there was even talk that Diana would make her a lady-in-waiting.

Fergie's father discounts that. 'She'd only known Diana for a year at the time,' he points out. That would not have mattered except that she was a little too inexperienced and, more pointedly, a little too exuberant for such a job.

Fergie was, however, asked to Diana's twenty-first birthday lunch at Buckingham Palace – the only non-family member to be invited.

This was a difficult time for the new and terribly young Princess of Wales. She had married a Prince but in this fairy-tale the Princess found herself increasingly confined in the ivory tower that constitutes royal life. The royal machine had cut her off from the few friends she did have and was slowly but inexorably starting to swallow her up.

Into this void had come Fergie who, as the daughter of her husband's polo manager, belonged ostensibly to Charles's circle and it was on Diana's insistence that she was invited to join the royal party at Windsor Castle for Royal Ascot. Which is where Fergie's romance with Andrew began over the profiteroles.

Diana did not push Andrew and Fergie together. But she did encourage their friendship. She invited them to tea at Kensington Palace and Highgrove in Gloucestershire.

She and Fergie started having luncheon together; sometimes at Kensington Palace, often – and to Diana's greater enjoyment – out at places like the restaurant in the Harvey Nichols department store in Knightsbridge.

And when romance developed into marriage, Diana was there to help Fergie with the ropes that she had had to learn by hard experience herself.

'She talked to Sarah about her life and that helped her enormously,' says Major Ferguson.

But if Diana was involving herself in the life of her new 'BF' – upper-class speak for best friend – and offering her what advice she could, Sarah, in her turn, was also having a considerable effect on Diana.

The Princess of Wales had come into the Royal Family a maiden barely out of her teens, gauche and immature. 'She came straight from the nursery school to the Palace,' Stephen Barry remarked.

Fergie's case was very different. She was twenty-six years old when she married. She had 'been around' – geographically, emotionally, sexually. Her personality had been formed and glazed in a wider world Diana had never known. She was, her father was fond of saying, 'streetwise'.

At first there was a reserve in her public approach to her new public role as a member of the world's most scrutinized, most public family. Being in their company and being one of them are very different things and the change from friend to Duchess in her own right was, as her father observed, 'daunting'.

Like her father, however, the Duchess of York has a character even the rigours of protocol cannot smother. Tall, attractive with a gruff exterior that only emphasizes a wicked sense of humour, the Major has never been anything less than outspoken.

'I am not bound by any rules or regulations, only by commonsense and loyalty to my daughter,' he says.

Unlike the family Sarah has married into, which makes it a rule never to answer back the criticism and speculation that showers its way, Ferguson – like the proverbial cavalry and in conscious rejection of Windsor protocol – is always ready to ride in to her defence. When she visited Canada in 1987 for instance, the local press accused her of being amongst other things 'a fat and frumpy, giggly disco queen.'

Said the Major, 'I should think those reports annoyed her intensely. But there is bottle behind Sarah's bounce and those reports made her go all out to prove that she is not what they said she was.'

It is an attitude that meets with Father's approval. For was it not Major Ferguson who turned to his daughter as they drove down the Mall in her wedding coach on her way to Westminster Abbey that morning in July 1986 and reminded her, 'Always be yourself'?

It is advice the Duchess of York has followed. She remains as friendly and as outgoing and as spontaneous as she ever was in those far off days in Verbier. She is still just as anxious to put people at their ease – a trait that has endeared her to the Royal Family in a way that Diana has never quite managed.

The Queen Mother, who can be quite cantankerous, adores her. 'She is so *English*,' she keeps saying, adding that she is free of those airs and graces 'we can't stand'.

She has also established a rapport with the Queen. It would not be accurate to say that the Queen and the future Queen do not get on. They do. But it is not a particularly close relationship. Fergie, however, has a great deal in common with her mother-in-law. They are both countrywomen by inclination, with a common interest in dogs and horses. And the Queen knows very well what it is like to be married to a young naval officer who is away much of the time as Andrew is. That is how she started her own married life after all.

When Andrew is on duty Sarah sometimes sees the Queen alone. They dine together, official engagements permitting, often on the card table in front of the television.

It is on occasions like these that Fergie's lack of those 'airs and graces' comes into play. If, for instance, the Queen offers her a glass of that sweet white German wine she likes so much – a taste few share – Fergie will drink it. Her more modern palate – like Diana's – much prefers the crisper sparkle of champagne or Chablis or an Italian Orvieto, but that is not the point, not for Sarah that is – she wouldn't dream of asking for a glass of champagne or even a glass of Perrier if it had not been offered.

Yet if this latest recruit to the Royal Family has won herself a high approval rating within the Firm, not everyone approves of the subtle but penetrating wind of change she has brought to the dusty recesses of royal life.

Some will argue, and argue forcefully, that the

changes she has wrought have not been all for the good. Indeed, that her influence on Diana, the woman who will one day be Queen, has in fact been positively harmful.

Princess Michael of Kent once told me, 'She is strong, she is independent. You watch – Fergie will change us all!'

And the person who has changed most is the Princess of Wales. The Shy Di of yesterday has gone, to be replaced by a woman who seems increasingly determined to enjoy herself even if it means going against the traditions of conservative decorum the British have come to expect from their reigning family.

In one sense the metamorphosis was, if not inevitable, then at least not unexpected. Married at twenty, a mother eighteen months later and again the following year, Diana never really had the chance to get out with people her own age and enjoy the things most other young people take, naturally and healthily, for granted. She has lived a life without dates or carefee holidays in the sun. Friends never simply 'drop round' to Kensington Palace for a cup of tea and when Diana went out it was always with a detective and, certainly in the early days of her marriage, only to places her husband had decided she should go.

If there was going to be a break-out it was going to happen then. Her sons had started school and for the first time in her marriage she found herself with time on her hands – and an understandable determination to get out and enjoy it.

Sarah showed her the way. She introduced her to a new and wider range of people drawn from her own age group and so very different from the conservative and intellectually intimidating circle Charles prefers.

She showed Diana that, notwithstanding her position, it is possible to have . . . fun.

The fun started almost straight away. For it was Fergie who persuaded Diana to make that foray into Annabel's disguised as a policewoman.

It was the night of Andrew's stag party and Fergie was convinced that he was holding a dinner party in the private room of that most exclusive nightclub in Mayfair's Berkeley Square. She was wrong but it was a reasonable guess: Annabel's has built its reputation on discretion and for twenty-five years the rich and the well-known have sought their relaxation there, secure in the knowledge that any word of their indiscretions would remain safely within the confines of its basement walls.

Opened by Mark Birley in 1963 and named after his then wife, the sister of the Marquis of Londonderry and now married to international corporate raider Jimmy Goldsmith, Annabel's is the place the younger members of the Royal Family go when they want to relax and let their hair down.

To call Annabel's a nightclub is something of an understatement. It is really an old-fashioned club with music and a dance floor at the back if you want it; a place to drop into to see friends and to dine on some of the finest food in London.

It is also a place of absolute discretion. After all, there are not many places where you could sip a Buck's Fizz standing next to the Princess of Wales and the Duchess of York disguised as policewomen and not be expected to bat an eyelid.

But that is Annabel's style. From the moment Nando the doorman takes your car keys – he never gives you a ticket, he *knows* who you are – you are back in an age of elegance and service.

The style is English country house – but on the grandest and most luxurious scale and much warmer than any of the Royal Family's homes.

In the ladies' cloakroom Mabel rules. She has been the confidante and romantic advisor to three generations of gentlewomen. Fergie knows her. She has been going to Annabel's since she was nineteen. Fergie introduced Diana to Mabel.

Then it is to the bar, an elegant wood-panelled room covered with the works of Sir Edward Landseer and Augustus John and Mark's own father, royal court painter Sir Oswald Birley.

This is not a place for gold chains or bleached blonde bimbos. At Annabel's the men wear suits. There has always been a duke, a cabinet minister or two, perhaps the Heir to the Throne gathering for a drink before moving on into the dining room where Louis reigns. The finest of *maître d*'s, Louis has an elephant's memory for faces and names.

This of course was no mean hurdle for the two young women to overcome. The club servants know Fergie. Diana is hardly unnoticeable. To get through the club and into the private room to the right across from the restaurant bar was clearly going to prove no easy matter.

This however is exactly the kind of merry jape Fergie had always enjoyed (and still does for that matter). And this was exactly the kind of night out Diana wanted to join in on.

Diana, Fergie, Pamela Stephenson and Renate, Elton John's wife, had been dining with Jane, the Duchess of Roxburghe. At about 10.30 Diana was ready to head off home for bed but Fergie had other ideas. She and Pamela had 'borrowed' some police uniforms from their friend Billy Connolly's theatrical outfitters.

With a great deal of giggling they dressed up and Pamela drove Diana's dark green Range Rover to Berkeley Square.

They left the Range Rover the other side of Berkeley Square, walked across it and into Annabel's, under the awning, down the stairs and into the club. City financier Paddy Dodd Noble, whose wife Julia is an old friend of Fergie's and once (in yet another circle within a circle that so marks London society) walked out with Andrew, signed them in.

As disguises go, policewomen's outfits are not the most unnoticeable in Annabel's. This is no speakeasy: the only police ever to be found in there are very senior members of the force and they arrive not in uniform but in well-cut Savile Row suits. Louis the manager was annoyed and told them to leave. 'You're upsetting the other customers,' he said, as they retreated to the front bar. But if the costumes did not for one moment fool the club servants, they certainly confused the members clustering in the outer sanctum. They looked and they stepped back, leaving the four women to make their way up to the bar where they dissolved in a most un-police-like fit of giggles.

Even that failed to provide the clue to one well-known Fleet Street journalist, a large bumptious man much the worse for alcoholic wear, who, oblivious to the scoop swimming before his eyes, staggered over to Diana to demand what a nice WPC like her was doing in a place like this.

He then proceeded to pinch the bottom of the Princess of Wales. Greater men have paid dearly for lesser crimes in times past, but in 1986 the covey of royal women simply giggled.

Then Fergie, who was wearing a wig and glasses, recognized two friends on the opposite side of the room. She winked. They looked blankly. She winked again. In confused disbelief the couple made their way through the crowd and offered them a drink.

'I don't drink on duty,' Diana said and dissolved into another fit of giggles, but both the girls finally accepted a Buck's Fizz.

By now the club's servants were in a state of some anxiety. A few members now knew the Princess of Wales and Sarah Ferguson were on the premises. Others believed they were kissogram girls. Most, however, were convinced that four policewomen were on the premises – an unheard of intrusion in a club where good behaviour is a requisite of membership. The joke was now perilously close to the precipice of farce.

By now Diana, Fergie and their 'minders' Pamela and Renate, knew that whoever else might be there, Andrew and his stag party were not. (They were in fact several miles away in a private house in Holland Park.) It was time to go.

They drank the last of their champagne and orange juice. They said a whispered farewell to the few who had recognized them. And then, still dissolved by the laughter that makes little sound but convulses the body, they made their way back up the staircase, past the trellis work and into the night. No nightingales sang; instead the air was rent with the sound of the giggling women.

Diana was last seen waddling across Berkeley Square – doing her impersonation of Charlie Chaplin – to the Range Rover and the drive back to Buckingham Palace and a confrontation with the very real policemen on the gate who, unaware of their identities, at first refused to allow them in.

Within twenty-four hours the story was front-page

news. The account of the royal party's nocturnal me-
anderings had sprinted down Society's bush telegraph
and into the social columns. As it was bound to. And
the reaction was just as predictable.

The sanctimonious mounted their high horses. Several MPs, their eyes firmly focused on their press
cuttings, demanded to know what action the police
intended to take against two young women who had
impersonated police officers in violation of the law
(the answer was none). Forests were felled as newspaper pundits, dipping their pens into the ink of light-
hearted controversy, scribbled their way into the
debate, some to defend the high jinks of youth, others
to condemn.

Fergie took the brickbats in her stride. It had, she
would say later, just been a bit of harmless fun; just the
kind of prank she had always indulged in and always
enjoyed. And why not? she would ask.

Diana was not allowed to dismiss the incident quite
so easily, however. The public, brought up to expect
the Royal Family to set a standard of stolid bourgeois
propriety, might excuse a bouncy 26-year-old her bit of
fun on the eve of her wedding. But Diana is different.
She is the mother of two small boys and the future
Queen. The suspicion was laid that the Princess of
Wales was travelling dangerously close to the edge of
the rails.

But if the public was concerned, Diana most decid-
edly was not. Early in 1987 she joined her husband on
their annual skiing expedition to Klosters in Switzerland. The Duke and Duchess of York were there too.
And one night in their chalet the two women put on a
cabaret act for their friends.

They put on headscarves and dark glasses and whatever other unlikely items of clothing they could find,

and in between fortifying gulps of gluwein – the potent mulled wine – they danced and sang and kicked their legs high in the air.

Prince Charles was not in evidence.

Once again Major Ferguson rides in to his daughter's defence. 'I am not aware,' he says, 'that Sarah has encouraged her (Diana) to meet anybody who is dubious. Why should she?'

As far as Diana was concerned it was all good clean 'hooray' relaxation. 'It was a wonderful holiday,' she said. 'And Fergie is such fun to be around.'

Prince Charles agreed – up to a point. He was thoroughly bored by that sort of impromptu entertainment and much preferred to devote his energies to a hard day's skiing on the slopes with his friend Charles Palmer-Tomkinson and take it easy afterwards with a hot bath, a book or a video. Nor did nightclubs hold much attraction for him and he let Diana go off dancing at Casa Antica with friends like brewery heir Peter Greenall and his wife Clare, while he stayed behind in the chalet, explaining that when he did go out, 'I get too tired as I like to start skiing early in the morning.'

'Sarah is a marvellous girl,' Charles has always insisted. But of all the members of the Family as they call themselves, the Prince is the most muted in his praise of the extroverted redhead who is now his sister-in-law. Her jolly hockey stick approach to life can grate on a man who is falling fast into a premature middle age and the tetchiness showed when the two royal couples gathered on the slopes one morning for a photocall.

Charles has always disliked the staged informality of these moments and as his relations with the travelling press corps that accompanies him everywhere continues its deterioration, he dislikes them even more. At best it is a duty but usually it is a chore. Diana, conversely, and despite her occasional moods, enjoys looking into a camera lens. It is one way this woman, who dreads public speaking and has only given one major interview (and that one, on television with Sir Alastair Burnet, was carefully pre-rehearsed), has to communicate. This morning she was in fine fettle, laughing and joking and clowning about with her new sister-in-law – her friend.

They started screaming at each other and trying to stuff snowballs down each other's ski suits. They started pushing and as their skis began sliding away from underneath, the photographers poised themselves for a money-earning picture of the Duchess and the Princess on the piste, collapsed like two melted snowmen.

Charles was not amused. 'Come on, come on,' he barked tetchily. Diana, for a moment, looked as if she was about to ignore her husband. Fergie did not. She took one look at the future King and promptly straightened up. She may be the life and soul of the party, but she also knows where to draw the line.

But if Fergie's sense of 'correctness' reined Diana back that day, they both crossed the line at Royal Ascot some months later.

As an 'incident' it was harmless enough. Diana and Fergie were walking back together from the Paddock, where they had been to see the horses being paraded before the next race, to the Queen's box in the Royal Enclosure. In front of them was Lulu Blacker, a cousin of Yorkshire landowner Earl Peel. She has been a friend of Fergie's since they were at Danes Hill School together and was once the companion of reformed drug addict the Marquis of Blandford, son and heir of the immensely grand Duke of Marlborough. She is now a friend of Diana's and was invited to join the royal party at Windsor Castle for Ascot Week.

Without thinking, Fergie and Diana started prodding Lulu in the backside with their umbrellas. They also prodded the Queen's former equerry, the late Hugh Lindsay. Both with the inevitable consequences. The photographers poised on the press balcony on the first floor of the grandstand had had their cameras trained on the royal twosome from the moment they left the Enclosure and all the way back again. Their shutters clicked, and yet again the Duchess of York and the Princess of Wales found themselves on the front pages in a situation that many – Prince Charles included – deemed less than edifying.

'It so happened that the person they jabbed was a very great friend of theirs,' Major Ferguson says. 'He was just in front of them and it was a natural reaction to have a bit of fun.'

In an interview in an American magazine, he added, 'The press says you can't behave like that, which is ludicrous.'

Not everyone is so convinced. 'Look, Fergie's wonderful and great fun and all that,' says an advisor to the Royal Family. 'But I am afraid that there are different rules in force when it comes to the Princess of Wales.'

That carefully weighted remark carries the implicit accusation that in some direct and specific way the Duchess of York is responsible for whatever changes have taken place in Diana over these past couple of years.

At a casual glance there might appear to be some truth in that. It is only since Fergie arrived on the royal scene that Diana has started behaving in such a light-hearted and, to the deeply conservative, frivolous way. It is also true that the more notable breakdowns in regal dignity have occurred when the Duchess of York has been in attendance.

To suggest, however, that in some bewitching way Fergie is the cheerleader egging Diana on, is to overstate the influence she exerts over the future Queen.

For above all, the Duchess of York is a team player and even in the intimacy of the Royal Family she always knows how far she can go. It is something she learned from her father who may resort to barrack-room language in the royal presence, but never forgets to call the Prince of Wales 'Sir'.

So it is with his daughter. If the Princess wants to sing or dance or get dressed up in funny clothes and hide under the sofa Fergie is delighted to join in. If the Princess decides to start a snowball fight, Fergie will throw one back. But she will always curtsy to the wife of the future sovereign when she comes into her presence. It is protocol and the Duchess of York knows the rules.

She does not compete with Diana in the fashion stakes – for one thing she does not have the money.

'Everyone thinks that because you're married to a member of the Royal Family you are rich beforehand and automatically become even richer,' says her father. 'That is ridiculous.'

Nor does she have the same model girl figure. In real life she is in fact quite trim and well groomed. And, with the help of Saint Laurent's French fashion house, who, free of charge, have provided her with a dozen high couture outfits (one evening gown alone cost $21,000), set off by that magnificent mane of red hair, she can look stunning. In the distortion of photographs, however, a figure which until she started dieting was Junoesque and even now could not be called svelte, tends to inflate – leading to those charges of dumpiness.

That is something Diana can never be accused of; even on a bad day when she is making a deliberate effort to dress down, she still carries herself with the kind of style that one can only be born with.

Says a friend of the Duchess, 'Sarah always treads carefully. They are genuinely the best of friends but Sarah knows when to stop fooling around; she never forgets that Diana is the Princess of Wales. It does not interfere with their friendship – it is so subtle that an outsider would never really notice. But it is there.'

But if the Duchess of York, out of breeding, protocol and an innate sense of what is right, makes it her business not to be seen to compete with the Princess of Wales, one cannot help but sense that Diana is in subtle competition with Fergie.

Before Sarah arrived on the royal horizon, Diana held unchallenged the high ground of attention. Now she finds herself constantly being compared to a woman who is at least her match in most things and her better in many. It must be galling to the Princess to see how well and without any apparent effort Sarah has slipped into the rhythm of the Family and the easy, unaffected way she has won the approval of her royal in-laws – something she herself has never quite managed to achieve.

And while Diana is an excellent swimmer and a superb dancer, Fergie is a black-run skier and a fine horsewoman (Diana after six years as a member of one of the most equestrian-minded families in the world still quakes every time she goes near a horse). Recently

Fergie qualified as a pilot in both fixed wing 'planes and helicopters and also 'can swim like a mermaid'.

She can tell risqué jokes that have her husband and her father-in-law Prince Philip roaring their heads off while Diana's own attempt at humour all too often falls on the fallow ground of bad taste. As it did – so the story goes – the day she asked her husband, who was deep in conversation at the time, what the definition was of 'confusion'.

When no reply was forthcoming, she gave the answer, 'Father's Day in Brixton'. The 'joke', needless to say, went down like a lead balloon.

Nor can the obviously tactile, physical nature of the Yorks' relationship and the obvious interest they have in each other have escaped Diana's notice.

Perhaps most irritating of all, even if only at a subconscious level, is the independence Fergie continues to enjoy. The Duchess can go around rapping with the Press, cheerfully advising a motley crew of paparazzi hiding behind a fence not to get 'too sunburnt'. She can pull faces. She can burst into tears, as she did when faced with a snake. She can put on a fur coat. Yet whenever Diana tries any of these things, she finds herself submerged under a bucket load of criticism.

When the Duchess of York's pregnancy was first announced in January 1988, the situation was reversed. She was criticized for flying a helicopter and continuing to go skiing. But unlike Diana, who suffered terribly from morning sickness throughout her pregnancies, Fergie felt terrific and wasn't going to be told what she could and couldn't do.

Motherhood has, however, brought the two women even closer. Diana adores baby Beatrice and although she is not a godparent spends as much time as she can with the latest addition to the family. While Fergie was pregnant and unable to fit into any of her designer clothes, Diana took advantage of the situation and was seen wearing one of the Duchess's Yves Saint Laurent couture ballgowns at a private party.

'Fergie lent me this because she can't fit into it any more,' Diana explained jovially to friends. But that choice of friends again underlines the different standards by which the two women are judged.

Fergie still keeps in close contact with the people she knew before her marriage – an eclectic group of well-heeled, upper-class socialites. She has introduced many of them to Diana. But while it is acceptable for Sarah to dash out to lunch with a girlfriend, and drop into Annabel's for a nightcap, it is not all right for Diana.

To argue that this is because Diana is the future Queen is an over-simplification. More than the roles marriage assigned to them, the real difference lies in the characters of the two women.

Fergie is doing what she has always done, behaving in the boisterous way she has always behaved. She is, as her father says, simply being herself. And why shouldn't she be? She was twenty-six years old when she got married, and old enough to know her own mind. And while her exuberance can occasionally get the better of her, it leaves no feeling that anything untoward is lurking in the psychological background.

Diana is different. Plucked unripe from the tree of her life, she has grown up in a cossetted, unexciting world, hidden away from modern life by a curtain of advisors and retainers and a protocol that can be frustrating and emotionally stifling.

That, she had come to accept, was the price she had to pay.

Then along came Fergie, full of pluck and spirit and determined to live her own life to the full, in her own way and getting away with it. It proved to be the catalyst in Diana's life.

14
Diana and her Friends

They drive through the gates in their Ford Escorts, Porsches, BMWs and Range Rovers. They are the Di-set, the Throne Rangers, that group of well-heeled upper-class men and women, who attend Diana's dinner parties at Kensington Palace, usually when Prince Charles is away. They escort her to the cinema, to lunch, on shopping expeditions, and sometimes back to their own homes in Fulham, Chelsea or Knights-bridge. (Throne Rangers seldom live north of London's Hyde Park, though they do sometimes venture south of the River Thames into Battersea and Clapham.)

Some of them have known Diana since her bachelor-girl days. Many belong to the new crowd, people who have known the Duchess of York for years and now know Diana. The men, some married, are mostly army, ex-army or 'something in the City'. Many have double-barrelled names – Wentworth-Stanley, Twiston-Davies, Holland Martin – and they address the Princess of Wales by the sobriquet of 'Duch', short for Duchess, the nickname her graces earned her as a child.

But even if the hairstyles have changed from the simple cuts of yesteryear and low-heeled Gucci court shoes and Cacherel shirts cuffed with gilded bracelets have been replaced by Bruce Oldfield and fine jewels, Diana remains the 'Sloane' she always was. And Diana for all her rank and privilege – and in a significant way in spite of them – still values the friendships she forged long ago in a flat near Earl's Court where she would wait in, hour after hour, sometimes for days on end, for a telephone call from the man who would one day make her a wife and princess.

'She's incredibly unpretentious,' says her old flat-mate, Caroline Bartholomew. 'I can pick up today where I left off with Diana.' Caroline, a godmother to Prince Harry, is now married to William Bartholomew, who owns Juliana's mobile discotheques, and forging a career for herself as an opera singer.

Diana, to supplement the allowance she received from her trust funds, washed shirts and baby-sat and worked as a daily maid. (A lowly occupation for an Earl's daughter, perhaps, but quite acceptable for those who did not have a proper job – provided of course, you were doing it for the right people.) One person she worked for was Phillipa Whitaker. She employed Diana as a temporary nanny at her home in Hampshire and remembers, 'if there was a job to be done, she'd do it'.

And once it was done there were dinners in local bistros and supper parties at home and rowdy skiing parties in Switzerland. And there were boyfriends to keep Diana company: men like Old Etonian Simon Berry, who took her to the tennis championships at Wimbledon and was a member of the chalet party during a skiing holiday in the French resort of Tignes, and George Plumptree, son of a Kent landowner. George, who is now happily married with two children, was supposed to take Diana to the ballet the day she got engaged to Charles. He didn't of course, but was invited to the wedding. She no longer sees him – he was a regular escort for almost a year – but she still keeps in touch with many others of the group including Phillipa Whitaker's brother, Willy van Straubenzee, whose shirts she once washed.

Diana was very popular. 'There was nothing hoity-toity about her,' Simon Berry remembers. 'We were all just friends together.'

There was a time, however, when she hardly saw anyone. Those early days in Buckingham Palace were lonely ones. With only a set of Walkman headphones for company she would roam the Palace corridors waiting for Charles to come home, and too unsure of herself and her new position to invite her old friends round. Suppose Charles didn't like them? It was worry based on reason. The Prince had little in common with Diana's easy-going friends, almost a generation his junior. Usually only when Charles was out did she invite them in, for small lunch parties, but her life was not her own. She wasn't even allowed to spend the night before her wedding with her friends.

Diana had wanted to invite her flatmate Carolyn Pride, secretary Anne Bolton, who is now married to Australian Noel Hill, and Virginia Pitman to a small supper party. She was staying at Clarence House that evening and for all her pleadings the Queen Mother refused her request, explaining gently there were some royal rules which could not be broken. Diana was told she must spend the last night of her spinsterhood with her family, not friends. Diana felt trapped, she was used to getting her own way and it was a long time since she had been told what she could do or whom she could see. Her father had seldom denied her anything – out of a feeling of guilt that in some way he had been responsible for the departure of their mother, he had tried to compensate by allowing his children a very free rein. And when Diana was told none of her flatmates could be bridesmaids she was even more upset. The only thing she could do was to ensure they had prime seats in St Paul's on the day, which she did.

It was all down to a question of confidence, and in those early days Diana, quite simply, did not have enough of it to claim vital territory as her own. She was not even mistress in her own home; it was Charles who organized their occasional dinner parties. And without a readymade 'Royal Bloomsbury Set' of interesting people to call upon, she found herself coming face to face, time and time again, with the same old collection of people whom Charles knew, but with whom she had little in common.

If dinners at home were difficult, official functions were worse. Her throat would dry up and she would find it impossible to eat. Her position prohibited her finding release in alcohol (she hardly drank, anyway, booze made her cheeks flushed), so formal, public luncheons and dinners, she said, were 'Yuk'.

It is not surprising she felt trapped. Understandably, she has started to break out. For Diana, for all that early demureness, is not the kind of woman to subserviate herself indefinitely to her husband, no matter how princely that husband may be. It is not in her character. And as Diana settled into her royal role that character started to reassert itself.

We have seen her grow in confidence and she has felt it herself. She has achieved her modest ambition, to be a wife and mother, and she is tackling the heavier task – of being herself. The process, because she is who she is, has caused ructions and unhappiness and concern. It has generated rumour and invited scurrilous speculation. But Diana, perhaps too isolated in the ivory tower of royalty at first to realize the reaction her behaviour would generate, has pursued her goal – of a life of her own filled with friends of her own choosing. She has now achieved it. And if Charles prefers not to be around when she entertains her own friends at 'KP', then so be it.

When Diana decides to have a dinner party, she will telephone friends like Mervyn Chaplin, who works for

Gerard Holdings in the city of London, and invite them around. She calls herself 'Diana' on the telephone and the switchboard operator will put her through, unaware of the identity of the voice on the other end of the line. Mervyn has been caught out on more than one occasion when friends, deciding to have a bit of fun with him, have telephoned imitating Diana's flattened vowels. 'Hi, Duch,' he will say, using the childhood nickname by which he and all her set call the Princess. 'Thought you looked wonderful in the papers this morning. But that dress – I nearly saw everything you had!'

Diana makes no fuss when her friends tease her, which they constantly do. It is what she wants. She finds all the adoration heaped on her shoulders very tiresome and embarrassing.

'There's far too much about me in the newspapers, far too much,' she says. Her friends agree and it is but rarely that her private entertainments make the popular print. When her friends dine at Kensington Palace they are secretive about it, never mentioning where they are going. These suppers are usually very informal and served in the small dining room or Diana's sitting room. The menu is equally simple – pasta and salad or lobster. Occasionally they will go to a movie first, but this is not easy for the woman with the most photographed face in the world. More usually they stay in Kensington Palace and watch the latest videos or Diana sometimes shows them the home movies she and Charles have made of the children. She claims she is not much good at photography – not true, she is very good – and she has hundreds of excellent snapshots, carefully pasted into leatherbound albums, which she will show to her guests. Wallace Heaton in Bond Street develop all the royal snaps including those taken by any of Diana's friends during skiing holidays or week-ends at Windsor Castle or Highgrove.

During the 1987 skiing holiday in Switzerland, all the guests dutifully gave their film to the royal detectives at the end of the holiday and had it returned processed but without negatives. The precaution is a sensible one: the daring snaps of Diana and Fergie dressed up in headscarves and T-shirts doing a risqué cabaret is not the image the Royal Family want to project. Informal pictures of Diana therefore are always at a premium and although the tiara and ballgown photographs no longer command the vast sums they once did, many magazines and newspapers will pay a great deal for off-duty snaps, a situation that caused Diana and her friends a great deal of aggravation in the latter part of 1987.

Diana had organized to go to a bridge party given by one of her friends, Kate Menzies, the heiress to a newsagent chain. As usual the weekly bridge party had been carefully planned; Kate had telephoned Diana and spoken with her secretary, who agreed a suitable date with the Princess and, for security purposes, a list of the other guests. Accompanied only by her detective, Diana drove to the South Kensington mews house Kate shares with her sister Sarah.

As the evening progressed, the players, who dined off Marks and Spencer lasagne, were unaware that a photographer was positioned outside the house, waiting for them to come out. Her detective that night, Ken Wharf, was in an adjoining room and also unaware. The photographer's long, cold wait did not go unre-warded and eventually Diana, wearing a satin bomber jacket and tight purple trousers tucked into boots, emerged from the house with Kate Menzies to say goodbye to one of the guests, Major David Waterhouse, a young officer in the Household Cavalry and an old friend of Diana's.

Stupidly perhaps, they started fooling around outside the house with masks and rubber noses and tried to put a rubber balloon over the exhaust of Waterhouse's car. Their howls of laughter drowned the click of the photographer's camera and he got the shot he wanted – the Princess of Wales larking about with a young man who clearly wasn't her husband. The photographer, who was hiding behind another car, was suddenly spotted and Diana leapt back on to the doorstep and shouted to David Waterhouse to drive off and let her detective handle the situation. Grabbing the photographer, 22-year-old Jason Fraser, Diana's bodyguard, Detective Sergeant Ken Wharf swiftly removed the film from his camera and told the photographer in no uncertain terms what would happen to him if he didn't leave immediately.

Brushing aside tears of frustration and rage, Diana explained to the young photographer that he and his sort were making her and her friends' lives a misery and that he had to give her his film.

'I've been working hard all week,' the Princess said. 'Katie fixed up a nice evening for me. She laid this whole thing on. It's very sweet and it's the only time I've been out all week. I've got so few friends left and this will only make things worse for me.'

The following day the photographer, who had given his name and address to the bodyguard Ken Wharf, was handed back the film, fully processed but without the negatives of Diana. It was an unfortunate incident, which highlighted the Princess's loneliness and frustration at not being able to keep her private life private. It also affected the Menzies sisters, who were hounded subsequently by photographers after the story broke.

But far from dropping Diana, her close-knit circle of friends rallied round and determined the press should not ruin her life – or theirs. But the situation worried them. It also worried her security advisors – what if instead of a camera the man had been carrying a gun? Her bodyguards and their superiors much preferred it when she confined her nocturnal outgoings to more conventional activities.

While Charles loves the opera and will often go to Covent Garden with the minimum of fuss, accompanied perhaps by Lady Susan Hussey, one of the Queen's ladies in waiting, with whom he is very close (her husband Sir Marmaduke Hussey, Chairman of the BBC is not an opera buff), Diana and her friends prefer to go to the theatre. They will drive to Kensington Palace and transfer to her car, arriving at the theatre with the detective a few minutes before the curtain goes up. The cast are informed of the Princess of Wales's arrival by the theatre manager, and if any of her showbusiness friends like Wayne Sleep or Michael Crawford are in the show, she might dine with them afterwards. Dinners are never completely impromptu as the chosen restaurant is always informed of her impending arrival and if the venue is new, it is checked out by a couple of detectives the day before. The detectives also dine in the restaurant at a couple of tables either side of the Princess and her party. It does not always work out that they can be seated exactly this way, hence a sneaky snapshot of Diana sharing a table with Lady Tryon on the occasion of their reconciliation lunch at San Lorenzo in Knightsbridge. The photographer who had discovered Diana was lunching with Lady Tryon managed to secure the adjacent table and take the clandestine shot without anyone noticing. Lady Tryon, however, was not displeased to be so publicly back in the royal fold from which Diana, jealous of the closeness of Kanga's friendship with her husband, had banished her. The friendship has not developed. Diana was not exactly delighted that the Australian Kanga spent so much of the autumn of 1987 at Balmoral with Charles, while she remained in London. The pair are no longer seen together in San Lorenzo, though Diana is often there with another of her girlfriends.

San Lorenzo is one of Diana's favourite lunchtime haunts. She loves the food and the hustle and bustle of the three-tiered restaurant. There are always plenty of 'faces' – a Sloane expression for famous people – and Diana sits with girlfriends like Caroline Twiston-Davies, who works in interior design in nearby Walton Street, gossiping about who is there and what they have both been doing. Another of Diana's favourite restaurants is Launceston Place, situated close to Kensington Palace and almost next to Lord Snowdon's London home. After lunch there Diana will sometimes go shopping in the maze of smart boutiques and children's shops nearby. She often lunches with her sister, Jane Fellowes, at Launceston Place or La Fontana, an unpretentious Italian restaurant in Pimlico. For show business friends Diana chooses haunts like the Groucho Club in Soho where she ate monkfish with Wayne Sleep or Luigi's in Covent Garden, where she joined Wayne and a crowd of ballet dancers for a pasta dinner.

Apart from Wayne Sleep with whom she shares a love of ballet, her lunches are strictly for the girls. Young men are only in attendance in private houses or one of the royal residences. The men, for their part, are understandably delighted to entertain the Princess to dinner, even if their homes are not particularly smart. Mervyn Chaplin lives in a mansion block of flats above

an arcade of shops in the Fulham Road. It is not grand,
but boasts a dark-green dining room, decorated with
hunting prints. Together with Humphrey Butler, who
works at Christies and Willy van Straubenzee, who
works at the merchant bank Morgan Grenfell, they will
invite Diana to dinner. The conversation is jovial and
Diana entertains her fellow diners with risqué jokes
and anecdotes about her children. She seldom mentions Charles, but doesn't mind being teased about her
latest nickname, hairstyle or outfit. When the press
called her 'Disco-Di', a reference to her late-night
dancing in a Swiss night club – she would ring up and
announce, 'It's Disco-Di from KP.'

In return she will invite them to Windsor for Royal
Ascot, where officially they are guests of the Queen.
Humphrey Butler, Willy van Straubenzee and several
girls from the set including, of course, Sarah Ferguson
before she was Duchess of York, have all been invited
to Windsor at Diana's suggestion. The Queen loves
having young people to stay during the racing week.
They make a good foil for some of her husband's
'boring' German relations and every evening each guest
has a card in their room informing them whom they
will be escorting in to dinner. After dinner the men
swop stories over port while the ladies retire to an
ante-room and decide the silliest party games they can
play. Dancing games such as Twister, which involves
trying to return to your original spot when the music
stops, are popular because everyone even the Germans
can understand the simple rules. The Queen usually
retires early followed by the Prince of Wales – Ascot is
a busy polo week for him and he practises in the
morning and plays every afternoon after the races.
Those who don't go to the polo return to Windsor
Castle and have a swim or play tennis before dinner.

The Duchess of York and Viscount Linley, Princess Margaret's son, who runs an extremely successful furniture business with his partner Mathew Rice, have been almost entirely instrumental in enlarging Diana's circle of friends. Before Sarah married in July 1986, her father gave a large party on the polo ground at Smiths Lawn, Windsor. It was an eclectic gathering mixing the Royal Family and Nancy Reagan with Paddy McNally, Sarah's former boyfriend and his jet-set group of friends. Diana had the time of her life; she boogied in the mobile discotheque organized by another of Fergie's mates, the dashing Angus Gibson, and danced with a host of attractive men she had never met before. Financier Charlie Carter was one. He had several dances with the Princess and when he returned to his table she invited him to dance again, which he duly did. They made an attractive couple as they are both excellent dancers and he found Diana 'charming and a terrific dancer'. They met again several months later at a charity ball and Charlie, who is happily married, asked Diana to dance. This time, however, a pair of mischievous press people were watching and the story duly found its way to the newspapers. For the next few weeks Charlie and his wife Tita had to put up with pressmen camping outside their Belgravia home, hoping to 'snatch' a picture of Charlie as he left for work. They didn't go unrewarded and caught him one morning when he left his house with a terrible hangover, his hair in his eyes and his tie askew.

'I can't understand them,' Tita exclaimed. 'All they had to do was ring on the doorbell and ask us if we minded posing for a picture.' She added, 'Both Charlie and I think the Princess of Wales is terrific but hardly know her apart from being Charlie's dancing partner on a couple of occasions.'

Charlie Carter is not the only one whose name has been linked with the Princess, merely because they shared a shimmy on the dance floor. Peter Greenhall who has a chalet in Klosters with his wife Clare, was another. He partnered Diana, who was dressed in sexy black leather trousers, to a local disco (where the Princess delighted the disc jockey by requesting Diana Ross's 'Chain Reaction').

'I asked if she still liked Duran Duran, but she wanted Diana Ross's hit "Chain Reaction",' DJ Martin Melsome explained. 'I obliged and she did a fantastic rock and roll solo to it. Then I had her in stitches by playing "Oh Diana".'

Diana was with a group of friends at the time, being carefully watched by three British detectives and two Swiss policemen. Charles was not part of the party but, said Melsome, 'she didn't look lonely or sad that her husband wasn't with her. In fact rather the opposite. She drank red wine and seemed to have a marvellous time.'

Diana's friends claim that there was nothing unusual about Charles letting Diana dance the night away without him. In Switzerland Charles loves skiing hard and starts early and therefore doesn't particularly want to spend his evenings in night clubs. Unlike Diana, Charles hates making an exhibition of himself on dance floors, as he revealed during their trip to Australia:

'I assure you it makes the heart sink, to have to make an awful exhibition of ourselves,' he explained as they started the dancing to the strains of Glenn Miller's 'In the Mood'. 'Having had a certain amount of practice in the last few years, each time I keep meaning to try to take lessons to learn the finer points of the tango, or the paso doble, or even break dancing.'

They began by dancing a formal quickstep and then

launched into their own medley – a personal jive when Prince Charles threw Diana to one side, while keeping hold of her with one hand. He then spun her around and around while he stood on the spot, causing her to call out, 'Steady, please slow down.'

Diana often gets the giggles when she dances with Charles and like many women prefers to dance with almost anyone other than her husband. At the wedding ball after 'Bunter' Worcester, the Duke of Beaufort's son and heir, married actress Tracy Ward, Diana never left the dance floor. She danced with Gerry Farrell, who runs a mail order art business, and David Ker, who owns an art gallery near Sloane Square. And she danced with Philip Dunne – again and again and again.

'It's all so innocent,' she told friends, 'and I don't intend to act like the guilty party.'

The gossip columns, which take a more cynical view of life, were not convinced. The speculation, however, only served to draw her circle tighter than ever. They included her in as many dinner parties as possible and Jules Dodd-Noble, known as 'Crown Jewels' because of her royal connections, and Antonia, Marchioness of Duro, encouraged Diana to join the Vanderbilt Racquet Club and play tennis with them. Diana is godmother to Antonia's daughter and both she and Charles spent a long weekend on the estate owned by her father-in-law, the Duke of Wellington, in Spain. She attended a David Bowie concert with Viscount Linley and a group of friends, including Major David Waterhouse. Photographers mistook the Major for Philip Dunne and the ensuing publicity forced the gallant Major, who was at Eton with Dunne, to speak up in the Princess's defence; so too did Kate Menzies.

Kate, who once enjoyed a brief liaison with Viscount Linley (they remain good friends), was introduced to

Diana through Susannah Constantine and Fergie. She has a company which arrange parties, outings and catering and lives with her older sister, Sarah, in an attractive South Kensington mews house. She is in a perfect situation to be able to gather all Diana's friends together and provide the Princess with a normal social scene so lacking in the early years of her marriage, and does so. But unfortunately for Diana, who loves giggling at the risqué jokes that fly around the dinner table and being teased about her wild dancing or sexy clothes, her position as Princess of Wales has to come first. Any breath of scandal, however unjustified, is harmful to her, her husband and the Royal Family.

When Diana took a breather from the Royal Box at Ascot last year and went for tea with her friends Clare Wentworth Stanley and her husband in the Turf Club, she was criticized, because she herself was not a member of the élite gentleman's club. And when she returned with Prince Charles the following day she spied her friend Ben Holland Martin holding a table she assumed was for her and Charles. Much to Ben's consternation it wasn't: he was holding it for Princess Margaret, who was due to appear, and the Prince and Princess were forced to move to another already crowded table. To make matters worse, Princess Margaret changed her mind and never appeared, leaving a red-faced Ben sitting at the empty table he had refused to the Prince and Princess of Wales.

Entertaining royalty is not easy, as Diana realizes, and when the pressure gets too great she will retreat back to the sanctuary of Highgrove and her husband. Charles and Diana do have a few mutual friends and they will occasionally be invited for weekends in Gloucestershire. (Charles is too busy with business dinners or official royal duties during the week to socialize much.) Sir Laurens van der Post sometimes visits so he can see his godson, William, and so do a group of Charles's hunting cronies like 'Milo' and Libby Watson: Miles, Lord Manton's son, is the brother of one of Charles's old flames, Fiona Watson. He and his wife Libby get along very well with Diana and love her wicked sense of humour. Catherine Soames, recently separated from her husband Nicholas, is also a regular guest; so is her former brother-in-law Rupert, who is now married to Philip Dunne's sister Millie.

Diana delights to see her friends get on with each other – better still, get on with Charles's friends. A close friend of them both was Major Hugh Lindsay, and his death in Klosters in March 1988 had a profound effect on both the Prince and Princess.

A former equerry to the Queen, Lindsay had met and married Sarah Brennan, a member of the loyal team of secretaries who work in the Buckingham Palace offices. His charm and easy manner endeared him to all the Royal Family and they remained friends even after he left the palace and returned to his regiment in Germany.

The horror of Lindsay's tragic death in the avalanche that engulfed his skiing party that sunny March afternoon has become a great mental burden for Prince Charles. Diana is worried that he is blaming himself unreasonably since the experts are unanimous that no possible blame can be attributed to him. Knowing that, but for a twist of fate, it might have been her husband who was killed, she has begged him to take fewer risks. She has lost a dear friend, and both she and Fergie have spent many sad hours discussing how it all might have been avoided.

Now that Fergie has her own home, Castlewood House, near Windsor, Diana sees less of her. But Diana does her best to persuade her friend to spend as many weekends with her as possible.

She is Diana's 'BF' and if Charles is in one of his tetchy moods, Fergie can usually chide and tease him out of it – something Diana cannot always do and she and Charles often find themselves rubbing each other up the wrong way. If Diana really wants to irritate her husband she will crack a stream of childish jokes about sex and race – guaranteed to drive Charles into a fury. He then refuses to speak to her and no amount of flirting and teasing will pull him out of his mood. Eventually, however, he will give in and sigh, 'Anything for a peaceful life' – one of his favourite phrases.

Charles may yearn for the peaceful life and Diana for the bright lights, but they have an amicable agreement to do their own thing. Charles is long-suffering, but he is also selfish and doesn't like his life being disrupted. After much consideration he allowed Palace officials to give Philip Dunne a gentle telephone call and inform him it would be far better for everyone concerned if he saw less of the Princess of Wales. By way of setting up a smoke-screen, several other people also received the call so that Dunne could not claim to have been singled out. It is the royal way of coping with a problem: Richard Meade, a one-time boyfriend of the Princess Royal received a similar call when Mark Phillips appeared on the romantic scene. He agreed to leave Anne alone and it was not until several years later when they were both married to their respective partners, that they became good friends again.

Obviously neither Diana nor Anne was happy with this kind of forceful alienation, but there was little either of them could do at the time, apart from sulk. Diana chose not to take this course of action and threw herself into her family life and socializing but she also had her brother to turn to. Since Viscount Althorp has been working for the American television network NBC, Diana hasn't seen so much of him, but they are close. Three years his senior she cared for him as a baby, then found him a 'pest' when he was a 'spotty ten-year-old creep' who spent his days following her and her friends around, but grew closer again when he matured. Today they are united by the love of their frail father, Earl Spencer, and contempt for their stepmother, Raine, who has gradually removed their heritage, by organizing the sale of certain family treasures.

Althorp is reluctant to discuss his favourite sister with anyone and when he was originally hired by NBC to commentate on the wedding of the Duke and Duchess of York in 1986, the only thing he let slip was that Major Ronald Ferguson had once proposed to his mother. He swallowed their referring incorrectly to his sister as Lady Diana and during all the speculation in 1987 when the major American networks ran stories on the state of her marriage, refused to comment.

'I'd never let her down in any way,' he said.

Intelligent and hardworking, he is highly regarded by his American employers. It took him a long time to shake off his 'Hooray Henry' image of the champagne-swilling hooligan, who liked to sit around in night clubs hurling abuse at those not so fortunate as himself, but he has finally succeeded and Diana is proud of him. She is, he claims, a good mixture of both his parents – she has his father's gentleness and his mother's single-mindedness:

'I think the combination's pretty good,' he says. 'And it's most obvious in Diana. She is exceptionally kind and thoughtful, but she's nobody's fool. She weeded out quite a few of the hangers-on that she found around her husband and his family in a subtle way.'

For all that and for all her insistence on developing her own circle of friends, Diana does do her best on occasions to include her husband in her activities. She was delighted when he agreed to host a pre-Christmas party for the stars who had worked so hard for his pet charity, The Prince's Trust, as a thank-you for their various appearances. Amongst the guests at the Kensington Palace bash were ex-Beatle George Harrison and his wife Olivia, Elton John and Renate, Paul Young, Kate Bush and Howard Jones. Diana had the carpet in their large reception room rolled back and persuaded Labi Siffre to play the piano. As always Elton John gave a rendering of some of his hit songs and everyone danced and sang. Diana was ebullient and while Charles aired his views on pop music with Ben Volpeliere of *Curiosity Killed the Cat*, she danced with as many of the famous guests as she could.

Ben Volpeliere later spoke about Prince Charles's views on pop music:

'He said he had the same views on modern music as he did on architecture. He thought much of it was soulless. I was surprised about his knowledge of the pop scene and how strongly he felt about it. He also told me that he and Diana sometimes fall about laughing at the chart hits.'

Diana's taste in pop music is middle of the road as her requests to DJ Graham Dene, whom she met at a cocktail party, reveal. He dedicated several records to 'Charlie's angel and her little goblins,' then played Paul McCartney's 'Once Upon a Long Ago', adding a cryptic message: 'If the Uptown Girl keeps listening there'll be something else she likes on soon.' And he then played Chris de Burgh's Christmas single.

Both Diana and Charles, stars themselves, are attracted to showbusiness folk and like to count them among their friends. Diana might prefer pop stars and TV heart throbs like 'Miami Vice' hero Don Johnson while Charles favours pretty actresses such as James Bond heroine Maryam D'Abo, whom he sat next to at the Cannes Film Festival dinner in 1987. It is a real affinity the Waleses feel with people who are in the public eye almost as much as the Royal Family, and know what it is like to be stared at all the time.

'You mustn't believe what you read in the papers,' Charles told Maryam D'Abo. 'I don't believe any of it, in fact I avoid reading them whenever I can.'

Ex-Goon Spike Milligan is a great friend of the Prince and they exchange a zany correspondence.

'He wrote to me by hand recently,' Spike explained, 'because he was het up about the plans for Paternoster Square near St Paul's, saying, "I need your support." I wrote back that I wasn't wearing one.' Spike loves what he calls 'loopholes' in the English language that enable him to play with words and he receives equally witty letters from the Prince of Wales, whom he sometimes entertains to dinner.

'Charles is a very ordinary person,' Milligan says. 'I wrote to him and asked if he and his wife would like to come for dinner. He turned up with an aide – I presumed she had another engagement. I was disappointed. I would like to have met her properly.'

One entertainer that both Diana and Charles love is Barry Humphries, who created the outrageous saliva-spraying slob, Sir Les Patterson, and Dame Edna Everage. At his charity show, Charles and Diana were both in fits of laughter at his blue jokes. After the show, dressed as Dame Edna Everage, Barry Humphries made an unabashed reference to the 'tip' of his gladioli being the most sensitive part.

The world has indeed changed. It would have been

unthinkable a few years ago for anyone – even an entertainer such as Humphries – to make such a lewd remark to a member of the Royal Family. But then Diana too has changed. Marriage may have made her a Princess, but it also deprived her of the irresponsible good times that are part of growing up. Instead of parties and dates and nightclubs, Diana had marriage, motherhood and the confines of royal responsibility.

She could not linger for hours in restaurants, dance the night away with a series of unlikely partners, or do anything quite mad and bad, just for fun. She had hardly experienced a normal life. Instead she had been wrapped in royal cotton wool. But then she started to break out, to lead her own life away from Charles and the confines of court. It led to gossip and speculation and reports of a serious rift in her marriage.

'I feel sorry for the Princess,' one of her girlfriends admits. 'She can't do anything without running into a mountain of criticism.'

But as Prince Charles says, 'The moment people have put you on a pedestal, along comes a separate brigade that likes knocking you off. It's human nature.'

The foundations of Diana's pedestal have taken a fair knocking recently. But she is determined to survive them and keep her seven-year marriage alive – with a little help from her friends.

Epilogue to the 1989 Edition

The time will come, unthinkably, but with mortal inevitability when, in a ritual as old as monarchy itself, Charles will be proclaimed King, his accession heralded from Friary Court, St James's Palace. The crowds will roar, trumpets sound and the band play the National Anthem while a salute of guns booms out over London from Hyde Park and the Tower – and Diana will be Queen.

It is not a role she was born to. It will be hers only by the right of marriage. It will bring her no Sovereign powers; she will have no papers of State to read, no Prime Ministers to advise her.

She will be Queen, therefore, in name only. Yet much, very much, will be expected of her – just as much as has been expected of her since that summer's day in 1981 when Prince Charles made her his Princess of Wales.

She was 'terrified', she said afterwards and sometimes still is. Only 20 years old at the time, she also admitted that she had no idea what being the Princess of Wales would be like. But then, no one did.

No royal personage has ever had his or her life so publicly analysed and held up to such public scrutiny as has Diana and even the old guard of Palace advisors were at a loss to know what to do and how to cope. It came as a shock to everyone. There was confusion and Diana was left with the struggle of trying to knit together into some passable harmony the essentially uncombinable; her private and her public lives.

In one she is a mother and wife with her own developing interests and, increasingly, her own circle of friends. In the other she is a Princess who will, by the dictate of public expectancy, one day be Queen. It is a two-dimensional role in which Diana is expected to be forever calm and beautiful and serene; without a hair out of place, without unseemly emotions and certainly without problems.

As Queen it will be the same, only more so. As the Princess of Wales she is a symbol of the future. As Queen she will become the embodiment of the present and there was a time when both her husband and her mother-in-law harboured grave doubts as to whether she had the character to cope with the strain and responsibility.

To be fair, it cannot have been easy for a woman so young, whose friends were off having fun and love affairs and carefree holidays, to come to terms with the fact that now and for the rest of her life she was going to be attending dreary official functions, making conversation with people she has never met before and will never meet again; forever on show with people poised to jump on the slightest indiscretion.

It is still not plain sailing. There have been problems in her marriage. As her father, Earl Spencer, pointed out, 'of course Charles and Diana have had their rows, what couple doesn't? What makes it so different for them is that they're on show the whole time. They might have had a disagreement, then they have to step out in front of the cameras and pretend that everything is going well and that's not easy.' Charles particularly has been infuriated by the public discussion of what he considers to be very much their private business and while Diana treats it more lightheartedly, this spotlight of unwanted attention has only compounded the difficulties they have faced.

For all her new found poise, she has yet to truly master the Royal art of public speaking, although, in 1988 she broke her silence several times. Encouraged by her recently appointed press officer, former broadcaster, Dickie Arbiter, she delivered a particularly well-received address to the Annual General Meeting of Barnardo's on the subject of family life. 'I know family life is extremely important,' she said. 'As a mother of two small boys I think we may have to find a securer way of helping our children, to nurture and prepare them to face life as stable and confident adults. The pressures and demands on all of us are enormous.'

It was the first time her comments had been treated more seriously than her clothes and praise for the speech and her professional delivery were heaped on the Princess. Yet a few weeks later she could not bring herself to say anything at a Birthright luncheon, after the television personality David Frost had presented her with a cheque for the million pounds he had helped raise. The Barnardo speech had been carefully polished and rehearsed. The Birthright luncheon called for a spontaneous response and Diana preferred to hide herself behind a silent smile.

Then there are always the inevitable family tensions to be faced. Her youngest son, Harry, had to undergo an emergency hernia operation in 1988 – and in painful reminder of her parents' bitter divorce, her mother, Frances, separated from her second husband, wallpaper heir Peter Shand-Kydd, for whom she had given up her reputation, her title and her young children. Also, Diana's relationship with her sister-in-law Anne has not warmed into friendship and the two women exchanged curt words with each other at Sandringham during the Christmas holiday.

The Princess Royal wanted to take her nephews, William and Harry out shooting to help pick up the pheasants as they had often done before. Diana refused to let them go. She was concerned by a repeat of the unfavourable public reaction when it was discovered she was allowing her children to take part in a 'blood sport'. She has not acquired the Royal Family's – in particular her sister-in-law's – indifference to criticism and the surprising amount of hate mail she receives can on occasion reduce her to tears.

But for all the turmoil and upsets, she has learned to cope remarkably well with the pressures of being the most famous woman in the world. Charles, now in his 40s, has still not fully resolved the dilemma of what to do in the years before he succeeds his mother on the last great throne of Europe. Not so Diana. Simply being the Princess of Wales is reward and role enough for a woman who never wanted much more than to be a mother and a wife. Being a princess as well is the fairy-tale bonus. However, she has discovered that it is a role with responsibilities and it was not just a husband she acquired in 1981, it was a life's work, with the most important part still ahead.

For it will be Diana who, unwillingly perhaps, certainly unconsciously, will be so important in establishing the style of her husband's reign. In premature middle age, Charles is displaying a cantankerous determination to involve himself in worthy causes which alas do not all necessarily capture the imagination of his future subjects.

Just as the Queen Mother – another 'commoner' – provided the tenable link to her husband, the shy and nervous George VI, so Diana, uncomplicated but caring, is the accessible totem of royalty in this generation. She has brought the gloss and international glamour to the altogether rather dowdy image of the Royal Family. At the same time she has added an extra dimension to Charles and the crowds rush to see her whenever she appears. She responds with an unaffected charm which impresses even those determined not to be moved by her. The fame and the homage may have moulded her, But they have not consumed her. She remains a caring and considerate woman, aware of her responsibilities and prepared to meet them – and that augurs well for the day when Charles is King and Diana is his Queen.

Appendix

Charities of which Her Royal Highness The Princess of Wales is President or Patron.

THE ALBANY
DR BARNARDO'S
BIRTHRIGHT
BRITISH DEAF ASSOCIATION
BRITISH LUNG FOUNDATION
BRITISH RED CROSS YOUTH
BRITISH SPORTS ASSOCIATION FOR THE DISABLED
THE COMMONWEALTH SOCIETY FOR THE DEAF
GLOUCESTERSHIRE COUNTY CRICKET CLUB
THE GUINNESS TRUST
HELP THE AGED
LONDON CITY BALLET
THE MALCOLM SARGENT CANCER FUND FOR CHILDREN
NATIONAL CHILDREN'S ORCHESTRA
NATIONAL HOSPITAL FOR NERVOUS DISEASES
NATIONAL RUBELLA COUNCIL
NORTHERN IRELAND PRE-SCHOOL PLAYGROUPS ASSOCIATION
PRE-SCHOOL PLAYGROUPS ASSOCIATION – WALES
PRE-SCHOOL PLAYGROUPS ASSOCIATION
ROYAL ACADEMY OF MUSIC
ROYAL COLLEGE OF PHYSICIANS AND SURGEONS OF
   GLASGOW
ROYAL SCHOOL FOR THE BLIND
SCOTTISH CHAMBER ORCHESTRA
SWANSEA FESTIVAL OF MUSIC AND THE ARTS
TURNING POINT

WALES CRAFT COUNCIL
WELSH NATIONAL OPERA LIMITED

Joint Patronage with the Prince of Wales:
THE CHILDREN'S MUSEUM EUREKA PROJECT
WISHING WELL APPEAL

Bibliography

Barr, Ann, and York, Peter, *The Official Sloane Ranger Handbook* (Ebury, 1982)

Barry, Stephen, *Royal Secrets* (Villard Books, 1985)

Barry, Stephen, *Royal Service* (Macmillan, 1983)

Burnet, Sir Alastair, *In Person: The Prince and Princess of Wales* (Michael O'Mara Books, 1985)

Burnet, Sir Alastair, *In Private – In Public: The Prince and Princess of Wales* (Michael O'Mara Books, 1986)

Courtney, Nicholas, *Royal Children* (Dent, 1982)

Courtney, Nicholas, *The Sporting Royals* (Hutchinson, 1983)

Geldof, Bob, *Is That It?* (Penguin, 1986)

Hall, Unity, *Philip: the Man Behind the Monarchy* (Michael O'Mara Books, 1987)

Hamilton, Alan, *The Royal Handbook* (Mitchell Beazley, 1985)

Hoey, Brian, *Princess Anne* (Country Life, 1984)

Hoey, Brian, *Monarchy* (BBC, 1987)

Hutchins, Phoebe, *The Royal Baby Book* (Octopus, 1984)

James, Sue, *The Princess of Wales Fashion Handbook* (Orbis, 1983)

James, Sue, *The Royal Baby Nursery and Fashion Handbook* (Orbis, 1984)

Junor, Penny, *Charles* (Sidgwick and Jackson, 1987)

Keay, Douglas, *The Press and the Palace* (Severn House, 1983)

Lacey, Robert, *Majesty* (Hutchinson, 1977)

Martin, Ralph, *Charles and Diana* (Grafton, 1985)

Menkes, Suzy, *The Royal Jewels* (Grafton, 1985)

Morton, Andrew, *Inside Kensington Palace* (Michael O'Mara Books, 1987)

Shute, Nerina, *The Royal Family and the Spencers* (Robert Hale, 1986)

Wade, Judy, *Inside a Royal Marriage* (Eden, 1987)

Whitaker, James, *Settling Down* (Quartet, 1981)

Index